macromedia®
FLASH™ 5
TRAINING FROM THE SOURCE

macromedia®
FLASH™ 5
TRAINING FROM THE SOURCE

Chrissy Rey

macromedia®
PRESS

Macromedia Flash 5: Training from the Source

  Published by Macromedia Press, in association with Peachpit Press, a division of Addison Wesley Longman.

Macromedia Press
1249 Eighth Street
Berkeley, CA 94710
510/524-2178
510/524-2221 (fax)
Find us on the World Wide Web at:
http://www.peachpit.com
http://www.macromedia.com

Printed and bound in the United States of America

ISBN 0-201-72931-8

9 8 7 6 5 4 3 2 1

CREDITS

Author and Instructional Designer
Chrissy Rey

Editor
Wendy Sharp

Copyeditor
Kathy Simpson

Production Coordinator
Kate Reber

Compositors
Rick Gordon, Emerald Valley Graphics; Debbie Roberti, Espresso Graphics

Indexer
Karin Arrigoni, Write Away

Cover design
Steven Soshea, Macromedia, Inc.

Technical Review
Jeremy Clark, Macromedia Flash Product Manager
Karen Cook, QA Manager Flash
Jared Loftus, QA Engineer Flash
Lily Khong, QA Engineer Flash
Lauren Park, QA Engineer Flash
Hiroko Takada, QA Engineer Flash
Jonathan Duran, Macromedia Flash Technical Support

This edition is based upon materials developed by:
Fig Leaf Software

Many thanks to everyone who helped me with this book: Tom Pizer, Jody Keating, Tracy Kelly, Branden Hall, Miles Windsor, Keenan Keeling, and Doug Clarke from Fig Leaf Software who all had a part in the original Flash 5 curriculum that this book was based on; Jon Spindler for providing a fresh perspective and making sure everything works; David Willis for being there from the beginning; Darwin, Jinx, Luna, and Gator for staying quiet long enough to let me work; the Flash community for all the inspiration and support; Brett Rampata, Todd Marks, Asako Nagata, Walt Rampata, Bill Murray, and Eddy from digitalorganism; Allise Berger and Tiffany Beltis from Macromedia; and most importantly, Wendy Sharp from Peachpit for her superhuman editing efforts.

This book is dedicated to Mom and Jon.

table of contents

LESSON 12 PUBLISHING AND EXPORTING   256

Using the Bandwidth Profiler
Optimizing a Movie
Creating a Preloader
Exporting a Movie
Publishing a Movie

introduction

Macromedia's Flash 5 is the professional standard for producing high-impact Web experiences. Macromedia Flash 5 delivers an intuitive, approachable authoring environment to enable both designers and developers to more easily create next-generation Web sites and applications.

The Macromedia Training from the Source course introduces you to the major features of Flash 5 by guiding you step-by-step through the development of several elements of a complex Web site. This 12- to 14-hour curriculum includes these lessons:

Lesson 1: Flash Basics
Lesson 2: Using Graphics and Text
Lesson 3: Using Symbols and the Movie Explorer
Lesson 4: Creating Animation
Lesson 5: Using Sound
Lesson 6: Adding Basic Interactivity
Lesson 7: Programming with ActionScript
Lesson 8: Adding More Complex Interactivity
Lesson 9: Using the Sound Object
Lesson 10: Processing Data Using Middleware
Lesson 11: Adding Generator Content
Lesson 12: Publishing and Exporting

Each lesson begins with an overview of the lesson's content and learning objectives and each is divided into short tasks that break the skills into bite-size units.

Each lesson also includes these special features:

Tips: Shortcuts for carrying out common tasks and ways you can use the skills you're learning to solve common problems.

Notes: Additional information or extra background about the tools or commands.

Menu commands and keyboard shortcuts: Alternative methods for executing commands. Menu commands are shown like this: Menu › Command › Subcommand. Keyboard shortcuts are shown like this: Control+Z (Windows) or Command+Z (Macintosh). The + between the names of the keys means that you should press both keys simultaneously and both Windows and Macintosh commands will always be included.

Appendices A & B contain quick lists of Flash's keyboard shortcuts. Appendix C is a guide to some handy Flash resources. Finally, Appendix D is a reference guide to the ActionScript used in the book, as well as additional ActionScript that may interest you.

As you complete these lessons, you'll be developing the skills you need to create your own Flash movies, complete with animation and interactivity. By the end of this book, you will have mastered the use of Flash's panels, commands, and interface, and grown familiar with Flash ActionScripting and animation and you'll be able to develop your own projects using the tools you've learned. For more on what you will learn, see the What You Will Learn list at the end of this introduction.

All the files you need for the lessons are included in the Lessons folder on the enclosed CD. Files for each lesson appear in their own folders, titled with the lesson name. You can use the files directly from the CD, or you can copy the Lessons folder to your hard drive for quicker access.

Each lesson folder contains two subfolders: Assets and Complete. The Assets folder includes any media files needed for the lesson, such as graphics, sounds or symbol libraries, as well as the initial Flash file for the lesson. The files that you will need are identified at the beginning of each lesson. The Complete folder contains complete files for each step in the project so that you can compare your work or see where you are headed.

You'll grow very familiar with the Neptune Resort Web site over the course of this book. Each lesson in the book is a piece of the site. At the end of the book, you'll put all the pieces together.

AUTHORIZED TRAINING FOR MACROMEDIA

Each book in the Macromedia Training from the Source series is based upon curriculum originally developed for use by Macromedia's authorized trainers. The lesson plans were developed by some of Macromedia's most successful trainers and refined through long experience to meet students' needs. We believe that Macromedia Training from the Source courses offer the best available training for Macromedia programs.

The lessons in this book assume that you are a beginner with Flash but that you are familiar with the basic methods of giving commands on a Windows or Macintosh computer, such as choosing items from menus, opening and saving files, and so on. For more information on those tasks, see the documentation provided with your computer.

Finally, the instructions in the book also assume that you already have Flash 5 installed on a Windows or Macintosh computer, and that your computer meets the system requirements listed on the next page.

WHAT YOU WILL LEARN

By the end of this course, you will be able to:

- Work with Flash's tools, panels, and commands to create Flash movies.
- Use symbols, the library, and the Movie Explorer to optimize your files and keep them organized.
- Create simple and complex animations, using frame-by-frame animation, motion tweening, and shape tweening.
- Add, modify, and customize sounds.
- Control sounds by adding them to buttons and by creating volume controls.
- Add basic interactivity by creating clickable buttons, and using actions to control the timeline.
- Use ActionScript to add drag-and-drop interactivity, dynamic text, and much more.
- Use other programs, such as ColdFusion, to process information.
- Publish, print, and export your Flash movies.

4

MINIMUM SYSTEM REQUIREMENTS

Windows

- 133 MHz Intel Pentium processor
- Windows 95/98, NT4, 2000, or later
- 64 MB of free available system RAM
- 48 MB of available disk space
- 256-color monitor capable of 800×600 resolution

Macintosh

- Power Macintosh with MacOS 8.5 or later
- 64 MB of free available system RAM
- 48 MB of available disk space
- 256-color monitor capable of 800×600 resolution

flash basics

LESSON 1

Before you're through with this book, you'll know how to use Flash to create complex Web movies with animations, buttons, and scripts. But every long journey starts with a single step—and in this case, your single step involves learning how to set Flash's preferences, how to customize its workspace for your use, and how to use some of the most straightforward of its tools and commands.

If you're familiar with other drawing or painting software—or any complex program that uses preferences and palettes—some of this lesson may seem to be too simple for you. Read through it anyway. Flash does a few things differently from other programs, and it's worth your time to learn about those variations.

You'll use Flash's drawing tools in this chapter to create some very simple movies.

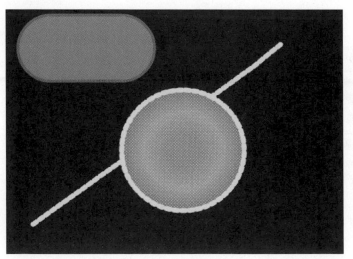

You'll experiment with Flash's panels and tools, creating a very simple movie.

WHAT YOU WILL LEARN

In this lesson, you will:

- Create a movie

- Customize Flash's preferences

- Work with panels to organize the workspace

- Modify the movie properties

- Draw and modify basic shapes by using various tools and panels

- Arrange, align, scale, and rotate elements on the stage

- Learn where to find additional help

APPROXIMATE TIME

It should take about one hour
to complete this lesson.

LESSON FILES

Media Files:

None

Starting File:

Lesson01\Assets\shapes.fla

Completed Projects:

myfile3.fla

pentool.fla

shapes2.fla

GETTING STARTED

Before you dive into building in Flash, you need to create a folder on your hard disk. You'll save your work to this folder as you work through the lessons in this book.

1) Create a folder called MyWork on your hard disk.

As mentioned in the introduction, this course assumes that you're familiar with the conventions of your computer. If you need help creating a folder, please refer to the documentation provided with your system.

After you create the folder, you're ready to open Flash—an important first step!

2) Double-click the Flash icon to open the program.

If this is the first time you have opened Flash, you should see something that looks like the figure below if you're working on a Windows machine or the figure on the next page if you're using a Macintosh. Notice that the two screens are very similar: there are very few differences between the Windows and Macintosh versions of Flash.

When Flash opens, by default the Info, Mixer, Character, and Instance panels are visible along the right side of the screen, and the toolbar (also called the toolbox or the Tools window) is visible along the left side. In the middle of the screen is a work area known as the *stage*.

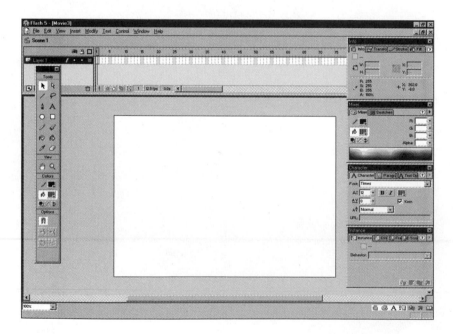

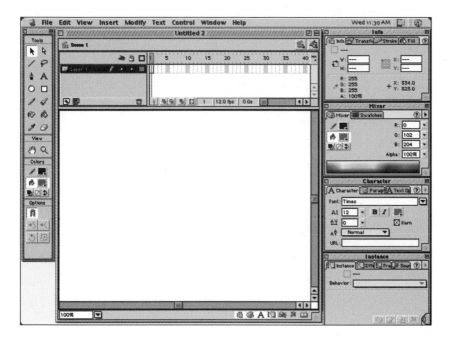

The blank document in the stage is a new movie. Every time you open Flash, the program automatically creates a new movie.

For the moment, you don't actually need to have a movie open. Before you start working on a movie, you're going to spend some time customizing the workspace and getting familiar with the program.

3) Choose File > Close.

The movie disappears. Your screen should now look something like the figure below.

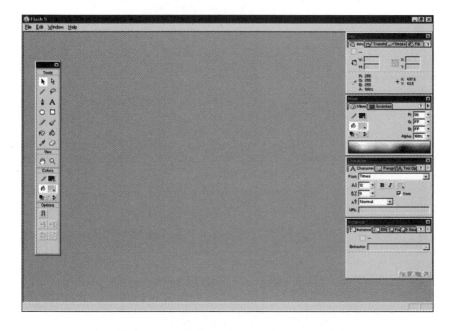

SETTING PREFERENCES

Flash has a wide range of preference settings that let you control everything from the number of Undos you can perform to the way objects are selected. At the moment, you'll just check to make sure that your preferences are set to Flash's defaults. And you'll make a single change that will make it easier for you to learn and use Flash.

1) Choose Edit > Preferences to display the Preferences dialog box. Click the General tab, and make sure that your preferences are set as shown below.

The options checked in the General panel of the Preferences dialog box are Shift Select and Show Tooltips. Shift Select allows you to add to a selection by holding down the Shift key when you click an object.

More important, Show Tooltips is a quick help system, handy for novices to the program. When Show Tooltips is checked, an icon label appears whenever you rest the pointer over an icon for a few seconds. You'll use this feature extensively in following sections.

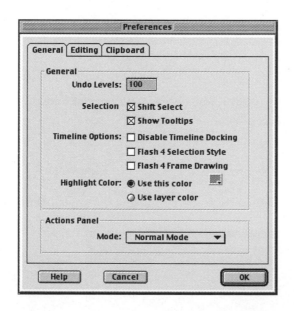

TIP *Undo Levels controls the number of steps that Flash remembers. If you need to make corrections to your work, Flash will be able to revert by the number of steps set in the Undo Levels field. At 100 steps, you should be able to undo almost any mistake. But you should also be aware that each level is saved in memory. With a high setting, your computer may start slowing after you complete several tasks. If you notice this and it's a problem, return to the Preferences dialog box and lower the Undo Levels setting.*

2) Click the Editing tab. In the Pen Tool area, check Show Precise Cursors.

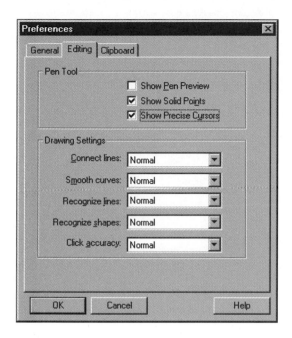

When you click the Editing tab, the Editing panel of the Preferences dialog box appears. Within this panel, you set options for the pen tool and settings for drawing controls.

Although you'll leave the drawing controls set on normal for now, checking the Show Precise Cursors option specifies that the pen tool appears as a crosshair instead of as the default pen-tool icon. This setting is useful because it lets you more precisely place lines drawn with the pen tool.

3) Click OK to close the Preferences dialog box.
Now that you've made some changes to your preferences, it's time to explore the Flash environment a little more.

WORKING WITH PANELS
Flash 5 organizes many of its tools and commands in panels, similar to the palettes in some other programs. Panels contain tools that allow you to view, organize, and modify elements in a movie. You can show, hide, and resize panels as you work in Flash. You can even combine panels to make it easier to work in Flash. Unlike dialog boxes, panels can remain on the screen while you work so you can easily use them to modify elements in your movie.

In the following exercise, you arrange the panels and then save this custom panel layout so you can use it later.

1) Choose File > New. Choose Window > Panels > Stroke.

When you choose File > New, a blank movie opens. The timeline and the stage are now visible, as well as the toolbar.

The Stroke panel is already on the screen, but you might not be able to see it; it is part of the group of panels that appears in the top-right corner of the screen. By default, this group includes the Info, Transform, Stroke, and Fill panels. When you choose Window > Panels > Stroke, the Stroke panel appears on top of the others in this group.

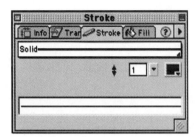

T I P *You can also click the tab of a panel to bring it to the front of the group.*

2) Click the tab at the top of the Stroke panel, and drag the panel to the left until it is no longer over any other panels.

As you drag, Flash displays an outline of the panel and its window. When you drop the panel, it appears in a new window by itself. You can drag any panel by its tab to separate it from the other panels.

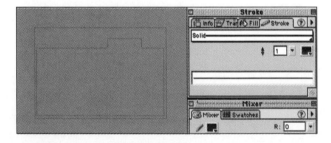

You could separate all the panels and fill your screen with individual windows, but that wouldn't make your work easier. On the other hand, it might come in handy to create a custom window that contains only the panels you need. You're now going to create a window that holds only the Stroke and Fill panels.

3) Click the Fill tab, and drag the Fill panel over the Stroke panel. Drop the Fill panel on the Stroke panel.

When you drag the tab of one panel to the tab of another panel, the two panels become grouped when you release the mouse button.

12

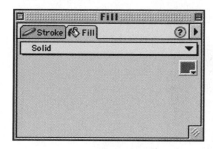

4) Close all the panel windows except the Stroke/Fill window by clicking the close button in the top-right (Windows) or top-left (Macintosh) corner of each window.

Your workspace should now be greatly simplified. Rather than multiple windows, each containing multiple panels, you should have a single panel window and the toolbar open.

This workspace would be useful for simple drawing tasks. But you wouldn't want to spend time re-creating it every time you need it. You can save custom workspaces so that you can re-use them. But you must have a movie open to save a workspace. In the next step, you'll open a new movie and save the panel layout.

5) Choose Window > Save Panel Layout.

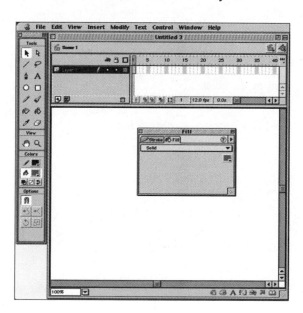

When you choose Window > Save Panel Layout, the Save Panel Layout dialog box appears.

6) Type *Basic Drawing Layout* in the Name text box, and click OK.

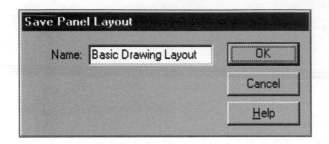

You've just saved your panel layout. That was pretty painless, wasn't it? Now you can open this panel layout at any time by choosing Window > Panel Sets > Basic Drawing Layout. If you decide that you'd prefer to use the default panel layout, you can switch back to that by choosing Window > Panel Sets > Default Layout.

MODIFYING THE MOVIE PROPERTIES

Before you start making a movie in Flash, you should think about its properties, such as the size, the frame rate, and the background. It's a good idea to decide what the properties should be before you start working with the movie, because it can be difficult to make changes after you've added artwork to the movie.

You can set the dimensions of your movie—as well as its background color, frame rate, and the units of measure of the stage's ruler—in the Movie Properties dialog box. In the following exercise, you'll modify the dimensions and background color of the movie that you opened in the preceding exercise.

1) Choose Modify > Movie to open the Movie Properties dialog box.

TIP *You can also open the Movie Properties dialog box by pressing Ctrl-M (Windows) or Command-M (Macintosh).*

In the Movie Properties dialog box, you can set the frame rate, dimensions (height and width), background color, and ruler units of your movie.

You can also use the Match buttons (Printer and Contents) to set the dimensions of the movie to match the current print size or the current contents of the movie (whatever you have drawn on the stage).

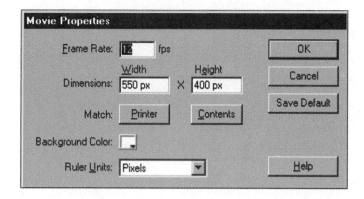

2) In the Width text box, type 600. In the Height text box, type 400.

By default, a new Flash movie has a width of 550 pixels and a height of 400 pixels. The minimum size of a movie is 18 by 18 pixels, and the maximum size is 2,800 by 2,800 pixels.

3) Click the Background Color color swatch.

The rectangle next to the Background Color label is called a *color swatch*. When you click the color swatch, the pointer turns into an eyedropper, and a pop-up window appears. The pop-up window contains all the available background colors. You can set the background color of your movie only to a solid color, so the window contains only solid colors.

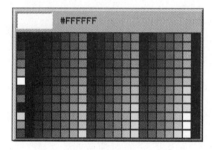

As you move the eyedropper pointer over the color swatches in the pop-up window, notice that the corresponding hex value appears in the top-left corner of the window. (*Hex* stands for *hexadecimal*—the code used to specify colors in HTML.) By default, only the 216 Web-safe colors appear in the pop-up window in the Movie Properties dialog box.

4) In the pop-up window, click a black color box. In the Movie Properties dialog box, click OK.

Clicking a black color box sets the background color of the movie to black. After you click the color box, the pop-up window sets the color and closes automatically.

Clicking OK in the Movie Properties dialog box applies your changes and closes the dialog box. Your movie dimensions and background color will change to the settings you specified.

TIP *If you continually change the default settings, you can save a new default. If you always change your screen size to 600 pixels by 400 pixels, for example, make that change in the Movie Properties dialog box, and click Save Default. The next time you create a new page in Flash, that page will have the new height and width.*

USING THE DRAWING TOOLS

Flash has a wide range of tools and commands that you can use to create your movies. Before you can start using them, you need to know where they are and what they are.

1) Move the pointer over the toolbar. Rest the pointer over a tool to see its name.

Remember when you checked to make sure that Tooltips was turned on? This is where that setting pays off. You can quickly and easily find out the name of any tool just by resting the pointer over it. After a second or two, a label with the name of the tool pops up.

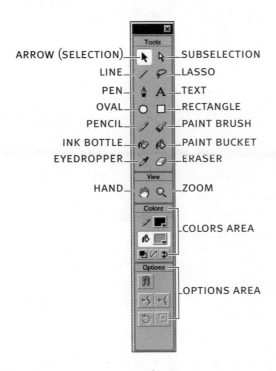

TIP *If the toolbar does not appear on your screen, you can open it by choosing Window > Tools.*

The toolbar contains Flash's drawing and transformation tools. It also contains additional settings for some of the tools. When you click the arrow, lasso, rectangle, pencil, brush, paint bucket, or eraser tool, icons appear in the Options area of the toolbar. If you move the pointer over the icons, you should notice that each one also has a ToolTip.

Spend some time moving the pointer over the tools and exploring the options. If you've used any other drawing, photo-editing, illustration, or paint programs, you're probably familiar with most of these tools.

2) Click the pencil tool to select it.

The pencil tool is useful for drawing lines and shapes. The shape created by the pencil tool is referred to as a *stroke*. Notice that when you click the pencil tool in the toolbar, the pointer changes to a pencil as you move it over the stage.

You can specify the straightness of the lines and shapes by changing the pencil mode in the Options section of the toolbar before drawing. Click the pencil-mode button until a pop-up menu appears. If you choose Straighten, Flash takes your freehand line and straightens it. If the line approximates a shape, Flash transforms your rough shape into a precise shape. If you choose Smooth, Flash smooths out the rough spots in your line. Choosing Ink leaves your line as you drew it. In the figure below, the squarish shape on the left was drawn in smooth mode; the one on the right was drawn in straighten mode.

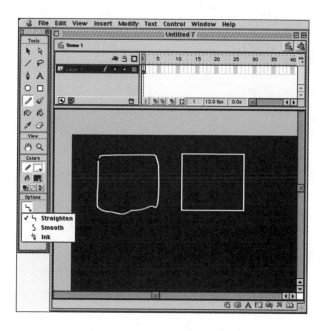

FLASH BASICS

3) In the Colors area of the toolbar, click the default-colors button; then click the swap-colors button. Drag the pencil tool across the stage to draw a single line.

When you click the default-colors button, Flash sets the stroke color to black and the fill color to white. By clicking the swap-colors button, you swap the stroke and fill colors. You want to do this because the movie's background color is black, and a black stroke would be impossible to see. Swapping the colors turns the stroke to white.

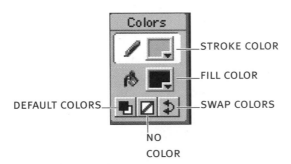

As you drag the pencil tool across the stage, you'll see a preview of the line you're drawing. When you release the cursor, the line appears on the stage, but it will look somewhat different from the preview, because Flash's default pencil mode is Straighten. Your line is straightened automatically unless you change the mode via the pop-up menu described in step 2.

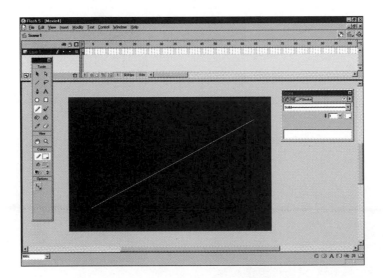

You can constrain the stroke drawn with the pencil tool to a straight line by holding down the Shift key as you drag the tool across the stage. You can also draw straight lines by using the line tool. You can constrain the line tool to 45-degree angles by holding down the Shift key as you drag across the stage.

4) Click the oval tool.

The oval tool is useful for drawing ovals and circles. In addition to creating a stroke, the oval tool can create a fill. A *fill* is a solid area of color that appears inside of the stroke created by the tool. You can use the oval tool to draw ovals and circles with both a stroke and a fill, a stroke without a fill, or a fill without a stroke.

TIP *When you draw with the oval tool, you can constrain the shape to a perfect circle by holding down the Shift key.*

5) In the Colors section of the toolbar, set the stroke color to green and the fill color to red.

The stroke-color and fill-color rectangles are color swatches, just like the one you used in the Movie Properties dialog box, and you set the color within those swatches the same way. Click the color swatch to make the color pop-up window appear; then click the color that you want to apply to your stroke or fill. It's simple.

If you want to be more precise in your color choice, you can type the hex value for the color in the text box at the top of the pop-up window. Pure green is #00FF00, for example, and bright red is #FF0000.

The pop-up window also has two small buttons in the top-right corner. The first allows you to set the color to none (no color); the second opens a Color Picker window to allow you to choose a color that is not in the color pop-up window.

TIP *Don't set both the stroke color and the fill color to no color! Although you can do so, it's not particularly useful to draw an oval that nobody can see.*

6) Click the stage, and drag with the oval tool to create an oval that covers some, but not all, of the line.

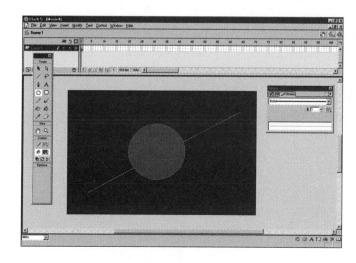

You don't need to be precise, but try to place the oval so that both ends of the line are uncovered. And remember, to create a circle, hold down the Shift key while you draw with the oval tool.

7) Click the arrow tool. Click inside the oval. Press the Delete or backspace key on your keyboard.

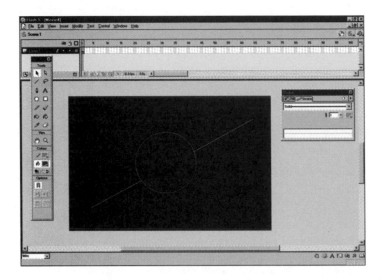

You should now have a drawing that looks something like the one above. If you're familiar with other drawing tools, you're probably somewhat surprised by your results.

Unlike many programs, in Flash, strokes and fills are separate entities. When you selected the oval by clicking it with the arrow tool, you selected the interior (the fill), but not the exterior (the stroke). If you use the arrow tool to select a fill and move it, the outline stays behind.

Another interesting behavior is that every time one shape overlaps another, the shapes are divided into segments wherever they intersect. So you might have noticed that when you deleted the oval's fill, the line that used to be behind it was no longer there. That's because drawing the oval on top of it removed the line from your drawing.

TIP *You can select a fill and its outline by double-clicking the fill with the arrow tool. If you'd like to test it out, choose Edit > Undo a few times to bring the oval's fill back; then double-click the fill. If the stroke that you drew with the pencil tool was the same color as the stroke that you drew with the oval tool, both strokes would be selected with this method.*

8) Click the rectangle tool. In the Stroke panel, set the stroke color to blue and the stroke height to 4. Drag the rectangle tool across the stage to draw a rectangle.

Your Stroke panel should still be open from earlier in the lesson. If it's not, choose Window > Panels > Stroke to open it. If the Stroke panel is behind the Fill panel, click the Stroke tab to bring it to the front.

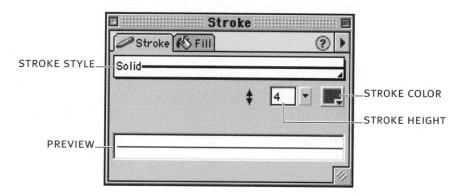

You can set the stroke color in the Stroke panel the same way you set it in the Colors section of the toolbar—just click the color swatch and choose the color that you want, or type the hex code in the text box at the top of the panel. You set the height of the stroke by typing a number in the text box or by dragging the slider to the right of the text box up or down until you get the right height. A line using the settings that you apply in the Stroke panel appears in the preview box, so you can see what the line will look like before you even draw it.

When you draw the rectangle with the rectangle tool, you can hold down the Shift key to constrain it to a perfect square. You can also control the corner radius (roundness) by pressing the up- and down-arrow keys on the keyboard as you draw the rectangle. This technique lets you draw rectangles with rounded corners.

You have created your first Flash movie. Just to get in the habit, finish the exercise by saving your work.

9) Choose File > Save. When the Save As dialog box opens, browse to the MyWork folder on your hard disk, type *myfile1.fla* in the File Name (Windows) or Save document as (Macintosh) text box and click Save.

You just saved your first Flash file to the MyWork folder. Congratulations!

MODIFYING BASIC STROKES AND FILLS

Now that you know how to draw some basic shapes, it's time to start modifying those shapes. You can use the paint bucket, ink bottle, eyedropper, and eraser tools to modify the strokes and fills that you draw. The paint bucket applies fills to shapes, and the ink bottle applies stroke attributes to lines and outlines. You can use the eyedropper to grab attributes from a shape or line so that those attributes can be applied to other shapes or lines, and you can use the eraser to erase portions of a drawing.

You can also make changes to existing strokes and fills by using the arrow tool to select the stroke or fill you want to modify and then changing the settings in the appropriate panel. Use the Mixer and Swatches panels to change the color of a selected stroke or fill. The Stroke panel lets you modify the style, thickness, and color of a selected stroke, and the Fill panel allows you to modify the type and color of a selected fill.

You should still be working in myfile1.fla, which you saved in the preceding exercise, as you continue with the following exercise.

1) Click the paint-bucket tool. In the Colors portion of the toolbar, set the fill color to purple (#CC00CC). Click inside the oval on the stage.
You can use the paint-bucket tool to apply fills to a closed outline, such as an oval. When you click inside the oval, the fill color that you selected should be applied to the oval.

NOTE *You must select a fill color to use the paint-bucket tool. Notice that the no-color button is not available when the paint-bucket tool is selected.*

TIP *Sometimes you click inside an object with the paint-bucket tool and nothing seems to happen. Your problem might be a gap in the outline of your object. You can change the gap size for the paint-bucket tool in the Options section of the toolbar; just click the gap-size button and then choose the Close Large Gaps option from the pop-up menu. Be aware, however, that what might be a large gap to you could be an enormous gap to Flash! So you might need to close some of the gaps in your outline on your own.*

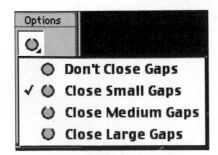

You can also change the color of a fill from the Fill panel. Let's give it a try.

2) Click the arrow tool; then select the fill inside the oval. In the Stroke/Fill window, click the Fill tab; and in the Fill panel, set the fill color to blue (#0000CC).
Make sure that you don't double-click the fill. (As you already know, that would select the outline as well.) You just want to select the fill for now.

When you change the fill color in the Fill panel, the fill in the oval changes to the selected color. You can use the Fill panel to modify the type and color of a selected fill.

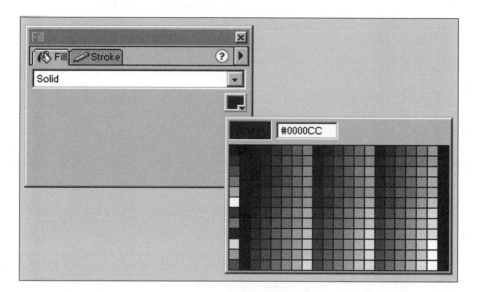

3) Select the eyedropper, and click the outline of the oval.
As you move the eyedropper over the outline, the pointer changes; a small pencil appears to the right of the eyedropper. If you move the eyedropper over the fill, a small paintbrush appears next to the pointer. These indicate the type of shape you are over: the pencil for a stroke, the paintbrush for a fill.

When you click the outline of the oval, the eyedropper picks up the attributes of the oval's stroke and changes to the ink-bottle tool. If you had clicked the fill, the eyedropper would have become the paint bucket.

4) Click a segment of the first line you drew.
When you click the line, the attributes of the oval's outline are applied to it.

5) Select the arrow tool in the toolbar, and double-click the oval's outline. Select any remaining line segments by holding down the Shift key and clicking them.

When you double-click the outline, not only is it selected, but the adjoining line that you just modified is also selected. If any line segments are not selected when you double-click, you can select them by holding down the Shift key and clicking them.

6) In the Stroke panel, change the stroke style to a dashed line, the stroke height to 8, and the stroke color to light blue (#3399FF).

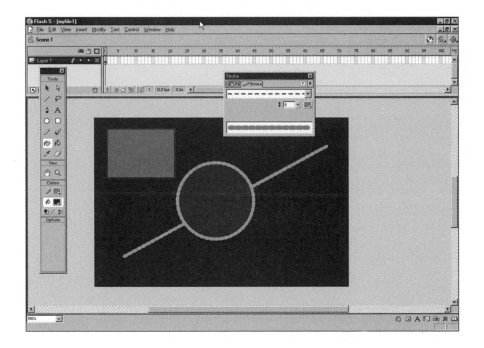

As you can see, the Stroke panel can be used to modify existing strokes, as well as determine what a stroke will look like before it's made.

7) Chose File > Save As, and save your file as myfile2.fla in the MyWork folder.

It's often a good idea to save your files with different names as you work through a project. This method allows you to go back a few versions if you ever need to.

APPLYING GRADIENT FILLS

So far, you've been working with solid colors for fills and outlines. Now it's time to get creative and try your hand at gradient fills. You can use gradient fills to create some great effects. Applying a gradient fill is very much like applying a solid fill, but more options are available to you with gradient fills. In the following exercise, you'll apply a gradient fill to one of your shapes; then you'll modify that fill by using the various options available in Flash.

1) Select the fill of the oval. In the Fill panel, click the fill-style pop-up menu and choose Radial Gradient.

There are two types of gradient fills: linear and radial. A *linear* gradient shades from one side of the filled area to the other in a straight line, and a *radial* gradient shades in a circular pattern.

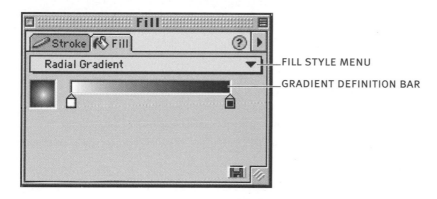

FILL STYLE MENU

GRADIENT DEFINITION BAR

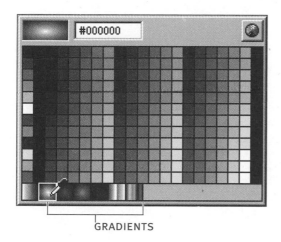

GRADIENTS

There are also two ways of selecting a gradient. You chose the gradient from the Fill panel's pop-up menu, but you could also click the fill color-swatch in the toolbar and choose a radial gradient in the pop-up window, as shown above.

2) In the Fill panel, drag the pointer on the right side of the gradient-definition bar toward the center of the bar.

When you move one of the pointers, you can change the look of the gradient fill. You can add additional pointers (up to a total of eight) to your gradient fill by clicking just below the gradient-definition bar. (To get rid of a pointer you've added, drag it off the bar; it'll disappear.)

3) Click one of the pointers and then click the gradient color-swatch to activate the color pop-up window. Choose a different color from the color pop-up window.

You can modify each of the pointers in the gradient this way to make some very interesting gradient effects.

4) Change the fill style of the selected oval to Linear Gradient.

The fill style menu in the Fill panel lists the following fill styles: None, Solid, Linear Gradient, Radial Gradient, and Bitmap. You can change from one type to another by choosing the new type from this menu. Notice that when you choose Linear Gradient from this menu, the colors in the fill don't change—just the style.

5) Save your file in the MyWork folder as myfile3.fla; then choose File > Close.

You're done with this file for now, so you can close it. If you want to play around with the tools you've learned so far, you can open this saved file later.

USING THE PEN AND SUBSELECTION TOOLS

The pen tool is a technical drawing tool that you use to create precise paths. If you've used the pen tools in Macromedia's FreeHand or Adobe's Illustrator, you'll find that the pen tool in Flash works in much the same way. If you've never worked with a pen tool before, getting used to it will take a little practice.

The subselection tool is used to display and modify the points on pen paths. (You can also display points on lines that you import or create with other Flash drawing tools, such as the pencil, brush, line, oval, or rectangle tool, to adjust those lines.)

TIP *When working with the pen and subselection tools, you'll do a lot of switching back and forth, so learn those shortcuts! The keyboard shortcut for the pen tool is **P**, and the shortcut for the subselection tool is **A**.*

1) Create a new movie (File > New). Select the pen tool in the toolbar. In the Stroke panel, set the stroke color to black, the stroke style to Solid, and the stroke height to 2.

Because you selected the Show Precise Cursors option in the Preferences dialog box earlier in this lesson, the pointer will change to an X when you select the pen tool. The center of this X is where the pen tool will draw your lines.

2) Click the stage. Move the pointer and click again. Click a third time at a different point.

Each time you click, you create a point for a new line. You can keep clicking the stage to draw more points.

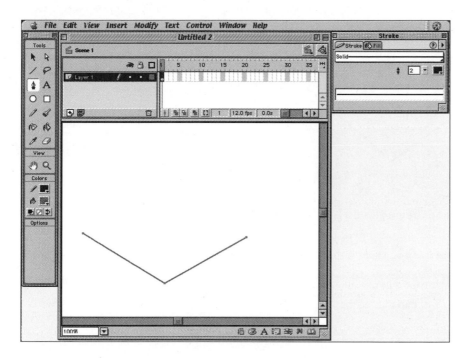

When you're ready to stop adding segments to a line, double-click the last point or deselect the pen tool by selecting another tool in the toolbar. You can also Ctrl-click (Windows) or Command-click (Macintosh) to stop adding segments.

3) Click the subselection tool in the toolbar.

If you completed your line in step 2 (by double-clicking, Ctrl- or Command-clicking, or selecting a new tool), you probably noticed that the line turned black. That happened because the line was no longer selected. When you click the subselection tool, all the line segments on the stage again become selected (highlighted blue). You should be able to see the points on the line; they are indicated by small squares, as you can see below. You can drag these squares around to reposition the points in your line.

POINT ON THE LINE

4) Select the pen tool. Click the stage and drag.

When you click and drag on the stage, you create a curve point. You'll notice something new here: when you create a curve point with the pen tool, you get handles around the point. The handles are known as Bézier handles, and you can move them with the subselection tool to modify the shape of your curve.

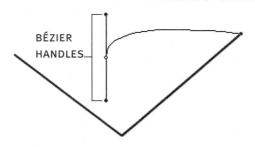

5) Click and drag a second time.

A curved line should appear between your two curve points. You can also create a curved line between a straight line segment and a curve point.

After you draw a curve, you can continue to add points to the line simply by clicking the stage. You can also add additional curves by clicking and dragging on the stage.

TIP *You can change curve points to corner points and vice versa. With the pen tool selected, move the pointer over the points in your line. When the pointer changes to a crosshair with a small carat next to it, it indicates that the point you are over is a curve point. Clicking a curve point with the pen tool changes it to a corner point. You can change a corner point to a curve point by clicking it with the subselection tool and holding down the Alt (Windows) or Option (Macintosh) key while you drag the point.*

6) With the pen tool selected, move the pointer over a point in your line until the pointer changes to a crosshair with a minus sign next to it. Click the point.

Clicking a corner point with the pen tool removes the point. The figures below show a line before and after having a point removed.

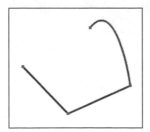 

7) Save your work as pentool.fla in the MyWork folder on your hard disk, and choose File > Close.

If you ever feel that you need some more practice using the pen and subselection tools, you can just open this file and play around some more. For the time being, you're done with this movie, so save a little memory and close it.

ARRANGING AND ALIGNING ELEMENTS

The Align panel lets you align selected elements on the horizontal or vertical axis. You can align objects horizontally and vertically along the edges or center of the selected elements; or horizontally and vertically along the edges or center of the stage. An element's edges are determined by the bounding boxes enclosing it. You can also use the Align panel to distribute selected elements so that their centers or edges are evenly spaced, and to resize selected elements so that the horizontal or vertical dimensions of all elements match those of the largest selected element.

1) Open shapes.fla from the Lesson01/Assets folder, and choose the arrow tool in the toolbar.

This file contains six colored circles. You'll arrange and align these circles on the stage.

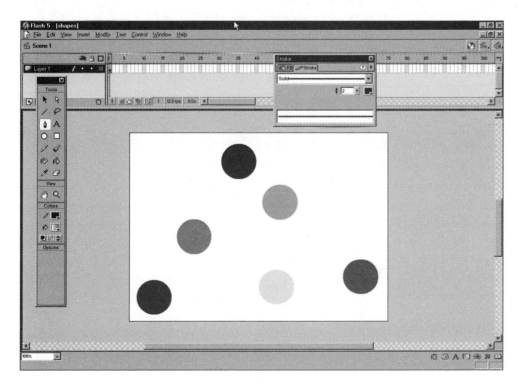

2) Open the Align panel by choosing Window > Panels > Align.

The Align panel consists of several buttons, which you can use to arrange and align selected elements. These buttons are arranged in groups, based on their function.

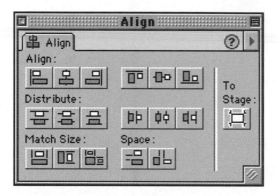

The Align and Distribute groups include buttons that let you align or distribute elements on the stage by their left edges, horizontal centers, right edges, top edges, vertical centers, or bottom edges.

There's also a Match Size group, which lets you match the width or height, or both, of elements. Finally, the Space group lets you space objects evenly, either vertically or horizontally.

In addition, the To Stage button lets you align or distribute elements in relation to the stage, rather than in relation to other selected elements.

3) Choose Edit > Select All to select all the circles on the stage. In the Align panel, click the button to distribute the horizontal centers of the elements.

If you can't figure out from the icons which button distributes the horizontal centers, use the Tooltips feature. Let the pointer rest over the icons one at a time until the labels pop up.

When you click the button to distribute the horizontal centers, the selected circles are spread out evenly, based on their horizontal centers. This distribution is based on the outermost elements.

4) In the Align panel, click the To Stage button to select it; then click the button to align the vertical centers.

When you click the To Stage button, the alignment effects that you apply are based on the bounding box of the stage, instead of the other selected elements.

5) Deselect all the circles by clicking the stage outside any circles. Use the arrow tool to select the red circle on the left side of the stage. In the Align panel, click the button to match the heights of the elements.

The Match Size: height button resizes the selected circle so that it matches the height of the movie, because you had the To Stage button selected when you made this modification.

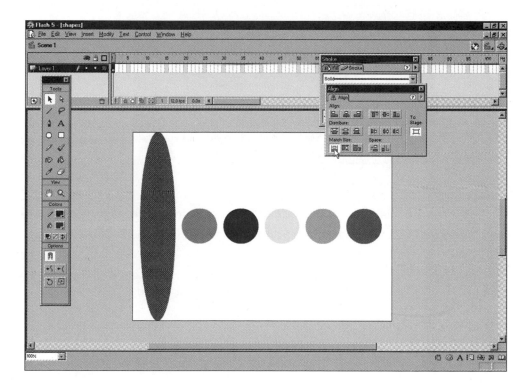

6) Save your work as shapes1.fla in the MyWork folder on your hard disk.

Keep this file open, because you're going to continue working with it in the next exercise.

ROTATING AND SCALING ELEMENTS

You can scale and rotate lines, fills, and other elements on the stage. By selecting a shape and choosing Modify > Transform > Scale, you can grab one of the handles bounding the fill or line to make the fill or line larger or smaller. By choosing Modify > Transform > Rotate, you can skew lines and fills and turn them in other directions. You can make numeric transformations by choosing Modify > Transform > Scale and Rotate to open the Scale and Rotate dialog box.

1) Make sure that you still have the file you worked with in the preceding exercise open. Choose Modify > Transform > Scale and Rotate.

The Scale and Rotate dialog box opens.

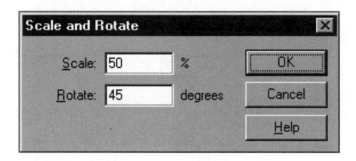

2) Use the arrow tool to select the red oval on the left side of the stage. In the Scale and Rotate dialog box, type 50 in the Scale text box and 45 in the Rotate text box; then click OK.

When you click OK, the dialog box closes. The oval becomes half the size it was before you applied the transformation (50%), and is rotated 45 degrees.

You can use the Scale and Rotate dialog box to apply precise transformations to elements on the stage. Also, you can scale and rotate an element at the same time when you use this dialog box.

TIP *Remember to double-click with the arrow tool to select both the fill and the stroke of the red oval. A single click selects only the fill.*

3) Select the blue circle near the middle of the stage. Choose Modify > Transform > Scale, or click the scale button in the Options area of the toolbar. Drag the handles that appear around the circle to make it taller.

A set of rectangular handles appears around the element. You can drag these handles to scale the selected element horizontally, vertically, or both. Just drag one of the corner handles to scale the selected element proportionally, or drag one of the center handles to scale the element horizontally or vertically.

32

**4) Select the magenta circle on the right side of the stage. Choose Modify >
Transform > Rotate, or click the rotate button in the Options area of the toolbar.
Use the handles that appear around the circle to skew it to the right.**

When you choose the Rotate command or button, a set of circular handles appears
around the element. Drag the center handles to skew the element, and use the
corner handles to rotate it. To skew the circle to the right, drag the top-center handle
to the right. You can see the results of your work in the figure below.

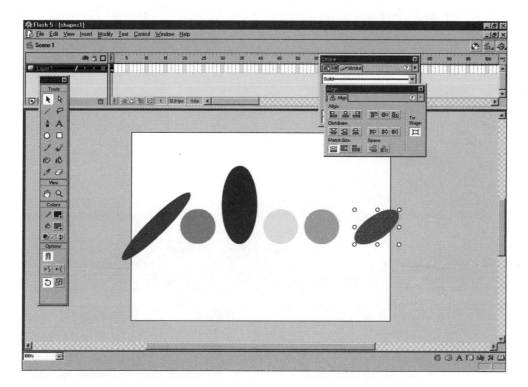

5) Save the file as shapes2.fla in the MyWork folder. Close the file when you're done.

You're done with this file, but if you want to practice modifying shapes later, you can
open this file and work on it some more.

GETTING HELP

Even after you finish reading this book, you might still need some extra help with
Flash. That should be no problem, because many resources are available. Some of
these resources come with Flash, and others are available on the Internet.

1) Choose Help > Using Flash to open the Flash help files.

The Flash help files will open in your browser. The help files include a simple tutorial that will give you even more practice using Flash. The topics in the help files are searchable, so you can easily find any topic that you might need additional help with.

2) Choose Help > Macromedia Dashboard.

This command opens Macromedia Dashboard for Flash, which provides access to resources within the Flash development community. If you're connected to the Internet, you can update the Dashboard with the latest information by clicking the Update button.

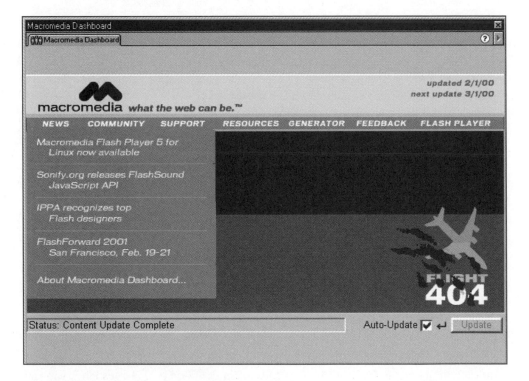

3) Open your browser, and visit the Flash Support Center at http://www.macromedia.com/support/flash.

The Flash Support Center is updated regularly and contains the latest information on Flash.

4) Browse to one of the Flash resource sites listed in Appendix C.

FlashLite, which is located at http://www.flashlite.net, is one example of the resource sites available. Flash developers around the world have taken the time to create sites with tutorials, source files, message boards, articles, and much more. Make full use of these resource sites, and you'll be working with Flash like an old pro in no time.

5) Sign up for one of the mailing lists listed in Appendix C.

Flashnewbie is a great mailing list for beginners—just go to http://chattyfig.figleaf.com to sign up.

WHAT YOU HAVE LEARNED

In this lesson, you have:

- Opened Flash and created a new movie (pages 8–9)

- Checked the settings of the Flash preferences and modified the pointer display (pages 10–11)

- Rearranged the panels to create a custom panel layout (pages 11–14)

- Used the drawing tools to create basic shapes (pages 22–24)

- Applied gradient fills (pages 24–26)

- Modified fills and strokes by using Flash's tools and panels (pages 26–29)

- Aligned and distributed shapes on the stage (pages 29–32)

- Rotated and scaled shapes on the stage (pages 32–33)

- Learned where to look for additional help (pages 33–35)

using graphics and text

LESSON 2

As your movies get more complex, you will want to use more complicated graphics and text. In this lesson, you'll learn how to import graphics into Flash, how to convert bitmap graphics to vector graphics, and how to use the text tool and Character panel to work with text.

But before you start adding graphic and text elements to your movies, you'll look at some of the tools Flash offers for controlling and modifying elements. Flash provides multiple tools to let you precisely control the placement of elements, including rulers, guidelines and the Info panel. In this lesson, you'll learn to use all three.

The abstract-looking dolphin was created using a photograph (a bitmap) which was converted to a vector graphic.

Site created by Fig Leaf Software

In addition, Flash uses layers and guide layers to let you control the way your elements interact. You'll add and modify layers, and you'll work with the layer display to show, hide, lock, and unlock different layers.

Throughout the lesson, your exercises will build upon one another to create a complex graphic that will be the first page of the Neptune Resorts Web site. You'll start simply, but by the time you complete this lesson, you'll have a page with graphics, text, and borders.

WHAT YOU WILL LEARN

In this lesson, you will:

- Use rulers and guide lines to position elements on the stage
- Use the Info panel to position elements on the stage
- Add and modify layers
- Import artwork
- Convert a bitmap graphic to a vector graphic
- Group elements
- Add and modify text

APPROXIMATE TIME

It usually takes about one hour to complete this lesson.

LESSON FILES

Media Files:

Lesson02/Assets/layout.swf
Lesson02/Assets/undersea.jpg
Lesson02/Assets/dolphin.jpg

Starting File:

Lesson02/Assets/neptune1.fla

Completed Project:

neptune8.fla

USING RULERS AND GUIDES TO POSITION ELEMENTS

When you are working in Flash, you can use rulers and draggable guides to position elements precisely on the stage. In Flash 5, you can even drag guides from the rulers onto the stage.

1) Open neptune1.fla. Choose View > Rulers to turn on the rulers. Choose View > Guides > Snap to Guides, and select Snap to Guides.

You can find neptune1.fla in the Lesson02/Assets folder on the CD-ROM that comes with this book.

When you choose View > Rulers, the rulers appear along the top and left sides of the stage. Like real-world rulers, the rulers show units of measure and are useful for positioning elements on the stage.

TIP *By default, Flash 5's rulers measure in pixels. If you'd rather see measurements in inches, decimal inches, points, centimeters, or millimeters, choose Modify > Movie, and in the Movie Properties dialog box, choose a different unit of measure from the Ruler Units pop-up menu.*

If there is a check next to Snap to Guides, it is already selected. Selecting Snap to Guides forces anything drawn near a guide to snap to the line. This option makes it much easier to position your elements at exactly the right spot.

2) Click the ruler at the top of the stage and, holding down the mouse button, drag to the stage.

When you click and drag the ruler, a green line appears on the stage. This is your guide.

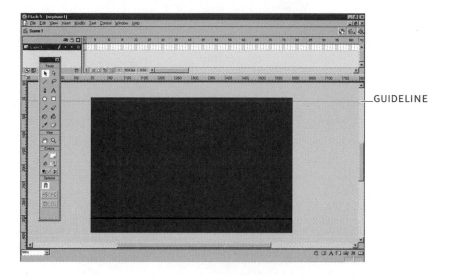

GUIDELINE

3) Position the guide at the 10-pixel mark. Then position three more guides at spots 10 pixels from the bottom, the right side, and the left side of the movie.

Use the rulers to help you place your guides properly. Each of the large, unnumbered hash marks on the rulers represents 10 pixels.

You should end up with four guides on the stage. They'll create a rectangle, which you'll use to draw a border for your movie.

TIP *To reposition a guide, select the arrow tool; then click and drag the guide. To remove a guide, use the arrow tool to drag the guide to the horizontal or vertical ruler.*

39

4) Select the rectangle tool. In the Options area of the toolbox, click the button to open the Rectangle Settings dialog box. In the Rectangle Settings dialog box, set the corner radius to 0. In the Color area of the toolbox, select the fill-color swatch, and click the no-color button.

You're going to use the rectangle tool to draw the border around your movie. Setting the corner radius of the rectangle tool to 0 ensures that the rectangle will have square corners, rather than rounded ones. Setting the fill to no color means that only the stroke (the outside edge) of the rectangle will appear.

But you're not finished defining the look of your rectangle.

5) In the Stroke panel, set the stroke style to Solid, the width to 1, and the color to white.

If the Stroke panel is not already open, choose Window > Panels > Stroke to open it.

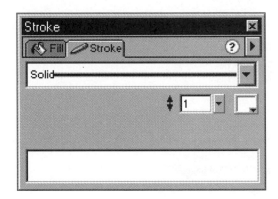

The Stroke panel lets you modify all the properties of the stroke. If you wanted to modify only the color of the stroke, you could also use the stroke-color swatch in the Color section of the toolbox, or the stroke-color swatch in the Mixer panel.

Can you picture your rectangle? In the next step, you'll see it.

6) Drag the rectangle tool over the stage, using the guides to help you.

Oops! You can't see the rectangle after all. The rectangle snaps right to the guides, and when you release the mouse button, the guides are hiding the rectangle.

If you're really curious, choose View > Guides > Show Guides to hide the guides. You should see a fine-lined white rectangle exactly where the guides were positioned. Choose View > Guides > Show Guides to turn the guides back on.

If you're less curious, you can just look at the following figure. If you followed all the steps, there is a rectangle on the stage.

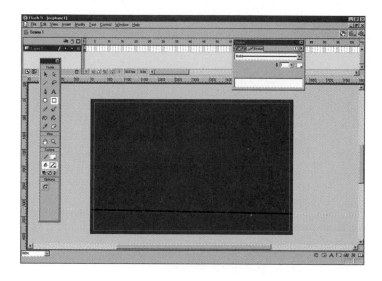

7) Drag another set of four guides onto the stage and line them up precisely with the outer edges of the movie. Without changing any settings, draw a second rectangle to form an outer border for the movie.

When you hide the guides, you should see a nice inner and outer border for your movie.

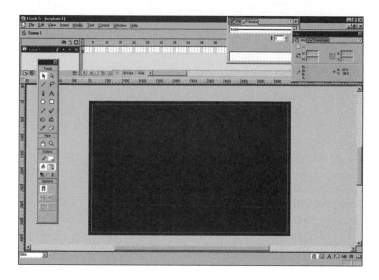

You're going to continue working with this movie, so now is a good time to save it.

8) Save your movie as neptune2.fla in the MyWork folder on your hard disk.

ADDING LAYERS

Layers act like a stack of transparent sheets. They are "stacked" on top of one another, and you can see their stacking order in the timeline. The layer on top is the highest in the stacking order, and the layer at the bottom is the lowest in the stacking order. Objects in a higher layer can obscure objects in a lower layer.

Layers are great for organizing content in your movie, because ungrouped objects on separate layers do not segment each other when they overlap. You can also name layers, hide their contents, and lock them so that they cannot be edited.

In the following exercise, you add a layer to your movie. You should still have neptune2.fla from the last exercise open.

1) Choose Modify > Layer. In the Layer Properties dialog box, type *Outlines* in the Name field, and click OK.

When you choose Modify > Layer, the Layer Properties dialog box opens.

As you can see in the layer section of the timeline, you have only one layer in your movie right now; it's currently called Layer 1. Because you have only one layer, the Layer Properties dialog box displays the properties of that layer.

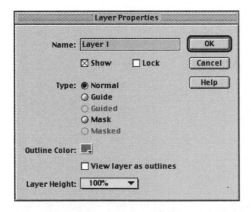

After you type *Outlines* in the Name field and click OK, the Layer Properties dialog box closes. The name of the layer changes from Layer 1 to Outlines.

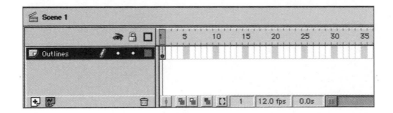

The more complex your movie is, the more layers it is likely to contain, and the harder it will be to keep track of which layer is which. It's a good idea to name all the layers. And try to give the layers meaningful names; that practice will make it much easier to find the layer you're looking for.

2) Choose Insert > Layer to add another layer to the movie.

The new layer is added above the Outlines layer, which means that it sits at the top of the layer stacking order. Whenever you add a layer to your movie, it's added above the currently selected layer. In this case, you have only one layer, so it's selected by default and the new layer is added above it. Objects in a higher layer can obscure objects in the layers below it, so if you add anything to this new layer, it may obscure the contents of the Outlines layer.

3) Click Layer 2 to select it, and choose Modify > Layer. In the Layer Properties dialog box, type _Navigation Bar_ in the Name field, and click OK.

The layer is now named Navigation Bar. As you start to add layers, you must remember to select a layer before you attempt to modify its properties in the Layer Properties dialog box.

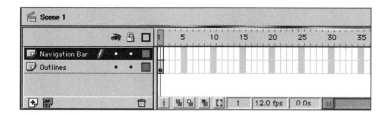

4) Save the file.

USING THE INFO PANEL

Rules and guides aren't the only way to position elements precisely. You can also use the Info panel. The Info panel allows you to specify exact coordinates for an element on the stage. It also lets you define an element's width and height.

In the following exercise, you'll use the Info panel to define and position a rectangle that will become the navigation bar. You should still have the file from the preceding exercise open. If not, start by opening it.

1) With the Navigation Bar layer selected, use the rectangle tool to draw a small rectangle in the center of the stage.

The rectangle tool's settings should be the same as they were for the first exercise in this lesson: a corner radius of 0, a fill that is no color, and a stroke that is solid,

43

1-point, and white. The dimensions and location of the rectangle don't matter, however, because you'll be modifying them later.

TIP *If you need to change the rectangle settings after you've placed the rectangle on the stage, use the arrow tool to select it. Remember, you need to double-click to select the whole rectangle. Then change the settings in the Stroke panel, Fill panel, or Color area of the toolbar.*

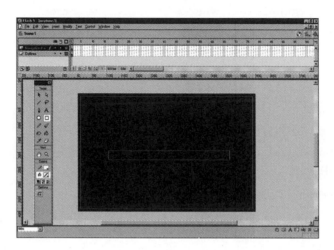

Because you drew the new rectangle in a different layer from your original rectangles, the new rectangle won't segment the border no matter where you place it. This will be very useful in later lessons, because you'll want to move the rectangle in the Navigation Bar layer separately from those in the Outlines layer.

2) Select the arrow tool. Double-click the outline of the rectangle to select it.
When you double-click the rectangle, the entire outline becomes selected. If you want to select a single segment of the rectangle, just click that segment. You can select multiple segments by Shift-clicking each segment.

TIP *You don't have to click the arrow tool to select it. On your keyboard, press V; the arrow tool is selected automatically. All the tools in the toolbox have shortcut keys like this. Just move your mouse over the tool, and you'll see the shortcut in the ToolTip that appears.*

3) Choose Window > Panels > Info to open the Info panel.
The Info panel lets you view and modify the dimensions and location (X and Y) of anything on the stage. Each setting is labeled: W (Width), H (Height), X, and Y. The name and type of the object selected are also listed in the Info panel. In this case, you have a shape selected, so a graphic indicating this fact and the label *Shape* appear in the top-left corner of the panel.

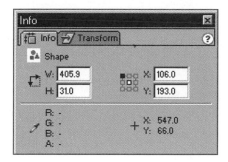

4) In the Info panel, set the Width (W) to 650, Height (H) to 24, X to –25, and Y to 260.

After you type each value in the appropriately labeled text box, press Enter (Windows), Return (Macintosh), or Tab to make the setting take effect. You'll see the changes take place immediately.

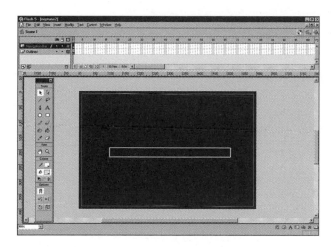

5) Save your file as neptune3.fla.

It's a good idea to save your file with a different name this time, just in case you need to go back to the file that you were working on in the preceding exercises.

USING A GUIDE LAYER

Not only can you use layers to organize your content, but you can also use special layers called *guide layers* as layout and drawing aids. Guide layers are not exported in your Flash Player movie and do not add any weight to your final file size. Guide layers are noted in your movie by a guide icon to the left of the layer name.

Guide layers are different from guides. Guides can be only straight lines, and they are not actually contained on a layer. Guide layers can contain graphics of any shape, which you can use as visual aids for drawing complex art in Flash.

In this exercise, you'll add a guide layer to your movie and then lock it.

1) Click the Show/Hide All Layers icon.
You can find the Show/Hide All Layers icon above the top layer in the layer section of the timeline. When you click it, Flash hides all the layers in the movie. In this case, everything in the movie is hidden. This feature is useful because it lets you draw a somewhat complex graphic without all the other elements getting in the way.

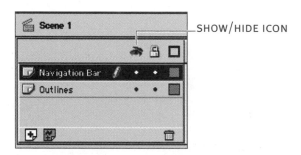

SHOW/HIDE ICON

2) Choose Insert > Layer. Name the layer *Layout Guide*.
Choosing Insert > Layer creates a third layer. It doesn't matter where in the layer stacking order this layer is added, because you're going to move it later in this exercise. Just remember that the layer will be added above whichever layer was selected when you chose Insert > Layer.

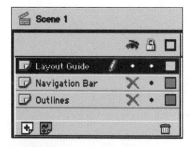

TIP *There's more than one way to change the layer's name. In earlier exercises, you chose Modify > Layer and typed the name in the Name field of the Layer Properties dialog box. But you can also double-click the layer name to highlight it and then type the new name over the highlighted name. Another method is to double-click the layer icon next to the name to open the Layer Properties dialog box and then change the name in the Name field.*

3) Select the Layout Guide layer, and drag it to the top of the layer stacking order.

You can move a layer by clicking its name and dragging it up or down. When you drag the Layout Guide layer to the top of the layer stacking order, it is listed first. This puts everything in the Layout Guide layer above the contents of every other layer. Remember, the layer on top is the highest in the stacking order, and the layer at the bottom is the lowest in the stacking order. Objects in a higher layer can obscure objects in a lower layer.

Depending on which layer was selected when you added the Layout Guide layer, the Layout Guide layer may already appear at the top of the layer stacking order.

Right now, there's nothing in this layer, but you're about to add a graphic to it. You will use this graphic as a guide to place elements in your movie.

4) Choose File > Import. Browse to layout.swf in the Lesson02/Assets folder, and select it. Click Open (Windows) or Add and Import (Macintosh).

Two green rectangles and some text appear on the stage.

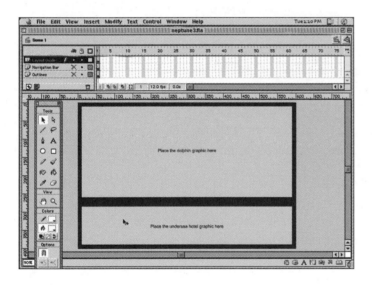

You just imported an SWF file, which was created in Flash by the artist who designed the Neptune Resorts site that you will be working on throughout this book. The rectangles appear in the position that they occupied in the Flash movie in which they were created. Later, you'll use this graphic to position elements in the movie.

5) Right-click (Windows) or Control-click (Macintosh) the Layout Guide layer name, and choose Guide from the pop-up menu.

When you right-click or Control-click a layer name, a contextual menu appears. Choosing Guide from this menu changes the layer into a guide layer. A bracket appears to the left of the layer name.

You can now use this guide layer to place elements in your Flash movie. The contents of the guide layer appear only while you are editing; they will not appear in the finished movie.

6) In the layer section of the timeline, click Layout Guide to select it. Next to Layout Guide, click the dot in the column below the padlock icon.

The padlock icon is the Lock/Unlock All Layers icon. When you lock a layer, you can no longer select anything in that layer, but you can still see its contents. You are also prevented from adding anything to the layer.

If you were to click the padlock itself, all the layers would be locked, and you would be unable to change anything in your movie without either adding a new layer or unlocking one of the old layers. When you click a dot in the column below the Lock/Unlock All Layers icon, a padlock appears in place of the dot. This padlock indicates that the individual layer is locked.

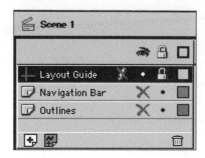

In the case of the Layout Guide layer, locking it is useful because you still need to use it as a guide to position elements in the movie, but you don't want to move anything in that layer accidentally.

7) Save your movie as neptune4.fla in the MyWork folder.
Because you just made a major change in your movie, now is a good time to save it.

IMPORTING ARTWORK

You are by no means limited to using artwork that you can draw in Flash. Use your favorite drawing program to make your artwork, or import existing artwork to use in your Flash movie. Flash will import different formats depending on whether QuickTime 4 or later is installed. Even without QuickTime 4, the following formats can be imported both in Windows and on a Macintosh: GIF, JPEG, PNG, Adobe Illustrator (EPS, AI, version 6.0 or earlier), AutoCAD DXF (DXF), FreeHand (FH7, FH8, FH9), FutureSplash Player (SPL), and Flash Player (SWF) files.

In Windows, you can also import Bitmap (BMP), Enhanced Windows Metafile (EMF), and Windows Metafile (WMF) files.

If QuickTime 4 is installed, you can also import MacPaint (PNTG), Photoshop (PSD), QuickTime Image (QTIF), QuickTime Movie (MOV), Silicon Graphics (SAI), TGA (TGF), and TIFF (TIFF) files.

Flash supports two types of image formats: vector and raster. *Vector* graphics are created with lines, curves, and descriptions of their properties. Commands within the vector graphic tell your computer how to display the lines and shapes, what colors to use, how wide to make the lines, and so on. You might have already used a vector drawing program, such as Macromedia FreeHand, to create such images. *Raster* images, also called *bitmaps*, are created with pixels. When you create a raster image, you map out the placement and color of each pixel, and the resulting bitmap is what you see on the screen.

In this exercise, you will import a graphic to add to your movie.

1) Select the Layout Guide layer, and add a new layer above it. Name the new layer *Undersea Hotel Graphic*.
This new layer is where you will place your imported graphic.

2) With the Undersea Hotel Graphic layer selected, choose File > Import. Browse to undersea.jpg in the Lesson02/Assets folder, and select it. Click Open (Windows) or Add and Import (Macintosh).

A bitmap graphic, undersea.jpg, appears on the stage. Though Flash is a vector-based authoring tool, you can also use bitmap images in Flash. Bitmap images are not created natively in Flash; you need to use an external application such as Macromedia Fireworks to create the files and then import them into Flash.

Unlike vector graphics, bitmap images are not very scalable. Simple bitmap images are often larger in file size than simple vector graphics, but very complex bitmap images (photographs, for example) are often smaller than comparable vector graphics. Bitmap formats that Flash can use include Bitmap (BMP), GIF Image, JPEG Image, PNG Image, Macintosh PICT Image, MacPaint Image (PNT), and TIFF Image.

3) Select the arrow tool, and double-click the graphic that you just imported. In the Info panel, set the Width (W) to 580 and the Height (H) to 105.

You can resize imported artwork just as you can resize artwork drawn in Flash, but be careful when you resize imported bitmap graphics. When you scale a bitmap, you can get *pixelation*, which means that parts of the graphic no longer appear smooth.

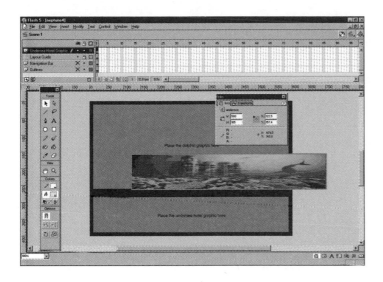

TIP *If the Info panel doesn't appear on your screen, choose Window > Panels > Info.*

Now you need to place the bitmap graphic in the correct position.

4) Use the arrow tool to drag the artwork to the position indicated by the graphic in the Layout Guide layer.

This step is where the guide layer comes in handy. You use it to position the graphic in the correct location.

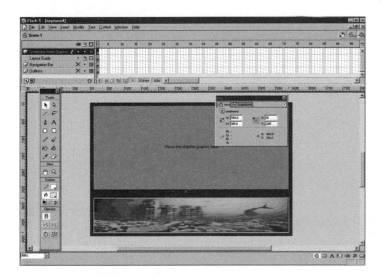

If you want the graphic to be placed even more precisely, you can use the Info panel to set the X to 10 and the Y to 285.

5) Lock the Undersea Hotel Graphic layer, and save your movie as neptune5.fla in the MyWork folder.

You're done with the Undersea Hotel Graphic layer, so you don't want to alter its contents accidentally. Locking it will prevent you from making unintentional changes.

CONVERTING BITMAPS TO VECTORS

One problem with bringing bitmaps into Flash is that they can substantially increase the size of the movie file. And because they are raster rather than vector graphics, you can't edit them in the same way that you'd edit a native vector graphic. In addition, bitmaps don't scale well. Fortunately, Flash lets you convert bitmaps to vector graphics by using the Trace Bitmap command.

Before you start converting every bitmap in sight to a vector graphic, you need to be aware of a few caveats. Complex images are not good candidates for converting to vector graphics unless you plan to reduce the number of colors substantially. (You would do this by increasing the Color Threshold. This change can produce an interesting "painterly" effect.)

In the following exercise, you will import a photograph into your page, and change it from a bitmap to a vector graphic.

1) In neptune5.fla, select the Undersea Hotel Graphic layer. Choose Insert > Layer, and name the new layer Dolphin Graphic.

Do you know why you started by selecting the Undersea Hotel Graphic layer? Doing so ensures that your new layer appears at the top of the layer stacking order. You could also simply add a new layer and then drag it to the top of the stacking order.

You will add an imported bitmap graphic to this new layer.

2) Select the Dolphin Graphic layer, and import dolphin.jpg (located in the Lesson02/Assets folder). Position the imported dolphin.jpg in the space indicated by the graphic in the Layout Guide layer.

Once again, the guide layer comes in handy. The graphic isn't the same size as the rectangle in the guide layer, but you can still use the rectangle as a guide for positioning the graphic.

3) Choose Modify > Trace Bitmap.

The bitmap should still be selected, with a gray outline around it, before you choose Modify > Trace Bitmap.

When you choose the Trace Bitmap command, the Trace Bitmap dialog box opens. You're about to turn dolphin.jpg into a vector graphic.

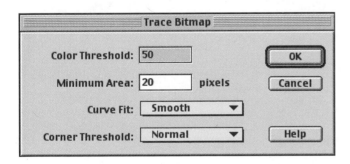

4) In the Trace Bitmap dialog box, type 50 in the Color Threshold field and 20 in the Minimum Area field. From the Curve Fit pop-up menu, choose Smooth; from the Corner Threshold pop-up menu, choose Normal. Click OK. Click the stage outside the graphic.

When you click OK, Flash converts the bitmap to a vector graphic. Clicking the stage outside the graphic lets you see the results.

When Flash converts a bitmap to a vector, it compares adjacent pixels in the bitmap. If the difference in the RGB values of the adjacent pixels is less than the color threshold, those pixels are considered to be the same color. Therefore, setting a lower threshold number results in a higher number of colors, and setting a higher threshold number results in a lower number of colors. The color threshold can be a value between 1 and 500.

The Minimum Area value determines the number of surrounding pixels to consider when assigning a color to a pixel and should be set between 1 and 1000. The Curve Fit setting determines how smoothly curves are drawn, and the Corner Threshold setting determines whether sharp edges are retained or smoothed out.

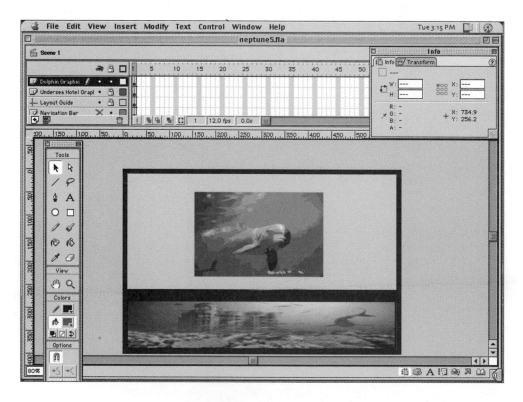

5) Save the movie as neptune6.fla in the MyWork folder.

WORKING WITH GROUPS

You can manipulate elements on the stage as a single object by grouping them. This capability can be very useful when you're working with a complex vector graphic, because as you learned in Lesson 1, each piece of a vector graphic is treated as a separate object in Flash. If you have a graphic that contains several pieces, manipulating all the pieces consistently can be difficult.

In this exercise, you will group all the different elements of the dolphin graphic. Start by making sure that all layers in neptune6.fla except the dolphin graphic layer are locked or hidden; if you've been following instructions, they should be.

1) Select the arrow tool, and click the traced bitmap.

When you click the traced bitmap, only a portion of it is selected. That's because each discrete area of color in the traced bitmap is a separate element. You can modify each individual element as you would modify any fill in Flash.

You're going to group all the elements in the graphic. Before you start, you need to select the elements that are going to be part of that group. In other words, you need to select everything in the Dolphin Graphic layer.

2) Choose Edit > Select All.

Everything that is on the stage in an unlocked and unhidden layer is selected.

3) Choose Modify > Group.

Everything that you had selected—the entire traced bitmap in the Dolphin Graphic layer—is now part of a group. A blue bounding box appears around the group, indicating that it is a single selected element.

4) Double-click the group.

In the top-left corner of the screen, just below the menu bar, a graphic appears, indicating that you are editing a group. Anything that is not part of the group becomes dimmed. You can now edit any part of the group without disturbing the rest of the movie.

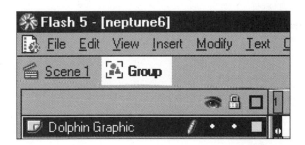

5) Drag a marquee across the top edge of the dolphin graphic. Press the Delete or Backspace key. Repeat for the left, bottom, and right sides of the graphic.

When you traced the bitmap, some of the edges might have become a little less than perfect. By selecting and deleting the edges, you ensure that they are completely straight.

TIP *If you accidentally select too much, just click outside the graphic to deselect and try again.*

The dolphin graphic should now have four clean edges.

6) Click the Scene 1 icon next to the Group icon.

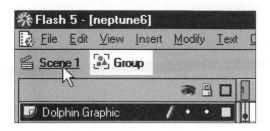

This step takes you back to the movie, so you are no longer editing the group. You can also go back to the movie by double-clicking anywhere outside the group.

7) Select the grouped dolphin graphic. In the Info panel, set the Height (H) to 580, Width (W) to 250, X to 10, and Y to 10.

The entire graphic reflects that changes you made in the Info panel. If you hadn't placed the vector graphic in a group, modifying those settings would have been much harder. Notice that the Info panel indicates that you have a group selected.

8) Save the movie as neptune7.fla in the MyWork folder.

ADDING TEXT

You can use the text tool to set the size, typeface, style, spacing, color, and alignment of text. And in Flash 5, you can use the Text Options panel to classify your text as static text, dynamic text, or input text.

1) Add a new layer, named Tagline, to neptune7.fla. Drag this new layer to the top of the layer stacking order.

The tagline is separate from the other elements in the movie, so you should add it to a separate layer.

2) Select the text tool. Choose Window > Panels > Character.

The Character panel lets you set the font, font height, tracking, character position, and text color for a block of text. You can also toggle the kerning, bold, and italic settings in the Character panel. Another great feature of the Character panel is the URL setting, which allows you to assign a URL to a block of text. You'll learn more about this feature in a later lesson.

3) In the Character panel, choose Arial from the Font drop-down menu. Set the font height to 18 and tracking to 10. Set the text color to pale blue.

For the moment, leave all the other settings in the Character panel in their default positions. Specifically, kerning should be selected, bold and italic should not be selected, the character position should be normal, and the URL text box should be empty.

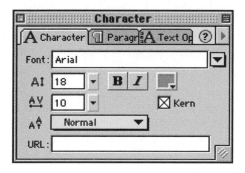

4) Click the stage and type *DIVE INTO PARADISE.*

When you click the stage, a text box appears. Anything that you type appears in that text box, using the properties that you set in the Character panel.

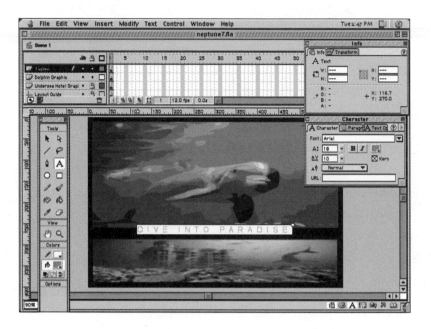

TIP *If your text doesn't look quite right, compare the settings of your Character panel against those in the figure on the previous page to confirm that your settings were at the defaults.*

5) Click the arrow tool. Click the text box to select it.

In this case, you can't just press *V* on your keyboard to switch to the arrow tool, because that will cause the letter *v* to appear in the text box. And if you don't switch to the arrow tool before you click the stage, Flash will create another text box.

If you accidentally double-click the text box that you just created, Flash will switch back to the text tool. Make sure that you click the text box once.

6) Use the Info panel to set the Y of the selected text box to 262.

The text box is now in the space between the dolphin and undersea-hotel graphics.

7) Choose Window > Panels > Align to open the Align panel. Click the To Stage button; then click the button to align the horizontal centers of elements.

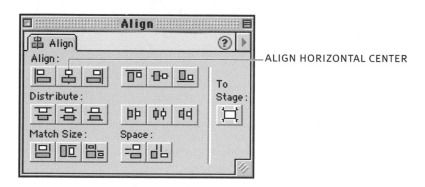

The text box jumps to the horizontal center of the stage. As you learned in Lesson 1, the Align panel lets you align selected elements in a variety of ways.

8) Unhide all the layers by clicking the Show/Hide All Layers icon twice. Drag the Outlines layer to the top of the layer stacking order; then drag the Navigation Bar layer above that.

When you click the Show/Hide All Layers icon a single time, all of the layers are hidden. Clicking a second time reveals all the layers.

Your movie now looks like something you can put on the Web. You've made some major changes, so make sure that you save the movie before you continue to the next lesson.

9) Save your movie as neptune8.fla in the MyWork folder.

WHAT YOU HAVE LEARNED

In this lesson, you have:

- Used rulers and guidelines to place a rectangle precisely in your movie (pages 38–39)

- Organized your movie's content by adding and modifying multiple layers (pages 42–43)

- Used the Info panel to modify the size and location of elements (pages 43–44)

- Added a guide layer (pages 45–49)

- Imported artwork (pages 49–52)

- Converted a bitmap graphic to a vector graphic (pages 52–54)

- Grouped elements to modify them (pages 55–59)

- Added and modified text (pages 59–62)

using symbols and the library

LESSON 3

You've learned to use Flash's tools and panels to create, modify, position, and import basic elements—such as text and graphics—for your Flash movies. But even when you're using simple elements, your movies can quickly become large and complex. In this lesson, you'll learn to use symbols, libraries, and the Movie Explorer to manage your movies and keep them small, fast, and organized.

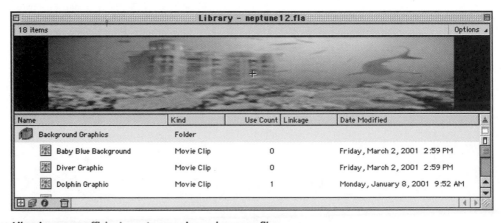

Libraries are an efficient way to organize and manage files.

WHAT YOU WILL LEARN

In this lesson, you will:

- Create a symbol

- Use and organize the library

- Use symbols from an existing movie's library

- Create and use a shared library

- Create a common library

- Use symbol instances

- Use the Movie Explorer

APPROXIMATE TIME

It usually takes about one hour to complete this lesson.

LESSON FILES

Media Files:

Lesson03/Assets/assets.fla

Lesson03/Assets/Neptune Resorts Assets.fla

Starting File:

Lesson03/Assets/neptune9.fla

Completed Project:

neptune13.fla

CONVERTING A GRAPHIC TO A SYMBOL

When you are working in Flash, each object you create increases the size of your final movie. What if you could reuse objects instead? You can. Any object that you intend to use more than once should be turned into a symbol.

Symbols reside in a Flash library. You can drag multiple copies of a symbol from the library to the stage. Each copy of the symbol on the stage is an *instance* of the symbol. Adding multiple instances of symbols to your movie does not significantly increase the movie size. Flash just records the properties of the new instance; its description already exists in the library. When you change an instance in the library, all instances on the stage are updated.

Instances of symbols can have different colors, sizes, and behaviors.

In this exercise, you'll convert a graphic to a symbol. Later in the lesson, you'll use this symbol in your Flash movie.

1) Open neptune9.fla in the Lesson03/Assets folder on your CD-ROM.

This file is similar to the movie that you completed in Lesson 2, with a few additional graphics and layers. If you'd like to try to make these changes yourself, just open the last version of the movie (neptune8.fla) from Lesson 2, and go for it. But read through this lesson first, because neptune9.fla contains some elements that you haven't learned how to make yet.

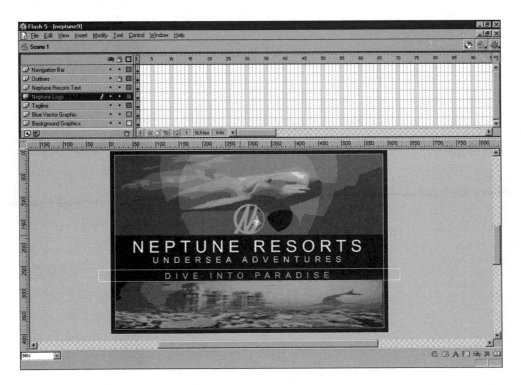

2) Select the graphic in the Neptune Logo layer. Choose Insert > Convert to Symbol, or press F8 on your keyboard.

When you choose Insert > Convert to Symbol, the Symbol Properties dialog box opens.

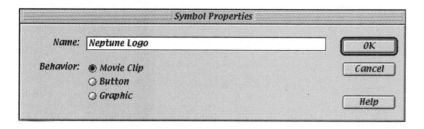

The Symbol Properties dialog box lets you set a name and behavior for a symbol. The name is important because it allows you to keep track of all your symbols; each symbol must have a unique name.

3) Type *Neptune Logo* in the Name text box. Set Behavior to Movie Clip and click OK.

When you click OK, Flash creates an instance of the new Neptune Logo graphic symbol. This new instance replaces the grouped graphic symbol that you selected before you chose the Convert to Symbol command. You can tell it's an instance of a symbol, because a small plus sign (+) appears in its center.

4) Save your file as neptune10.fla in the MyWork folder.

You've just created a symbol, which joins several existing symbols in the library. Before you start to play around with these symbols and the library, it's a good idea to save your movie.

USING THE LIBRARY

All symbols and any bitmaps or sounds that you import are stored in the movie's library. You can take an instance of anything in the library and place it on the stage. The Library window has many useful features that allow you to organize your movie's assets (such as symbols, bitmaps, and sounds).

In this exercise, you'll explore some of the library's features. Before you begin, make sure that neptune10.fla, the file you saved in the last exercise, is open.

1) Open the Library window by choosing Window > Library or by pressing Ctrl+L (Windows) or Command+L (Macintosh).

The Library window appears.

TIP *You can also open the library by clicking the book icon in the Launcher bar that appears at the bottom of the main Flash window. The Launcher bar contains buttons that let you quickly open the Info, Mixer, Character, Instance, and Actions panel, as well as the Movie Explorer and the library.*

The name of your current Flash movie should appear at the top of the Library window. Remember this, because you will be able to open libraries from other movies, and it's important to know which library you are using.

2) Select the Neptune Logo symbol in the Name column.

If you don't see the Neptune Logo symbol, you might need to scroll through the library to it by using the scroll bar on the right side of the window.

When you select the symbol, a graphic representation of that symbol appears in the Library window.

3) Expand the Library window by clicking the wide window button on the right side of the window.

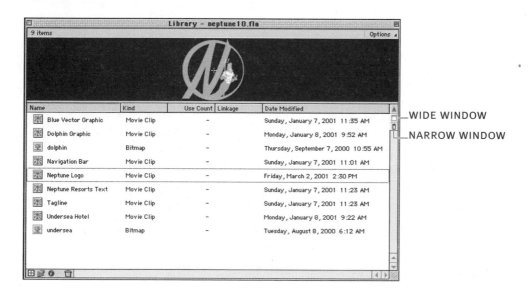

WIDE WINDOW

NARROW WINDOW

You should now be able to see the Kind, Use Count, Linkage, and Date Modified columns in the Library window, in addition to the Name column.

4) Sort the symbols by kind by clicking the heading of the Kind column.

You can use each of the column headings to sort the contents of the library. You can reverse the sort order by clicking the sort-order button on the right side of the Library window.

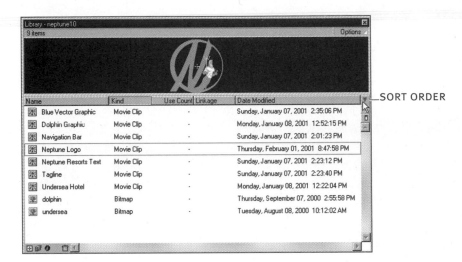

SORT ORDER

5) Sort the contents of the library so that the names are in alphabetical order by clicking the appropriate column heading (Name).

Use the sort-order button, if necessary.

The Blue Vector Graphic symbol should be listed first; you might have to scroll up in the Library window to see it.

6) Select the dolphin bitmap, and delete it by clicking the delete button (the trashcan icon) at the bottom of the Library window. When a dialog box opens, asking whether you want to delete the selected item, click Delete.

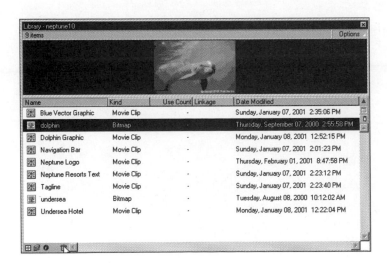

70

You don't need the dolphin bitmap anymore, because you converted it to a vector graphic in Lesson 2, but do not delete the undersea bitmap. That bitmap is still intact inside the Undersea Hotel symbol, and Flash still needs to refer to the bitmap. Make sure that you don't delete anything you still want, because you can't undo the deletion.

7) Choose Library > Options > Keep Use Counts Updated.

The Use Count column is updated. Everything that is used in the movie should have a number next to it.

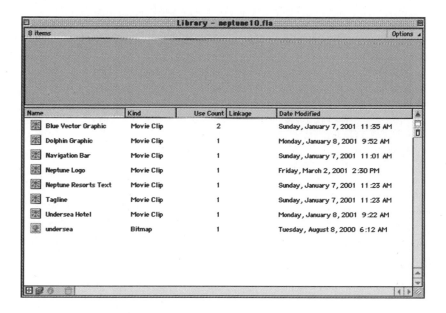

8) Click the narrow window button.

The Library window returns to its default width.

ORGANIZING THE LIBRARY

Many of your Flash movies will contain lots of symbols, and remembering what everything is for might be difficult. To prevent this problem, you should use folders in the library. Just as you can create folders in a Web site to organize your files, you can create folders in a Flash library to organize your symbols, bitmaps, and sounds.

To create a folder, click the new folder button in the bottom-left corner of the Library window. You can also choose Library > Options > New Folder. After a folder has been created, you can drag symbols, bitmaps, and sounds into it.

In this exercise, you'll organize the library for the Neptune Resorts site. Make sure that you have the library for neptune10.fla open before you begin.

1) Click the new folder button, which is located in the bottom-left corner of the Library window.

A new folder appears in the Library window, with an editable name.

NEW FOLDER

2) Type *Background Graphics* in the space provided, and press Enter (Windows) or Return (Macintosh).

The folder is sorted in alphabetical order automatically with the rest of the contents of the library, because you previously sorted everything by name.

3) Create another new folder and name it Header Graphics.

You can create this folder the same way that you created the Background Graphics folder, or you can choose Library > Options > New Folder.

4) Select the undersea bitmap in the library, and drag it into the Background Graphics folder.

72

The Background Graphics folder opens. The undersea bitmap name and icon appear, indented below the folder.

5) Drag the Dolphin Graphic and Undersea Hotel symbols into the Background Graphics folder, and close the folder by double-clicking it.

You now have several items inside the Background Graphics folder. When you place items in folders, you not only organize the contents of your library, but also make the list of items more compact so that it's easier to find everything.

6) Drag the Blue Vector Graphic symbol into the Header Graphics folder, and close the folder by double-clicking it. Save your movie as neptune11.fla in the MyWork folder.

Now if you need any background graphics or header graphics later, you know exactly where to find them. If you add symbols or bitmaps that fall into either of these categories, you should place them in the appropriate folder.

OPENING AN EXISTING MOVIE AS A LIBRARY

You are not limited to using the internal library of a Flash movie; you can open other Flash movie libraries by using the Open As Library command (File > Open As Library). You can drag items from one library to another, or you can drag items onto the stage.

73

1) Choose File > Open as Library. When the Open As Library dialog box opens, browse to the Lesson03/Assets folder, and select the assets.fla file. Click Open.

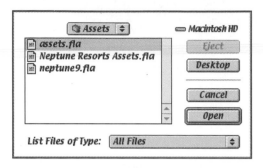

The library for assets.fla opens. If you have not moved your original Library window, the new window might open on top of the old one. Just drag the new window until you can see both windows. Notice that the newly opened assets.fla library is gray, which indicates that it is not the current library for the file you are editing.

2) Select the Baby Blue Background symbol in the Background Graphics folder of the assets.fla library. Drag the symbol to the Background Graphics folder in the neptune11.fla Library window.

Make sure that you look for the name of the library before you start dragging. The name appears across the top of the window. Each Library window that you open is named after its movie.

The Baby Blue Background symbol should appear indented below the Background Graphics folder.

3) Repeat step 2 for Diver Graphic, Reservations Graphic, and World Map, placing each of these symbols in the Background Graphics folder of the neptune11.fla library.

The Background Graphics folder should now contain several symbols and bitmaps.

4) Drag the Whale Shark symbol from the Header Graphics folder in the assets.fla library into the Header Graphics folder of the neptune11.fla library.

If you can't see a file, make sure that the folders in the assets.fla library are open by double-clicking them.

You've just added another symbol to the Header Graphics folder.

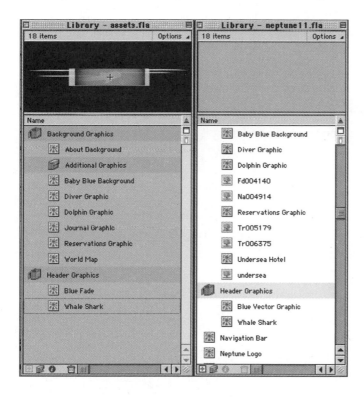

5) Close the assets.fla Library window. Make sure that the Library window for neptune11.fla is still open, because you're going to use it again. Save your movie.

When you're done using a library, it's a good idea to close it so that it doesn't get in the way.

USING A SHARED LIBRARY

Shared libraries are new to Flash 5. Now several Flash movies can use symbols from the same library. This arrangement enables you to keep your file sizes small by storing assets such as sounds and fonts outside your main Flash movie. The beauty of shared symbol libraries is that teams can share a standard set of artwork across multiple movies. Any final tweaking of a symbol can be done in the shared library. After the shared library has been published, any other movies that use the library are updated automatically.

Shared symbols need to be downloaded only once and can be used across any number of files that refer to the shared symbol. This setup dramatically reduces download time and leads to a faster viewing experience. You can include font symbols, buttons, graphics, movie clips, and sounds in a shared library.

1) Create a new Flash movie (File > New). Save the movie in the MyWork folder as shared.fla.

This new movie is going to contain your shared library.

2) Open the library for your shared.fla movie. Switch to the neptune11.fla Library window, select the Neptune Logo symbol, and drag it into the shared.fla Library window.

This step creates a copy of the Neptune Logo symbol in the shared.fla library. This symbol and the symbol in the neptune11.fla library are not linked in any way at this point–editing one will not affect the other, because the symbols are in separate files. But you're going to turn the library for shared.fla into a shared library, so you will be able to link these two symbols.

3) Select the Neptune Logo symbol in the shared.fla Library window, and in the Library window's Options pop-up menu, choose Linkage.

The Symbol Linkage Properties dialog box opens. You can use this dialog box to tell Flash to export the symbol even if it isn't used in a movie, which is exactly what you need to do when you create a shared library. Normally, a symbol is not exported if it is not used in the movie.

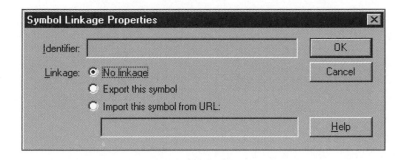

4) Set Linkage to Export This Symbol, and type *NeptuneLogo* in the Identifier text box. Then click OK.

When you export a symbol for use in a shared library, you need to give it a name, or identifier. That way, Flash knows which symbols to link.

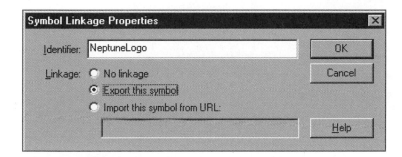

5) From the main menu, choose Control > Test Movie.

Before you can use a shared library, the library file must be published as a .swf file—a Flash Player movie. Choosing Control > Test Movie command is a quick and easy way to do this. The SWF file is saved in the same folder in which you saved the shared.fla file.

6) Close the movie. Save and close shared.fla.

Now that you have a shared library to work with, you have to go back into neptune11.fla and link to it.

7) Locate the Neptune Logo symbol in the neptune11.fla Library window. Right+click (Windows) or Control+click (Macintosh) this symbol, and choose Linkage from the pop-up menu.

When you choose the Linkage command, the Symbol Linkage Properties dialog box opens. You are going to use this dialog box to link the symbol in the neptune11.fla library to the same symbol in the shared.fla library.

8) Set Linkage to Import This Symbol From URL, and type *shared.swf* in the text box below this option. Type *NeptuneLogo* in the Identifier text box, and click OK.

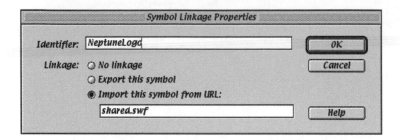

This step tells the movie that it should link to the symbol identified as NeptuneLogo that is exported in shared.swf (from the shared.fla library). If you decide to change the Neptune Logo symbol, you must make the change in shared.fla and then export the movie as shared.swf again.

9) Save your movie as neptune12.fla in the MyWork folder.

CREATING A COMMON LIBRARY

Flash 5 comes with several common libraries (Window > Common Libraries) preinstalled: Buttons, Buttons-Advanced, Graphics, Learning Interactions, Movie Clips, Smart Clips, and Sounds. You can add your own permanent libraries of symbols to Flash 5. This capability can be very useful when you need to use the same sets of symbols for several projects.

1) Open Neptune Resorts Assets.fla from the Lesson03/Assets folder.
You're going to turn this file into a common library. It contains several symbols that you're going to use in later lessons.

2) Choose File > Save As. When the Save As dialog box opens, browse to the Macromedia/Flash 5/Libraries folder on your hard disk, type *Neptune Resorts Assets*, and click the Save button.
The Macromedia/Flash 5/Libraries folder is located wherever you installed Flash 5 on your computer. On a Windows computer, a common location for this folder might be C:\Program Files\Macromedia\Flash 5.

When you save a .fla file in the Macromedia/Flash 5/Libraries folder, it becomes available in the Window > Common Libraries submenu.

3) Choose Window > Common Libraries.

The Neptune Resorts Assets library should appear in the Common Libraries submenu. If it's not there, close and reopen Flash; the library should appear. You don't need to open the Neptune Resorts Assets library at this time, but you will use it in the next exercise, so remember where it is.

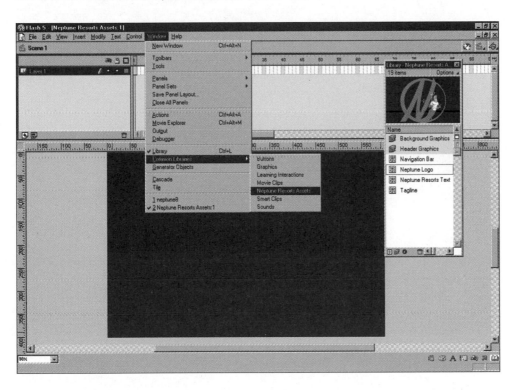

USING SYMBOL INSTANCES

Each instance of a symbol has its own properties. By using various panels, you can change the appearance of individual instances while they remain one symbol. The best thing about this capability is that you can change the original symbol (the one that lives in the library) and affect all instances on the stage.

1) Choose File > New.

You've just created a new movie.

2) Choose Window > Common Libraries > Neptune Resorts Assets. Locate the Neptune Logo symbol in the Neptune Resorts Assets library. Add an instance of the symbol to the stage by selecting its name and dragging it onto the stage.

Each copy of the symbol that you add to the stage is called an instance. Every instance of a symbol has its own properties, such as width, height, and alpha. You can use panels such as the Info, Effect, and Transform panels to modify the properties of each instance. Although each instance has its own properties, it is linked to the original symbol in the library. Any changes that you make in the original symbol affect all instances on the stage and inside other symbols.

3) Use the arrow tool to select the instance of the Neptune Logo on the stage. Open the Info panel (Window > Panels > Info), and set both the width (W) and height (H) to 200.

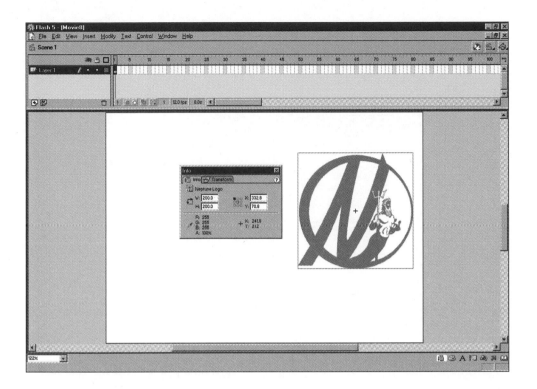

You aren't applying the change in width and height to the original symbol; rather, you're applying it to an instance of the symbol. The information about the new width and height is saved with the instance of the symbol, but all the other information—such as how the symbol looks and what its behaviors are—is kept with the original symbol. This means that Flash has to export only minimal information with each instance of the symbol, which keeps file sizes small.

4) Close the Neptune Resorts Assets.fla library, and open the library for the current movie (Window > Library). Add another instance of the Neptune Logo symbol to the stage.

It doesn't matter where you place the second instance of the logo. You can always move it later by using the Info panel.

5) Use the arrow tool to select the second instance (the smaller one). In the Effect panel, choose Alpha from the pop-up menu, and type *50* in the text box.

You can open the Effect panel by choosing Window > Panels > Effect.

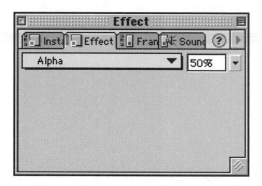

You can use the Effect panel to make changes in the color properties (brightness, tint, and alpha) of an instance. You choose the property that you want to modify from the pop-up menu in the panel. You can choose None, Brightness, Tint, Alpha, or Advanced. None removes all color effects from an instance. Brightness modifies the relative lightness or darkness of the image, measured on a scale from black (-100%) to white (100%). Tint colors the instance with the same hue. Alpha adjusts the transparency of the instance, from completely transparent (0%) to completely opaque (100%). Advanced adjusts the red, green, blue, and transparency values of an instance separately.

When you choose the Brightness and Alpha options in the Effect panel, a slider and text box appear on the right side of the panel. You can drag the slider up and down to modify the brightness and alpha settings, or you can type a value from –100 to 100 in the text box to modify the brightness or 0 to 100 to modify the alpha.

Choosing the Tint option also causes a slider to appear. This slider allows you to set the saturation of the hue that you want to apply. The hue is determined by the R (Red), G (Green), and B (Blue) settings. You can set the R, G, and B in several ways: by dragging the R, G, and B sliders up and down; by typing a number between 0 and 255 in each of the text boxes; by clicking the color swatch next to the Tint Color label and choosing a color from the resulting pop-up color swatch palette; or by picking a color from the Color Picker.

The Advanced option is, to put it mildly, much more advanced. You can use this option to modify the color and the transparency of the instance in relation to the original symbol. Typing a number in, or dragging a slider next to, the percentage boxes multiplies the color or transparency value by a percentage of the original. If the instance was pure red, for example, changing the B (blue) percentage value would cause no change, but changing the R (red) percentage would reduce the intensity of the red. Typing a number in the addition box (or dragging the slider next to it) would add or subtract the relevant saturation or transparency from the entire instance. Using the same pure-red instance and typing a positive number in the B addition box would result in a shade of purple, for example.

Take some time to play with the Advanced option of the Effect panel—it's a lot of fun and much more obvious in action than in explanation.

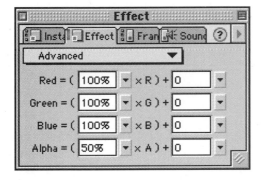

6) Double-click an instance of the Neptune Logo symbol on the stage to open this symbol in symbol-editing mode.

You can tell that the symbol is in symbol-editing mode because its name appears just below the main menu. When you open a symbol in symbol-editing mode, you can edit the original symbol. Any changes that you make in the original symbol are reflected in every instance of that symbol used in the movie.

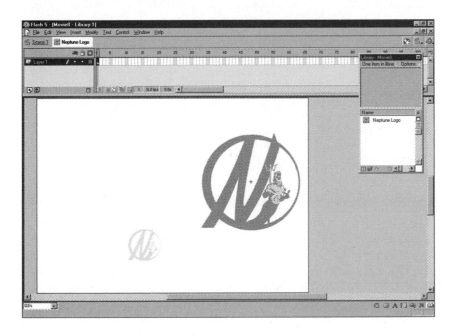

7) Choose Edit > Select All to select the contents of the symbol. Use the Fill panel to change the color of the graphic to red (#FF0000). Return to the movie by choosing Edit > Edit Movie.

The color change that you made in the original symbol has taken place across the board. All the instances of the Neptune Logo symbol now appear red. When you edit the original symbol, all changes made in that symbol affect every instance of the symbol.

8) Save and/or close the file.

You're done with this file for now; it was just for practice. If you'd like to play around with adding and editing symbols some more, you can save the file and return to it. Otherwise, simply close the file.

USING THE MOVIE EXPLORER

In earlier versions of Flash, keeping track of the structure of your Flash movie was difficult, especially when you were using ActionScripts or nested symbols. The Movie Explorer puts an end to the confusion. The Movie Explorer provides a hierarchical tree view of every element in your Flash movie. You can search, replace text and fonts, and find every instance of any symbol. You can also copy the contents of the Movie Explorer as text to the Clipboard or print the display list in the Movie Explorer.

1) Open neptune12.fla from your MyWork folder. Choose Window > Movie Explorer.

You open the Movie Explorer by choosing Window > Movie Explorer. The Movie Explorer window consists of a display list (the contents of the movie), a row of filtering buttons, and a Find text box. Like many other windows or panels in Flash, the Movie Explorer window has an options button in the top-right corner.

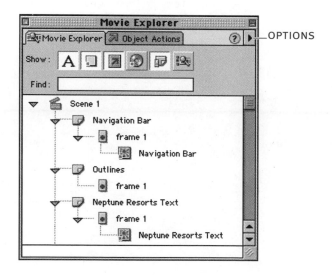

2) Deselect all the filtering buttons.

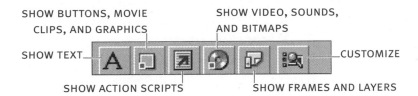

There are five filtering buttons, plus a customize button that you can use to customize which items to show. Click a filtering button to toggle it off or on. Filtering is on when the button appears to be pressed in and the background is white. (Filtering is off on all of the above buttons.)

You can view the hierarchical tree in two contexts: by movie elements, which are organized by scenes; and by symbol definitions. Currently, you have one scene, so the only movie element is Scene 1.

3) Click the first filtering button: the Show Text filter.

Text is embedded in a symbol in two places: the Tagline symbol and the Neptune Resorts Text symbol. These two symbols appear in the Movie Explorer.

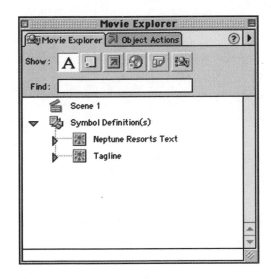

TIP *You may also need to show the symbol definitions, by clicking on the Options button and choosing Show Symbol Definitions from the pop-up menu. If there's already a check next to this menu item, it's selected and you don't have to do anything.*

4) Click the plus sign (+) (Windows) or the expand triangle (Macintosh) next to the Neptune Resorts Text symbol.

When you click a plus sign or expand triangle in the Movie Explorer, the item next to the plus sign expands, and you can see the filtered contents of that item. In this case, you're filtering for text, so you'll see information about the text in the Neptune Resorts Text symbol. To collapse a symbol definition, click the minus sign (–) or triangle next to the expanded definition.

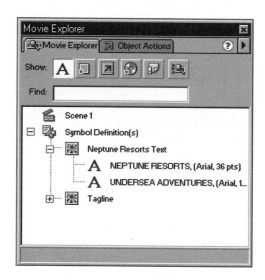

5) Double-click the UNDERSEA ADVENTURES text in the Movie Explorer. When the text becomes editable, change it to AQUATIC ADVENTURES, and press Enter (Windows) or Return (Macintosh).

You can change the text in the symbol from within the Movie Explorer. When you modify the text, the change takes place not only in the Movie Explorer, but also on the stage. You can modify the properties of just about anything in the Movie Explorer. If you decide that you'd like to use a different font, for example, you can select the text in the Movie Explorer and then change the font in the Character panel.

TIP *After you select an item in the Movie Explorer, you can open all panels relevant to the item quickly by choosing Panels from the Options pop-up menu in the Movie Explorer window.*

6) Save the movie to your MyWork folder as neptune13.fla.

WHAT YOU HAVE LEARNED

In this lesson, you have:

- Converted a graphic to a symbol (pages 66–67)

- Used and organized the library (pages 67–73)

- Opened an existing library (pages 73–75)

- Used a shared library (pages 76–79)

- Used and revised symbol instances (pages 79–84)

- Used the Movie Explorer (pages 84–86)

creating
animation

LESSON 4

Animation is the process of creating a change over time. Animation can be an object moving from one place to another or scaling from one size to another. A change of color or transparency over time is animation, too. The change also can be a morph from one shape to another. Any change of position or appearance that occurs over time is animation.

In Macromedia Flash, you achieve animation by changing the contents of successive frames over a given period. This change can include all the changes discussed in the preceding paragraph, in any combination.

In this lesson, you will animate the Neptune Resorts logo, the stylish N in a circle at the upper-left of this screen.

Flash provides two methods for creating an animation sequence in the timeline: *frame-by-frame animation* and *tweened animation*. To create Flash animation frame by frame, you change the contents of successive frames. In frame-by-frame animation, you create the image in every frame, although your modifications may be barely noticeable between frames. In tweened animation, you create starting and ending frames and let Flash create the frames in between. Because of its interactive capabilities, Flash is also capable of creating dynamic animation that is controlled with ActionScript.

WHAT YOU WILL LEARN

In this lesson, you will:

- Create a frame-by-frame animation

- Use a mask

- Create a motion tween

- Use a motion guide

- Make a movie clip with a shape tween

- Use a movie clip to create an animated button

APPROXIMATE TIME

It usually takes about one hour to complete this lesson.

LESSON FILES

Media Files:

None

Starting Files:

Lesson04/Assets/neptune13.fla

Completed Project:

neptune19.fla

CREATING A FRAME-BY-FRAME ANIMATION

The most basic form of animation is frame-by-frame animation. Because this type of animation employs unique artwork in each frame, it is ideal for complex animations, such as facial expressions that require subtle changes. Frame-by-frame animation can also be useful for making dramatic changes in a short period of time—in a slide show, for example.

Frame-by-frame animation does have drawbacks. Drawing a unique image for each frame of the animation can be tedious and time-consuming. And all those unique drawings contribute to a larger file size.

Let's start things off with a simple frame-by-frame animation.

1) Open neptune13.fla from the Lesson04/Assets folder. Lock the Outlines and Blue Vector Graphic layers.

This file is nearly identical to the one that you completed in Lesson 3. The only changes are that the *AQUATIC ADVENTURES* text is centered inside the Neptune Resorts Text symbol, and the Neptune Logo symbol is unlinked.

You have finished using these layers and don't want to move things around accidentally, so it's best to lock them.

2) Select frame 2 of the Blue Vector Graphic layer, and insert a frame by choosing Insert > Frame. Repeat this step for frame 2 of the Outlines layer.

You can select a frame by clicking it in the timeline. When you select a frame, it becomes highlighted.

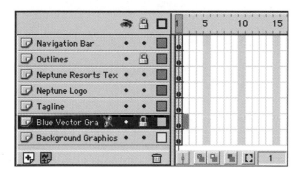

Inserting a frame does not change the animation in a layer; it only extends the animation for a longer period. The contents of the frame that you just added are identical to those of the preceding frame in the same layer.

Up until this point, you've known the timeline as the place where Flash keeps all your layers, but it's really much more than that. Layers contain the actual content of your movie, but the timeline is where you animate the content of the movie. The timeline enables you to create an animation by changing the contents of the stage over time.

The major parts of the timeline are layers, frames, and the playhead. Frames in a Flash movie represent time. The playhead shows you which frame is currently visible on the stage.

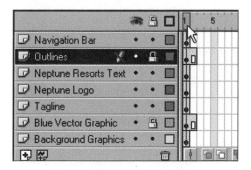

The playhead is the red rectangle above the timeline. It moves through the timeline to indicate the current frame displayed on the stage. To display a frame on the stage, you move the playhead to the frame on the timeline. Drag the playhead back and forth between frames 1 and 2 to see what you accomplished in this step. Notice that

91

in frame 2, only the graphics from the Blue Vector Graphic and Outlines layers appear; these are the only layers in the timeline with frames at this point. You should also notice that the contents of these layers have not changed.

TIP *You can also insert a frame by pressing F5 on your keyboard.*

3) Select frame 2 of the Navigation Bar layer, and insert a keyframe by choosing Insert > Keyframe. Select the instance of the Navigation Bar symbol that's on the stage, and use the Info panel to move it to X: –25 and Y: 85.

A keyframe marks a point on the timeline where the contents of a layer may change. A black dot should appear on the timeline in frame 2 of the Navigation Bar layer. This black dot signifies a keyframe at this point in the timeline.

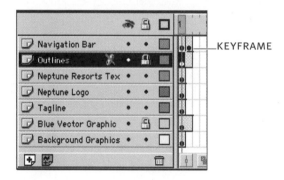

TIP *You can also insert a keyframe by pressing F6 on your keyboard.*

4) Select frame 2 of the Tagline layer, and insert a blank keyframe by choosing Insert > Blank Keyframe.

In frame 1 of the Tagline layer, you have an instance of the Tagline symbol. In frame 2 you have nothing, because the keyframe you inserted was blank. Drag the playhead back and forth between frames 1 and 2 to see the difference.

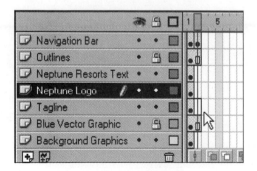

92

5) Insert another blank keyframe at frame 2 of the Background Graphics layer. Open the library, and drag an instance of the Diver Graphic from the Background Graphics folder onto the stage, using the Info panel to position it at X: 10 and Y: 110.
This time, you inserted a blank keyframe but then put something in that keyframe. Once again, a change has been made in your animation. Drag the playhead between frames 1 and 2 to see the change.

6) Insert a keyframe at frame 2 of the Neptune Logo layer, and use the Info panel to move the instance of the Neptune Logo in that keyframe to X: 19 and Y: 15.
Once again, you're animating a layer—this time, the Neptune Logo layer. Drag the playhead between frames 1 and 2 to see the change.

TIP *If you're having trouble seeing the changes, click the show/hide layers button (the eye icon in the layers area of the timeline) to hide all the layers. Then click on the dot below the eye icon next to the layer you want to see.*

7) Insert a keyframe at frame 2 of the Neptune Resorts Text layer. Select the instance of the Neptune Resorts Text symbol in frame 2 of that layer and use the Transform panel to make it 80% of its original size. Then position this symbol next to the Neptune Logo.

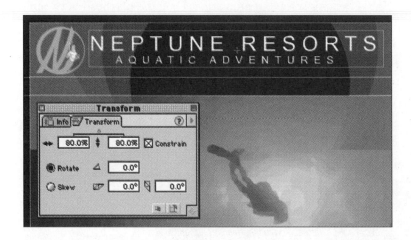

You can accomplish transformations quickly by using the Transform panel. Also, you can click the reset button in the Transform panel to undo the last transformation. You can apply the transformation to a duplicate of the shape, leaving the original shape intact, by clicking the copy and apply button. You can check the Constrain checkbox to ensure that the height and width of the instance are scaled to the same percentage.

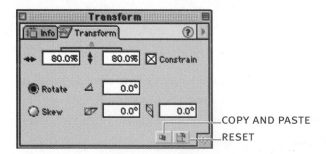

COPY AND PASTE

RESET

8) Save your file as neptune14.fla in the MyWork folder.

Congratulations! You just made your first animation. That wasn't so tough, was it? Now let's move on to something a little more complicated: masking.

USING A MASK

You can use a mask layer to create a hole through which the contents of one or more underlying layers are visible. You can group multiple layers below a single mask layer to create sophisticated effects. You cannot mask layers inside buttons.

In the following exercise, you'll use a mask to mask the contents of two of your movie's layers. You should still have neptune14.fla open from the preceding exercise.

1) Click the lock/unlock all layers button (the padlock icon) at the top of the timeline to lock all the layers in the movie.

You took the time to set up your animation and place your symbols precisely, so you don't want to mess them up. Locking all the layers will prevent anything from happening to your project while you work with other layers.

2) Select the Blue Vector Graphic layer, and choose Insert > Layer. Name the new layer Header Mask, and insert a blank keyframe at frame 2 of this layer.

You are going to use this new layer to create a mask for what will become the header of your movie. The header will include the contents of the Blue Vector Graphic layer and another layer that you'll add soon.

3) In frame 2 of the Header Mask layer, draw a rectangle with no stroke, bright green fill, and a corner radius of 0. Use the Info panel to set the width to 580, the height to 100, and the X, Y coordinates to 10, 10.

TIP *If you need to open the Stroke, Fill or Info panel, choose Window > Panels, and choose the appropriate panel from the submenu. Remember, though, that you can also change the stroke and fill from the Colors area of the toolbar.*

This rectangle is going to be your mask. It doesn't matter what color the fill is, but this exercise uses a very visible color so that you can see it among all the other elements on the stage.

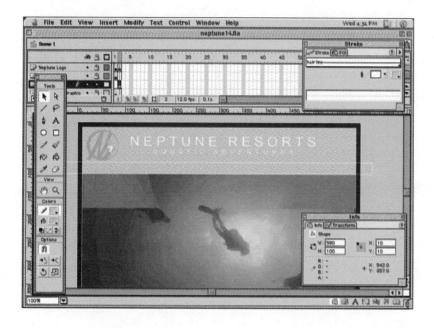

4) Right+click (Windows) or Control+click (Macintosh) the name of the Header Mask layer, and choose Mask from the contextual menu.

This step turns the Header Mask layer into a mask for the layer below it, which is the Blue Vector Graphic layer. Only the area covered by the rectangle in the Header Mask layer (the mask layer) shows through in the Blue Vector layer (the masked layer). Flash locks the mask and masked layers automatically. Icons identify the mask and masked layers in the timeline.

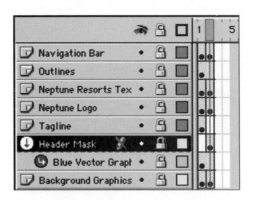

5) Select the Background Graphics layer, and choose Insert > Layer. Name the new layer Header Graphic. Insert a blank keyframe at frame 2 of this new layer.

You are going to add some content to this new layer, which is destined to become part of the header.

6) Drag an instance of the Whale Shark symbol from the Header Graphics folder in the library onto the stage; place it in frame 2 of the Header Graphic layer. Use the Info panel to position the symbol at X: -435 and Y: -15.

At this point, the instance of the Whale Shark symbol looks horrible; the effects used to create it run off the edge of the graphic. You don't want your users to see that, so you're going to mask its layer so that only the important stuff shows through.

7) Select the Header Graphic layer, and choose Modify > Layer. In the Layer Properties dialog box, click the Lock checkbox and the Masked radio button; then click OK.

You used the Layer Properties dialog box in Lesson 2, so it should look familiar.

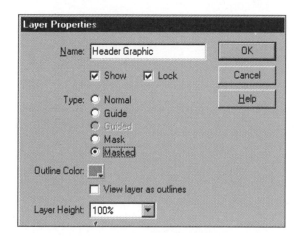

After you modify the Layer properties and click OK, the layer becomes masked by the Header Mask layer. The edges of the Whale Shark graphic are now hidden, giving your developing site a nice clean look.

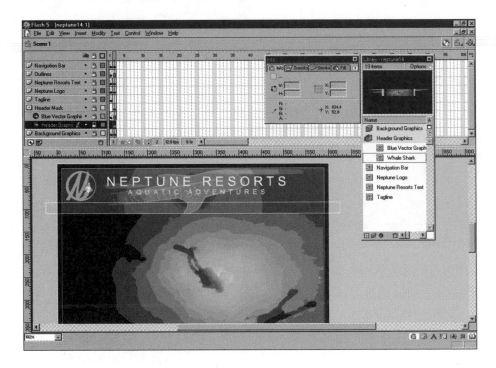

8) Save your movie in the MyWork folder as neptune15.fla.

Your movie is coming along nicely. Now it's time to make things move around a bit.

CREATING A MOTION TWEEN

Motion tweening is useful for animating symbols. As its name suggests, motion tweening typically is used to move an element from one place to another, but it can do more than that. You can use motion tweening to scale, rotate, and skew elements, and to change the color settings and transparency of a symbol over time. You can apply motion tweening to only one element on a layer, so when you must tween multiple elements, you need to use multiple layers.

Right now, you have a fairly simple frame-by-frame animation for the two screens in your site. This animation is good enough for a simple site, but wouldn't it look better with some transitions—things moving, things fading in and out, and all the other stuff that makes a site interesting? That's exactly what you're going to do next. You're going to make the Navigation Bar move from its location in the first screen to its location in the second screen. Instead of having it jump there, as it does currently, you're going to make it move smoothly from place to place.

1) Drag the playhead over frame 1 in neptune15.fla. Click the playhead to make sure you don't have any frames selected, and add 13 frames to every layer after frame 1 by pressing the F5 key 13 times.

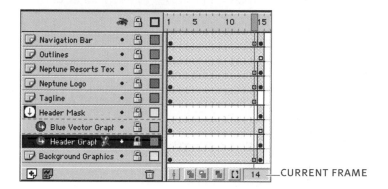

CURRENT FRAME

You're going to add some motion to the movie, so you need to give it a few extra frames over which to perform that motion. When you added 13 frames after frame 1, the contents of frame 2 moved to frame 15. The contents of frames 2 through 14 are identical to those of frame 1, because all you did was add some frames. Remember that frames only increase the time in your movie; they don't change the animation (except for expanding the time).

TIP *You can tell exactly which frame the playhead is located on by checking the current frame box at the bottom of the timeline. In the preceding figure, the frame is 14, and the box is located at the far-right side of the screen.*

2) Select the Navigation Bar layer, and drag the playhead to frame 10. Insert a keyframe at frame 10 by choosing Insert > Keyframe or pressing F6. Select this new keyframe, and choose Insert > Create Motion Tween.

A small arrow appears between frames 10 and 15 of the Navigation Bar layer to indicate that a motion tween has been created. The frames in the motion tween are shaded.

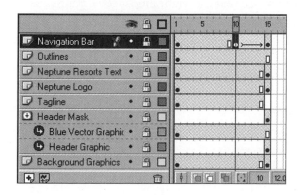

When you create a motion tween, you must have at least two keyframes. The first keyframe contains the initial state of the symbol to be animated, and the last keyframe contains the final state of that symbol. To create the motion tween, Flash interprets the state of the symbol in the in-between frames. In this case, you have an instance of the Navigation Bar symbol in the middle of the stage in frame 1 through 10; you have another instance of the same symbol near the top of the stage in frame 15. Flash generates the intermediate positions of this symbol for frames 10 through 15.

3) Drag the playhead to frame 1, and play your movie by choosing Control > Play.
The first 10 frames are static, but the Navigation Bar moves to a new position over frames 10 to 15. You didn't have to put a keyframe in each frame to make this transition, because Flash did all the tweening work for you.

4) Save your movie in the MyWork folder as neptune16.fla.
Keep the file open for the next exercise; you're going to add more to it.

USING A MOTION GUIDE

You can use a motion guide to force a tweened symbol to follow a specified path. This technique is great for simulating motion along a curved or irregular line. All you have to do is select the layer you want to guide and then choose Insert > Motion Guide.

In the following exercise, you'll learn how to create a motion tween that follows a path, or motion guide, to move the Neptune Logo to the top of the stage. You'll also learn how to use onionskinning to see multiple frames of your animation at the same time.

1) Select the Neptune Logo layer, and drag the playhead to frame 10. Insert a keyframe at frame 10, select this new keyframe, and choose Insert > Create Motion Tween.
This step should be a piece of cake for you, because you did the same thing in the preceding exercise. This time, you're going to spice things up a bit by adding a path for the animated symbol—in this case, the Neptune Logo—to follow. You can drag the playhead between frames 10 and 15 to see that the Neptune Logo currently just zooms to the top-left corner of the stage. You're going to make it follow a curved path.

2) Right+click (Windows) or Control+click (Macintosh) the Neptune Logo layer, and choose Add Motion Guide from the contextual menu.

A new layer called Guide: Neptune Logo appears above the Neptune Logo layer. A motion-guide icon appears to the left of the name, and the Neptune Logo layer is indented below it.

MOTION GUIDE ICON

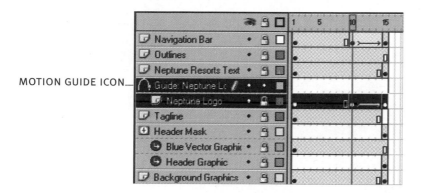

3) Insert a keyframe at frame 10 of the Guide: Neptune Logo layer.

You're going to add a motion guide to this layer, but first, you have to see the whole animation that you want to place in the motion guide. To do that, you turn on onionskinning.

4) Unlock the Neptune Logo layer, and click the onionskin outlines button at the bottom of the timeline.

ONIONSKIN   ONIONSKIN OUTLINES

CENTER FRAME —   — MODIFY ONION MARKERS

EDIT MULTIPLE FRAMES

Flash's onionskin feature lets you view multiple frames at the same time. The onionskin outlines feature lets you see only the outlines of the selected frames. But before you can really use this feature, you need to specify which frames you want to view. The onionskin markers appear at the top of the timeline. These markers show you which frames are included in the onionskin.

5) Drag the left onionskin marker to frame 10 and the right onionskin marker to frame 15.

OUTLINE
COLOR   ONIONSKIN MARKERS

The outlines of the contents of frames 10 through 15 should be visible. If you wanted to view the actual contents of each frame instead of outlines, you could have clicked the onionskin button in step 4. As it is, you can see the outlines of the contents of each of these frames at the same time.

You can see which color will be used for the onionskin outline to the right of the layer name in the timeline. This color is set in the Layer Properties dialog box as the Outline Color.

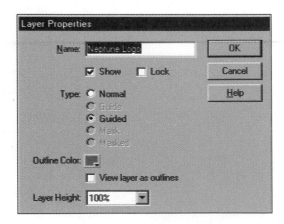

6) Select the line tool, and set the stroke color to red (#FF0000).

You're going to create a line that will be your motion guide.

TIP *When you create a motion guide, it's wise to make the line height 4 or larger, so that it's easier to see the line on top of everything else.*

7) Select frame 10 of the Guide: Neptune Logo layer. Draw a line from the center of the Neptune Logo in the center of the stage to the center of the outline near the top-left corner of the stage.

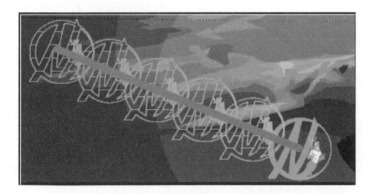

The Neptune Logo in the center of the stage is in frame 10; the outline of the logo in the corner of the stage represents the logo's place in frame 15. The line between these two points is the motion guide. The motion guide currently is straight, which won't change the animation (because the animation was already moving in a straight line), so you need to make it a curved line instead.

8) Use the arrow tool to drag the line into a curve.

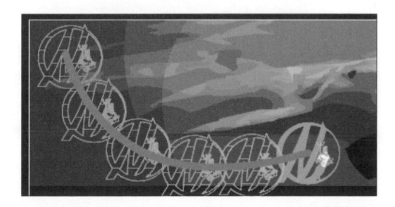

The path of the outlines should change with the shape of the line. If it doesn't, make sure that the center point of the instance in each keyframe is on the line. If you're having trouble making your symbol follow the path, lock the Guide: Neptune Logo layer, make sure that Snap to Objects is selected in the Options section of the toolbox, and drag the instance of the Neptune Logo around the stage by its center. As you drag, you should notice a small circle. Drag that circle near the line, and the symbol should snap to the line automatically.

Make sure that you perform this step for each instance of the Neptune Logo symbol. You have one in frame 10 and another in frame 15.

9) Drag the playhead to frame 1, and play the movie. If you like what you see, turn off the onionskin outlines feature, and save the movie in the MyWork folder as neptune17.fla.
You can turn off onionskin outlines by clicking the onionskin outlines button in the timeline again.

Now that you have motion tweening down, it's time to make a complex animation for your movie. You're going to make this animation inside a movie clip, and while you're at it, you're going to learn what a movie clip is.

CREATING A SHAPE TWEEN

Shape tweening is useful for morphing shapes between end points. Flash can shape-tween only shapes, not groups, symbols, or editable text. If you want to tween a group, symbol, or editable text, you must first turn it into a shape by breaking it up completely (choose Modify > Break Apart until everything has been turned into a shape).

You can shape-tween multiple shapes in a layer, but for the sake of organization, putting each shape in its own layer usually is easier.

You should still have neptune17.fla open as you begin this exercise.

1) Choose Insert › New Symbol. When the Symbol Properties dialog box opens, name the new symbol *Animated Text: Reservations*, set the Behavior to Movie Clip, and click OK.

You're going to make an animated movie clip for use in a button. When you choose Insert > New Symbol, Flash creates a new empty symbol and takes you into symbol-editing mode. Flash adds the symbol to the movie's library automatically.

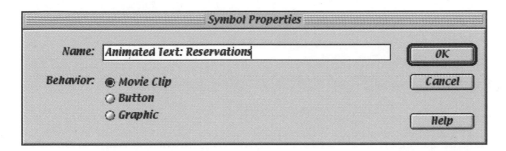

2) Select the text tool in the toolbox, and create a text box on the stage. In the Character panel, set the font to 18-point Arial in cyan (#33FFFF). Type Reservations in the text box.

Leave the other settings in the Character panel at their defaults. Font tracking should be set to 0, kerning should be on, and the character position should be Normal.

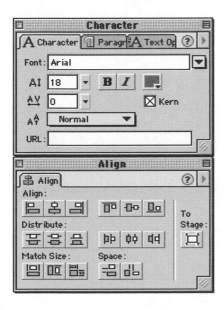

3) Use the Align panel to center the text box horizontally and vertically on the stage.

Make sure that the To Stage button is selected when you click the Align Horizontal Center and Align Vertical Center buttons in the Align panel. If it's not, the text box won't move.

4) Choose Modify > Break Apart.

The text box should still be selected. If it's not, use the arrow tool to select it before choosing Modify > Break Apart.

When you break text apart, you turn it into its component shapes, which is what you need to do to create a shape tween. You cannot shape-tween symbols, editable text, groups, or anything else that has a solid bounding box. You can shape-tween only shapes.

5) Select frame 5, and choose Insert > Blank Keyframe. With the oval tool, draw an oval with no stroke and a cyan fill.

Now you need to position this oval in the correct place on the stage.

6) Select the oval. In the Info panel, set the width to 130 and the height to 20. Center the oval horizontally and vertically on the stage.

This oval is the shape into which your text is going to morph.

TIP *Use the Align panel to position the oval. This method is easier than trying to specify a location in the Info panel.*

7) Select frame 1. In the Frame panel, choose Shape from the Tweening pop-up menu.

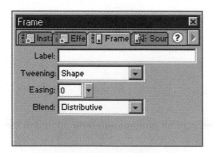

You now have a shape tween between frames 1 and 5 of the movie clip. When you set the tweening to Shape, the affected frames are highlighted green to indicate that a shape tween occurs there. If you drag the playhead back and forth between frames 1 and 5, you should see that Flash created several intermediate shapes between the Reservations text in frame 1 and the oval in frame 5.

106

Now you have to make the oval turn back into text.

8) Select frame 1, and choose Edit › Copy Frames. Then select frame 10, and choose Edit › Paste Frames. Select frame 5, and set the tweening to Shape in the Frame panel.

The shape tween is complete. The animation starts with some text in frame 1, tweens the text into an oval by frame 5, and then tweens back to the text by frame 10.

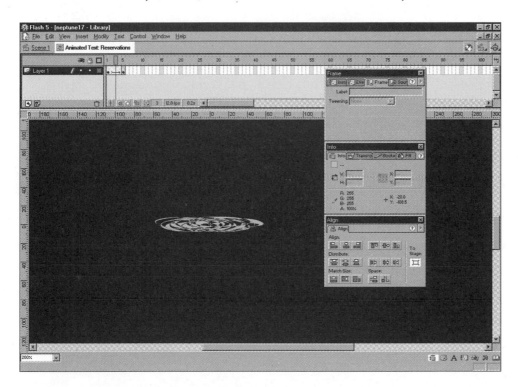

9) Save your movie as neptune18.fla in the MyWork folder.

You're done making your shape-tween. Now you're going to take the movie clip that contains the shape tween and add it to a button.

USING A MOVIE CLIP TO CREATE AN ANIMATED BUTTON

Movie clips are essentially movies inside other movies. They're good for animations that run independently of the main movie's timeline. Movie clips can contain interactive elements (*actions*), other symbols, and sounds. They can also be placed inside other symbols and are particularly useful for creating animated buttons. You created a movie clip in the preceding exercise; now you'll put that movie clip in a button to animate the button.

You should still have neptune18.fla open from the preceding exercise.

1) Choose Insert > New Symbol to create another new symbol. In the Symbol Properties dialog box, type Reservations Button in the Name text box, select the Button radio button, and click OK.

You just made an empty button. Notice that the button's timeline is significantly different from the other timelines you've seen. A button has four states: Up, Over, Down, and Hit. Each state is defined in a frame of the same name.

The Up state is how the button appears on the screen when it first appears. The Over state becomes visible when you move the mouse pointer over a button on the stage. When you click a button, the Down state is revealed. The Hit state is not visible in your movie; it defines the active area of a button. The active area can be larger or smaller than the visible button and can even have a different shape. Button symbols can have graphic symbols, movie clips, and sounds in the first three frames.

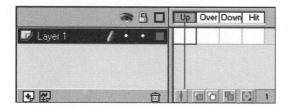

2) Select the Up frame. Use the text tool to create a text box containing the word *Reservations*. Center the text box horizontally and vertically on the stage.

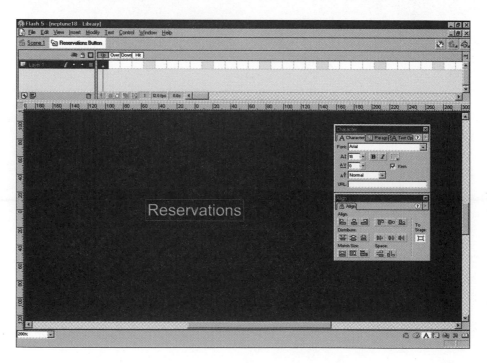

Use the Character panel to set the font to Arial, font height to 18, font tracking to 0, and font color to cyan (#33FFFF). If you haven't made any changes in the Character panel since the preceding exercise, these settings should still be there.

3) Select the Over frame, and choose Insert > Blank Keyframe. Drag an instance of the Animated Text: Reservations movie clip onto the stage and center it horizontally and vertically on the stage.

Remember that the Animated Text: Reservations movie clip is a symbol. Like all symbols, it's stored in the library.

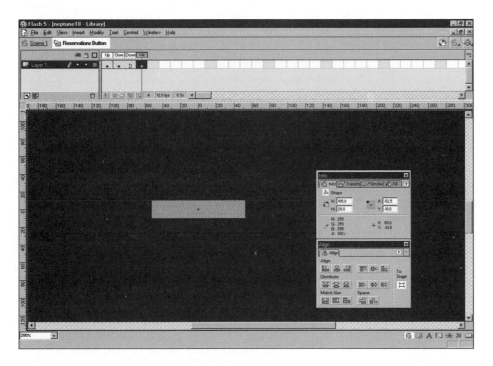

You've added an animation to the button. When you add the button to a movie, that button responds to mouse actions. Initially, you see only the text *Reservations*. But when you move the mouse over the text, you see the Animated Text: Reservations movie clip.

You have to add only one more thing to your button to make it work perfectly: a Hit state.

4) Select the Hit frame, and choose Insert > Blank Keyframe. Draw a rectangle, and set its width to 105 and its height to 20. Center the rectangle horizontally and vertically on the stage.

Without a Hit area, you'd have a hard time clicking the button. The Hit state is not visible in your movie, so the color of the rectangle doesn't matter. The only thing that matters is the size of the rectangle, because it acts as the hit area for the button.

You're done making your button. Now you have to add it to the movie.

5) Choose Edit > Edit Movie. Insert a new layer, named Navigation Buttons, to the top of the layer stacking order. Insert a keyframe at frame 15 of this new layer.
This keyframe is where you're going to add the button that you just made.

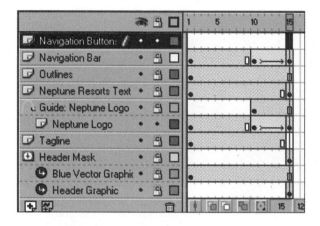

6) With frame 15 of the Navigation Buttons layer selected, drag an instance of the Reservations Button symbol onto the stage. Use the Info panel to position it at X: 15 and Y: 85.

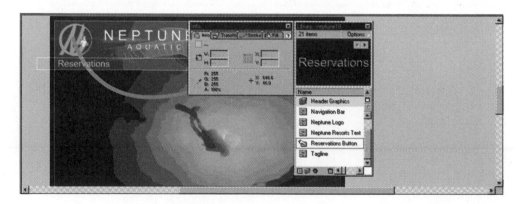

The button is now on the stage, but you can't preview it in all its animated glory without testing the movie. The reason is that the button contains a movie clip for its animated Over state, and you cannot preview movie-clip animations in movie-editing mode.

7) Choose Control > Test Movie. When the exported movie appears, choose Control > Loop to keep it from looping through the animation repeatedly. The movie will stop. Move the mouse over the Reservations Button symbol to see the animated button state.

When you move the mouse over the button, you should see the animated movie clip that you created. The clip will loop continuously, which is what movie clips (and movies in general) do by default.

8) Choose File > Close to close the test-movie window. Save the movie as neptune19.fla in the MyWork folder.

You're done with the movie for now. In the next lesson, you'll learn how to add sound to your movie.

WHAT YOU HAVE LEARNED

In this lesson, you have:

- Created a simple frame-by-frame animation (pages 90–94)

- Used a mask to create a polished image (pages 94–98)

- Animated a symbol by using motion-tweening (pages 98–100)

- Used a motion guide and onionskin outlines to modify your animation (pages 100–104)

- Used shape tweening to morph a shape (pages 104–107)

- Created a movie clip (pages 105, 107)

- Animated the button by using the movie clip (pages 107–110)

- Created a button (page 108)

- Added the animated button to the movie (pages 110–111)

using sound

LESSON 5

The use of sound in Flash movies will enhance your presentations (think silent movie versus talkies). Although it is not always necessary, sound adds another dimension to your presentation and, when used effectively, can make the viewer's experience more enjoyable.

You'll learn in this lesson how to modify sound files by using the edit envelope.

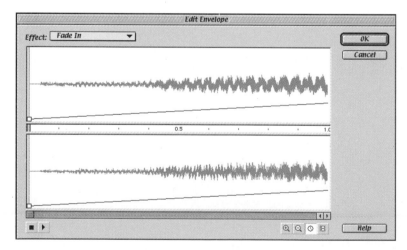

The Edit Envelope window shows sound in both the right and left channels.

WHAT YOU WILL LEARN

In this lesson, you will:

- Import sounds

- Add sounds to a movie

- Modify the sound settings

- Add a sound to a button

- Customize sound effects

- Modify sound compression settings

APPROXIMATE TIME

It usually takes about 30 minutes to complete this lesson.

LESSON FILES

Media Files:

Lesson05/Assets/sounds.fla

Lesson05/Assets/loop.mp3

Starting File:

Lesson05/Assets/neptune19.fla

Completed Project:

neptune25.fla

IMPORTING SOUNDS

Before you can include sound files in your Flash movie, you need to import them into the library just as you would import artwork. When you import a sound, it gets added to your current movie library. You can use numerous instances of the same sound throughout your movie, just as you would use multiple instances of a symbol.

1) Open neptune19.fla in the Lesson05/Assets folder.

This file is the one that you finished with in Lesson 4. If you want to use the file from your MyWork folder instead of this one, go ahead; it should be exactly the same as the neptune19.fla file in the Lesson05/Assets folder.

2) Insert a new layer, name it Soundtrack, and drag it to the bottom of the layer stacking order.

Putting your sounds on a separate layer usually is a good idea; they're easier to find and modify that way.

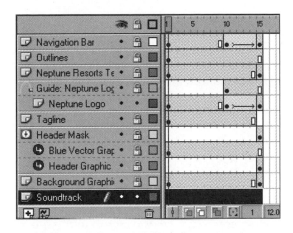

3) Choose File > Import. When the Import dialog box opens, browse to the Lesson05/Assets folder, and import loop.mp3.

The sound file is imported directly into the current Flash library—not added to the stage, as an imported graphic would be.

TIP *You can also bring the loop.mp3 file into your movie by opening sounds.fla in the Lesson05/Assets folder as a library.*

4) Open the library, and locate the loop.mp3 sound.

You can preview your sound before you add it to the movie by clicking the play button in the top-right corner of the Library window.

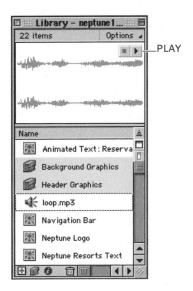

5) Save your movie in the MyWork folder as neptune20.fla.

ADDING SOUNDS TO THE TIMELINE

Importing only adds the sound to the library. For the sound to play in your movie, you must place it on the timeline. Adding a sound to your movie clip is relatively easy, but it is important to make sure you place the sound clip in the frame where you want the sound to begin. You should create a new layer for each sound you want to play in your movie to prevent one sound from overwriting another.

1) Select the Soundtrack layer of neptune20.fla, and drag a copy of loop.mp3 from the library to the stage.

The sound is added to the first, and only, keyframe of the Soundtrack layer. You can see that the sound is there because a graphic representation (waveform) of the sound appears in the timeline. The sound doesn't actually appear on the stage, but you have to drag it there to add it to the movie from the library.

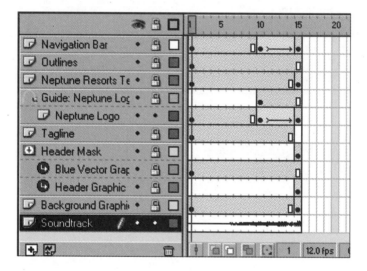

2) Choose Control > Play.

When you play the movie, you can hear the sound play once.

3) Save your movie in the MyWork folder as neptune21.fla.

Next, you're going to make the sound fade in and loop a few times.

MODIFYING SOUND PROPERTIES

After you have a sound in your movie, you can use the Sound panel to apply a preset sound effect or customize a sound effect by using Flash's basic editing capabilities. The Sound panel is also where you define the sound type as a streaming or event sound.

116

Streaming sounds are synchronized with the timeline. Each piece of the sound is linked to a specific frame in the movie. *Event sounds* are synchronized with a specific keyframe or event, such as clicking a button. An event sound plays independently of the timeline. You'll learn more about the different types of sound synchronization as you work through this exercise.

1) Select frame 1 of the Soundtrack layer, and choose Window > Panels > Sound to open the Sound panel. Make sure that loop.mp3 is selected in the Sound pop-up menu.

You can pick any sound that you've imported into the movie. To remove an existing sound from a frame, choose None from the Sound pop-up menu.

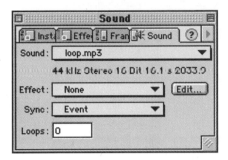

2) From the Effect pop-up menu, choose Fade In.

Choosing Fade In gradually increases the sound over its duration. (Fade Out does the opposite, gradually decreasing the sound.)

If you wanted to remove an effect, you could choose None from the Effect pop-up menu.

Left Channel/Right Channel applies the sound to only the left or right channel, so that it seems as though the sound is coming from only one speaker. Fade Left to Right/Fade Right to Left shifts sound from one channel to the other. You can specify Custom to create your own effect, using the edit envelope (see "Customizing Sound Effects" later in this lesson).

3) From the Sync pop-up menu, choose Stream.

The Sync setting can be set to Event, Start, End, or Stream. Event synchronizes the sound to an event, such as clicking a button or reaching its keyframe in the timeline. An event sound plays for its entirety and independently from the timeline. If you need the sound to play exactly with the timeline, do *not* choose this option. Event sounds play each time they are triggered, so they can overlap.

Start is similar to Event, but sounds play to the end before playing again if they are triggered. End stops every occurrence of a specific event or start sound at the frame in which the stop is located. To use this feature, create an additional layer; insert a keyframe where you want the sound to end; insert the sound you wish to stop into that keyframe; open the Sound panel; and set Sync to End. Because Event sounds run independently of the timeline, this procedure is the only way to guarantee that an event sound will stop at a specific frame.

Stream synchronizes the sound with the timeline. Streaming sounds end when there are no more frames in the timeline. Streaming sounds can be helpful for use as background sounds and for synchronizing a voice with animation.

4) Set Loops to 0.

Finally, you set the number of times you want the sound to repeat in the Loops setting. A sound cannot be looped forever, but it can be looped 99,999 times.

TIP *Looping a streamed sound is not wise. If a streamed sound is set to loop, the size of the file increases to accommodate the additional frames of the looped sound.*

5) Drag the playhead to frame 1, and choose Control > Play.

When you play the movie, the sound fades in. But as soon as the animation reaches frame 15, the sound stops, because the streaming sound is synchronized with the movie's timeline. When you run out of frames, the sound ends.

6) Select frame 1 of the Soundtrack layer. In the Sound panel, choose Start from the Sync pop-up menu, and type 3 in the Loops text box. Play the animation again.

This time, the sound plays all the way through three loops. When you set Sync to Start, the sound starts playing in the frame in which it's triggered and keeps playing until it's completed or stopped.

7) Save the movie in the MyWork folder as neptune22.fla.

You have a nice looping sound in your movie. You'll learn how to control the volume of this sound in Lesson 9. Now it's time to look at how to add sounds to buttons.

ADDING SOUNDS TO BUTTONS

Adding sounds to buttons is similar to adding sounds to the timeline. By adding a keyframe and inserting the sound into that state of the button, you can place a sound in any of the three active states of the button: Up, Over, and Down. In the following exercise, you will add a sound to the Reservations button that you created in Lesson 4.

1) Open the Reservations Button symbol in neptune22.fla in symbol-editing mode. Name the existing layer Graphics, and add a layer named Sounds.

The simplest way to open a symbol in symbol-editing mode is to double-click the symbol's icon in the library. (You must click the icon, not the name; double-clicking the name just highlights it.) Another method is to select the symbol's name in the library and then choose Edit from the Library window's Options menu. Or you can choose Edit > Edit Symbols and then select the symbol in the library.

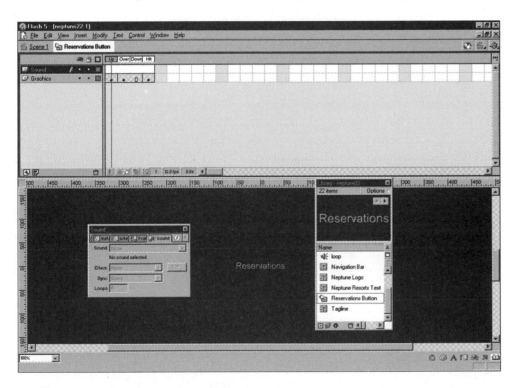

2) In the timeline, click Over, and insert a keyframe.

Clicking Over in the timeline selects the Over state and lets you add a sound that plays only when the mouse is over the button.

3) With the keyframe that you just added selected, open sounds.fla in the Lesson05/Assets folder as a library. Locate bubble.mp3 in the library, and drag it onto the stage.

This sound is the one you will hear when the mouse is over the bubble. If you'd like to test the sound, click the play button in the top-right corner of the Library window.

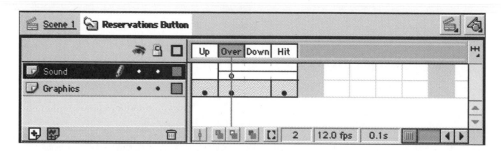

4) In the Sound layer, select the Over state, and open the Sound panel. From the Sync pop-up menu, choose Event.

Remember that because event sounds play each time they are triggered, they can overlap. Each time you move the mouse over this button, the sound plays.

5) Choose Edit > Edit Movie. When Flash switches to movie-editing mode, choose Control > Enable Simple Buttons, and move the mouse over the instance of the Reservations Button symbol on the stage.

If you move the mouse over the button once, you hear the sound once. If you keep moving the mouse back and forth over the button, the sound starts to overlap, because it keeps getting triggered.

6) Open the Reservations Button symbol in symbol-editing mode, and change the Sync of the sound in the Over state to Start. Return to movie-editing mode, and move the mouse over the button.

Sounds that have a sync setting of Start play all the way through when they are first triggered. If a sound of this type is triggered again before it finishes playing, it won't play. So you can keep moving the mouse back and forth over the button, but the sound will not overlap.

7) Save your movie in the MyWork folder as neptune23.fla.

Working with sounds in Flash has been fairly painless so far. Now you're going to get into something more complicated: customizing sound effects.

CUSTOMIZING SOUND EFFECTS

Clicking the Edit button in the Sound panel opens the Edit Envelope dialog box, where you can modify existing sound effects and create your own custom effects. By using the Edit Envelope dialog box, you can change the in point and out point of the sound, as well as control the volume of each sound channel. If you hope to do to something more complex with sound, you'll need another program. Macromedia's SoundEdit and Sonic Foundry's Sound Forge can assist you in creating complex sound edits.

1) Select frame 1 of the Soundtrack layer in neptune23.fla, and click the Edit button in the Sound panel.

The Edit Envelope dialog box opens. This dialog box has several controls that you can use to customize your sounds, as well as three windows. The top window controls the sounds for the left channel. The bottom window controls the sounds for the right channel. The center window—a bar between the channel windows—is the timeline for the sound.

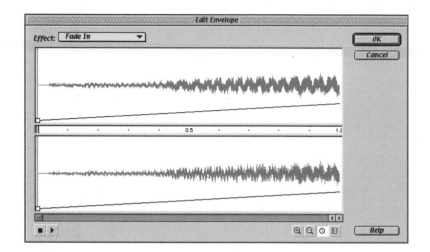

2) Click the zoom-out button in the bottom-right corner of the Edit Envelope dialog box until you can see one complete loop of the sound file.

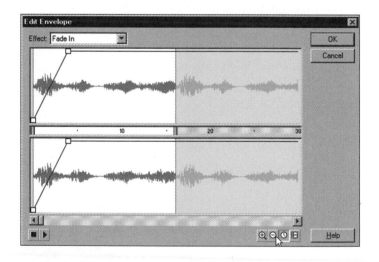

The end of the loop is marked by a vertical line. Right now the sound fades in, starting at no volume and ending at full volume. This setting is indicated by a solid black line (the envelope line) that goes from the bottom of each channel up to the top. The line indicates the volume of the sound in that channel. Each line features two white squares, which are called envelope handles. You can move the envelope handles to change the volume in each channel.

3) From the Effect drop-down menu, choose Fade Left to Right.

The envelope handles move to new positions. The first envelope handle in the left channel is now at the top of that channel's window, indicating that the left channel starts at full volume. The line in that channel slopes down and eventually meets the bottom of the window, indicating that over the course of the first loop, that channel fades out to no volume. The opposite is true of the right channel; it starts at no volume and moves up to full volume. You can click the play button in the bottom-left corner of the dialog box to test the sound.

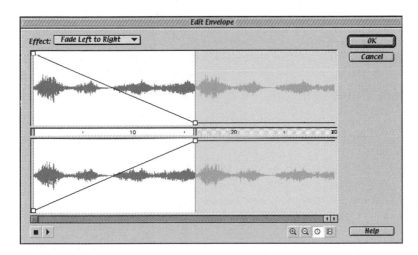

4) Drag the first envelope handle in the right channel window to the top of that channel's window. Do the same for the second envelope handle in the left channel window.

Now both channels start at full volume, and continue to play at full volume for the duration of the sound. You can click the play button in the Edit Envelope dialog box to make sure.

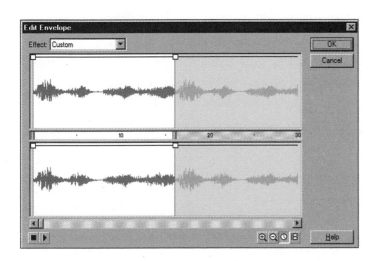

123

5) Click the envelope line between the existing envelope handles in the left channel.

When you click the envelope line, Flash adds another handle to both channels. You can have up to eight envelope handles in each channel.

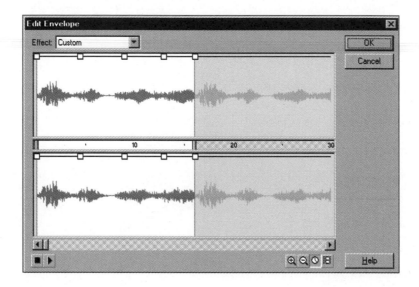

6) Drag the envelope handle that you just added off the top of the left channel window.

When you drag an envelope handle that is not an end point (the first or last envelope handle) off the channel, it removes that envelope handle from both channels.

7) Click OK, and save your movie as neptune24.fla in the MyWork folder.

Now that you're a sound-effects pro, it's time to look at sound compression. Because Flash is used primarily for the Web, it's very important that you keep your movies small, and sound compression is one way to do that.

MODIFYING SOUND COMPRESSION

Flash 5 lets you export sound in three formats: ADPCM, MP3, and Raw. If you are using Windows, Flash can also export sounds in WAV format. By setting the export properties for each sound individually, you can control the quality of each sound file by choosing how small (compressed) to make the file. The files that need to be clearest can be compressed less so that they are truer to the original file. Experiment with these settings to balance the overall file size with sound quality.

1) Open the library for neptune24.fla, and locate the loop.mp3 sound. Right+click (Windows) or Control-click (Macintosh) the sound, and choose Properties from the contextual menu to open the Sound Properties dialog box.

You can set compression settings for each sound individually in this dialog box.

2) From the Compression pop-up menu, choose MP3.

You have several choices for this setting.

ADPCM sets compression for 8-bit or 16-bit sound data. Use ADPCM when you are exporting short event sounds, such as button sounds. A setting of 22 kHz is standard for Web publishing and half the standard CD publishing rate of 44 kHz.

MP3 exports sounds with MP3 compression. Use MP3 when you are exporting longer and streamed sounds, such as music soundtracks. Change the Bit Rate and Quality settings, and notice how the sound file size is reduced or increased. Choose a bit rate higher than 16 Kbps for better sound quality.

Raw exports sounds with no sound compression. A setting of 22 kHz is standard for Web publishing and half the standard CD publishing rate of 44 kHz.

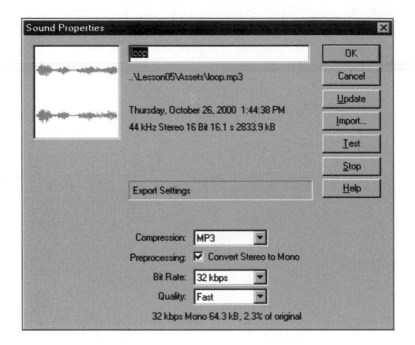

3) Set the bit-rate to 32 Kpbs and the quality to Fast.

A higher bit-rate results in a higher-quality sound with less compression. The quality setting affects the speed at which the sound is compressed. Fast yields the fastest compression with lower sound quality. Medium yields slower compression with higher sound quality. Best yields the slowest compression with the highest sound quality.

TIP *When you are exporting music, set the bit-rate to 16 Kbps or higher for the best result.*

4) Click the Test button.

The sound should play, using the compression settings you specified. You can see how the compression settings affect the size of the sound at the bottom of the window. Play around with the compression settings until you get a sound quality that works for you.

5) Click OK, and save your movie as neptune25.fla in the MyWork folder.

That's it for sound right now. You'll learn how to make a volume control in Lesson 9, and you'll learn more about compressing sound in Lesson 12.

WHAT YOU HAVE LEARNED

In this lesson, you have:

- Imported sounds into a library (pages 114–115)

- Added sounds to the timeline (page 116)

- Modified sound properties (pages 117–118)

- Attached a sound to a button (pages 119–120)

- Experimented with the Edit Envelope dialog box (pages 121–126)

adding basic interactivity

LESSON 6

Up until this point, you have created a movie with a timeline that plays sequentially, one frame after the other. That's all well and good, but you're probably impatient to get to all this interactivity stuff you keep hearing about. Not to worry, that's the subject of this lesson.

You will add simple actions to the Reservations, Activities, Games, Journal, and About buttons in this frame of the Neptune Resorts movie.

In Flash, you can set up your movie to be interactive. When you reach a particular frame, click a button or move the mouse pointer over it, press a key, or enter information in a text box, an event is triggered. To make interactivity possible, you assign actions to a frame or an object, such as a button or movie clip. *Actions* are sets of instructions written in ActionScript, Flash 5's full-fledged scripting language.

WHAT YOU WILL LEARN

In this lesson, you will:

- Explore the Actions panel

- Use actions to control timelines

- Add actions to button instances

- Create a form in Flash, using text boxes and SmartClips

- Create a link to another Web page with the Get URL action

APPROXIMATE TIME

It usually takes about one hour to complete this lesson.

LESSON FILES

Media Files:

Lesson06/Assets/assets.fla

Starting File:

Lesson06/Assets/neptune26.fla

Completed Project:

neptune32.fla

EXPLORING THE ACTIONS PANEL

You can attach actions to buttons, movie clips, or frames by using the Actions panel. In this exercise, you discover what's available in the panel.

1) Choose File > New. Select Frame 1, and choose Window > Actions.

You've just created a new movie and opened the Actions panel.

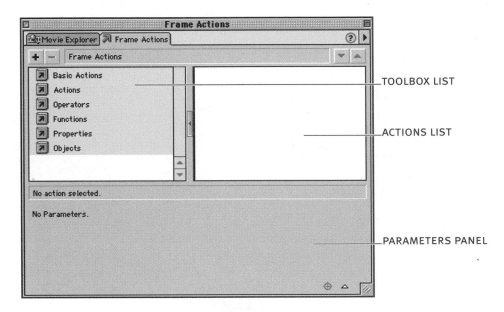

On the left side of the Actions panel is the toolbox list. The toolbox list contains all the pieces of ActionScript that you can add to your movie. On the right side of the Actions panel is the actions list. The actions list is where your script is created. When you double-click an item in the toolbox list, it appears in the actions list. (You can also drag items from the toolbox list to the actions list.) Below the two list windows is the parameters pane. When you're editing in normal mode, the parameters pane prompts you for the parameters (arguments) needed for each action.

You are not restricted to using the toolbox list or even scripting only in the actions list. In expert mode, you can import an external file into the actions list or write your own script directly in the actions list. You can also export the ActionScript in the actions list to an external file.

NOTE *The name of the Actions panel varies depending on whether you're working with a frame or an object. You'll see that it is sometimes called the Frame Actions panel and sometimes called the Objects Actions panel. However, both of these panels are opened by choosing Window > Panels > Action or by clicking the actions icon in the launcher toolbar, so we use the generic name* Actions panel *when referring to either panel.*

2) If necessary, click Basic Actions in the toolbox list to expand the category.

The toolbox list is divided into categories: Basic Actions, Actions, Operators, Functions, Properties, and Objects. For now, you're going to work with the items in the Basic Actions category.

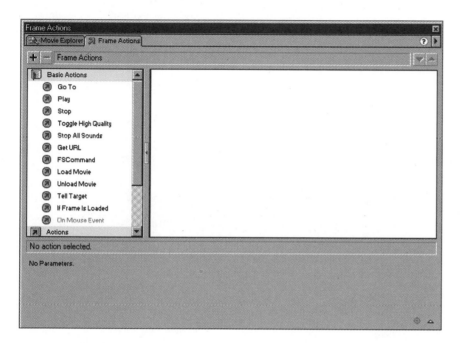

3) In the Basic Actions category, select Go To and drag it to the actions list, or double-click it.

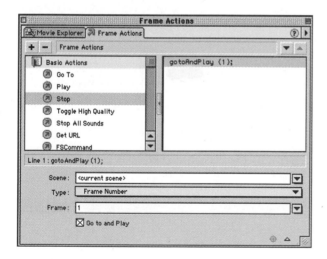

When you drag an item from the toolbox list to the actions list, that item is added to your ActionScript. In this case, you added the Go To action, which controls the movement of the timeline. The actual ActionScript reads `gotoAndPlay (1);`

Look at the parameters pane. Some actions in the toolbox list have parameters associated with them. The Go To action is one of those actions. You can see in the parameters pane that this action has Scene, Type, and Frame parameters. There's also an option called Go To and Play. The parameters can tell you what the line of ActionScript will do; this line tells the movie to go to Frame 1 of the current scene and play.

4) In the toolbox list, double-click the Stop action.

The Stop action is added to the actions list. It looks like this: `stop ();`

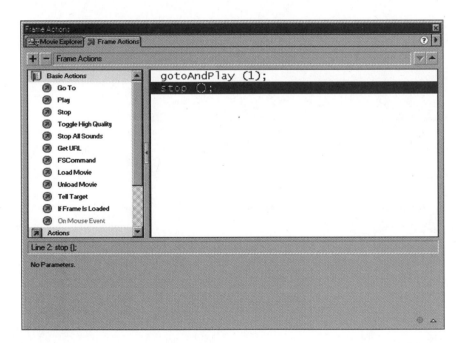

5) Choose File > Close.

You don't need to save the file; this exercise was just for practice. Now it's time to add some actions for real.

USING ACTIONS TO CONTROL THE TIMELINE

You're ready to start adding some interactivity to your Flash movie. You'll start by adding a couple of Stop actions. This may sound like un-interactivity, but it's a good first step.

1) Open neptune26.fla in the Lesson06/Assets folder.

This file is very much like the movie you ended up with in Lesson 5, but it contains a few more frames and keyframes, some additional symbols, and a better-organized library.

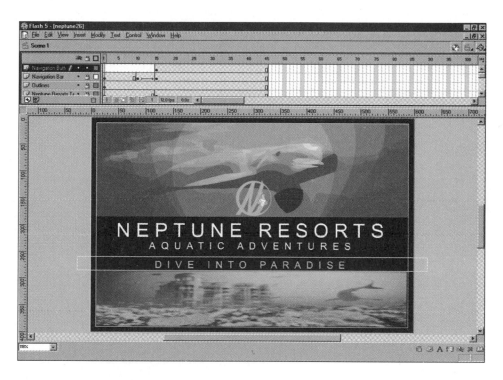

2) Choose Control > Test Movie.

When the test movie appears, your almost-finished Neptune Resorts site opens. The site looks great, but right now it just flips through each of the sections very quickly. You need to add some actions to prevent that from happening.

3) Close the test-movie window. In neptune26.fla, add a new layer to your movie. Name the layer Actions and Labels, and drag it to the top of the layer stacking order.

It's a good idea to keep all your frame actions in the same layer. This practice makes troubleshooting and editing much simpler.

4) At frame 15 of the Actions and Labels layer, insert a keyframe. Select the keyframe, and open the Actions panel.

You're going to add an action to this keyframe.

5) In the Actions panel's toolbox list, double-click the Stop action.

The Stop action is added to the actions list.

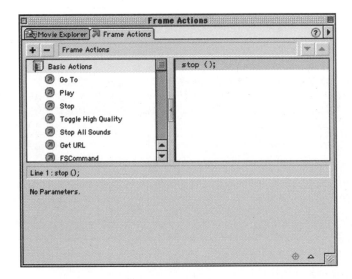

6) In the Actions and Labels layer, insert keyframes at frames 20, 25, 30, 35, and 40. Add a Stop action to each keyframe. Choose Control > Test Movie.

When the movie plays, it should now stop at frame 15. You'll add more ActionScript later in this chapter to make the movie jump to the other sections of the site.

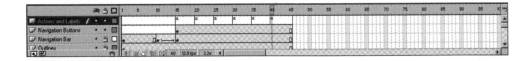

7) Save your movie in the MyWork folder as neptune27.fla.

In the following section, you add buttons to the movie to make it jump to the various sections of your site.

CREATING AN INVISIBLE BUTTON

Sometimes, you don't want your button to be visible in the movie; you just want existing content to be clickable. In Flash, you easily can create an invisible button for this purpose.

TIP *The most obvious way to create an invisible button is to set the transparency (alpha) of an existing button to 0. Don't do the obvious! Flash has to render graphics with an alpha of 0, which slows the movie. Instead, use the method outlined in this section.*

As you begin this exercise, you should still have neptune27.fla open.

1) Choose Insert > New Symbol. In the Name text box, type *Invisible Button*. Click the Button radio button, and click OK.

You're going to make a new symbol for the invisible button. When you click OK, Flash automatically switches to symbol-editing mode.

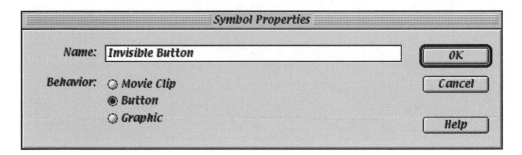

2) Select the Hit state, and choose Insert > Blank Keyframe.

When you create an invisible button, all you have to do is define a hit area. Simple, isn't it?

3) On the stage, use the oval tool to draw a circle with no outline (just a fill). In the Info panel, set the circle's height and width to 75 each. Center the circle horizontally and vertically on the stage.

Make sure that the Hit state is still selected before you begin to draw. (It should be.) The invisible button will take the shape of the circle.

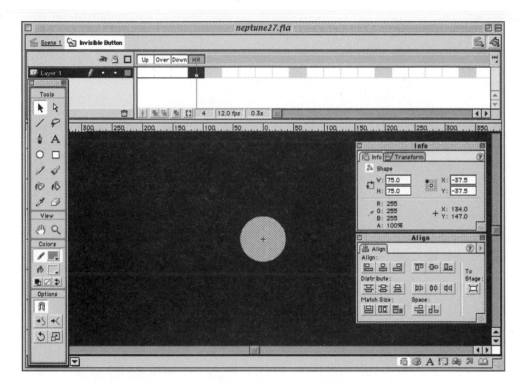

4) Choose Edit > Edit Movie.

You need to exit symbol-editing mode to add the invisible button to the movie.

5) Select frame 15 of the Navigation Buttons layer, open the library, and drag an instance of the Invisible Button symbol onto the stage. Position it directly over the Neptune Logo symbol.

You are going to use the Invisible Button symbol to act as a hit area for the Neptune Logo symbol. When you add the button to the stage, it should show up as an aqua circle. The color indicates that this button has a Hit state but not an Over state. If you want to position the button precisely with the Info panel, you can set its X coordinate to 15 and its Y coordinate to 11.

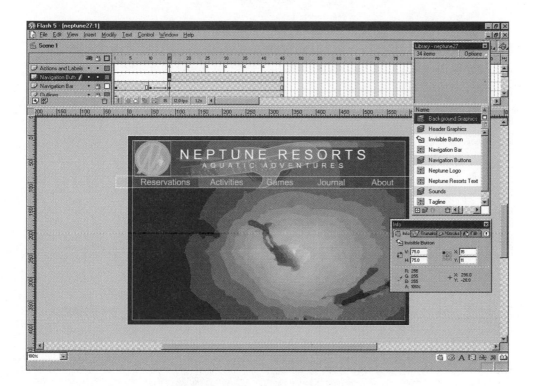

6) Save your movie in the MyWork folder as neptune28.fla.

Now you need to add some interactivity to the button, along with all the other buttons in the Navigation Buttons layer.

ADDING ACTIONS TO BUTTON INSTANCES

You already know how to stop the movie. In this section, you'll use actions to activate the buttons in the Navigation Buttons layer so that you can navigate to each section of the site.

1) Select frame 15 of the Actions and Labels layer in neptune28.fla, and open the Frame panel.

You used the Frame panel in Lesson 4 when you applied tweening to some frames. Now you'll use it to apply labels to keyframes in the Actions and Labels layer. Each keyframe in this layer marks a new section of the movie.

2) In the Label text box, type *Home*.

Frame 15 is essentially the home page of your developing movie. When you set the label in the Frame panel, you should be able to see it in the timeline as well, provided that enough frames follow the labeled frame for Flash to display the label.

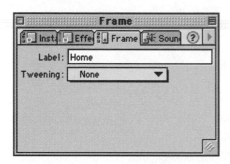

3) Select frame 20 of the Actions and Labels layer. In the Label text box of the Frame panel, type *Reservations*. Use the Frame panel to set the following labels for each of the other keyframes in this layer: frame 25 to Activities, frame 30 to Games, frame 35 to Journal, and frame 40 to About.

Each section of your movie is now labeled. By labeling the sections, you can add actions that refer to specific sections, rather than frames. That way, if you wanted to add more frames between sections (to add more animation, for example), you would still be able to refer to the labeled section.

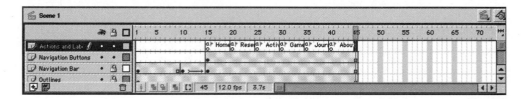

4) Select frame 15 of the Navigation Buttons layer; then select the instance of the Invisible Button. In the Frame Actions panel, locate the Go To action in the toolbox list, and add it to the actions list.

The following ActionScript is added to the actions list:

```
on (release) {
 gotoAndPlay (1);
}
```

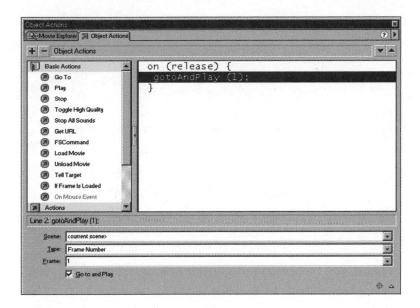

The first line of this ActionScript tells Flash to do something on (release), which means that when the mouse button is pressed and released, everything inside the curly braces ({}) should happen. The next line tells Flash to gotoAndPlay (1);— specifically, to go to frame 1 and play the movie from there.

5) Select the line that says gotoAndPlay (1);**. In the parameters pane, set the type to Frame Label and the frame to Home, and deselect the Go To and Play option.**

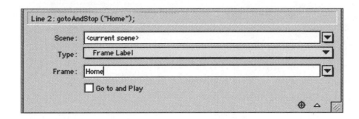

Your ActionScript should now look like this:

```
on (release) {
gotoAndStop ("Home");
}
```

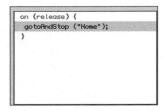

With just a few simple changes, you modified the ActionScript so that when the mouse button is released, the movie goes to and stops at the frame labeled Home.

The Frame setting has a drop-down menu containing all of the labeled frames in the movie, so you can select the necessary frame label from that menu.

6) Repeat steps 4 and 5 for each of the other buttons in the Navigation Buttons layer, setting the frame to the label that corresponds with the button.

Just select each button in turn, and apply the Go To action to it. Make sure that you set the type to Frame for each button, and set the frame to the appropriate frame for the button. The Reservations button goes to the Reservations frame, the Activities button goes to the Activities frame, and so on.

7) Close the Actions panel, and choose Control > Enable Simple Buttons. Click each of the buttons in the Navigation Buttons layer to see what the movie does.

If a check appears next to the Enable Simple Buttons command, it's already selected, so you don't have to select it again. When you click each button, the movie should jump to the appropriate frame. You should be able to see the playhead move to each frame.

8) Save your movie as neptune29.fla in the MyWork folder.

You're done adding buttons for now. In the next part of this lesson, you'll work with a different sort of interactivity: creating forms in Flash.

USING TEXT BOXES

Flash's text boxes let you create graphically appealing forms and surveys. You can use these text boxes to collect information about your users, give users a means of logging into your Web site, create order forms, and much more.

In this exercise, you will use the text tool and the Text Options panel to create some text boxes for your reservations form.

1) Open assets.fla as a library.

You can find assets.fla in the Lesson06/Assets folder. You are going to use some assets from this library throughout this exercise.

2) In neptune29.fla, select frame 20 of the Background Graphics layer. Locate the Form Background Graphic symbol in the assets.fla library, and drag it onto the stage. Position it at X: 20 and Y: 120.

This symbol will act as the background for the text boxes that you're going to add to the movie. Unlike HTML, Flash allows you to get very creative with your form backgrounds.

3) Add a new layer to the movie, name it Form Elements, and place it just above the Background Graphics layer in the layer stacking order. Insert blank keyframes at frames 20 and 25 of the Form Elements layer.

You are going to add text boxes to frame 20. The blank keyframe in frame 25 is to prevent the text boxes from appearing there.

4) Select frame 20 of the Form Elements layer. Select the text tool, and open the Character panel. Set the font to _sans, font height to 12, and font color to White.

As you did when you used the Character panel earlier in this book, make sure that the other settings are at their defaults: tracking at 0, character position at Normal, and bold and italics turned off.

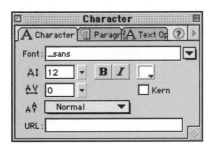

Before you create the text box, it's a good idea to set the options for the appearance of the text. Setting the font to _sans establishes that the text box will use the default sans-serif font on the user's computer.

In the next step, you'll add the functionality that makes this box a text box.

5) Open the Text Options panel. From the top pop-up menu, choose Input Text. From the second pop-up menu, choose Single Line. Create a text box on the stage by clicking and dragging to the desired width.

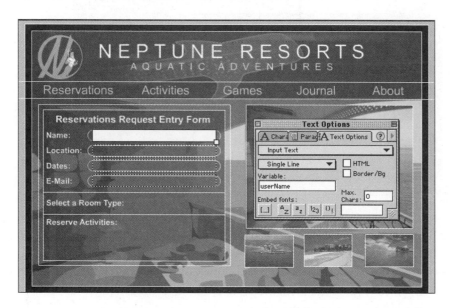

Make the text box about the same width as the area labeled Name in the Form Background Graphic. These labeled areas will be called text-box backgrounds throughout the rest of this lesson.

6) Use the arrow tool to select the text box that you just drew. Position the text box so that it's in the text-box background labeled Name. In the Text Options panel, type *userName* in the Variable text box.
When you switch to the arrow tool, the text box is selected automatically.

You now have an text box that can hold a variable called userName.

7) Create additional text boxes for the text backgrounds labeled Location, Dates, and E-mail. Set the variable names to *location*, *dates*, and *userEmail*, respectively.
You should end up with four text boxes, each of which has a different variable name. It's very important that you give each text box a different variable name. If you

accidentally use the same variable name for more than one text box, both text boxes will end up with the same text.

8) Choose Control > Test Movie. When the movie opens, click the Reservations button, click inside one of the text boxes you just made, and start typing.

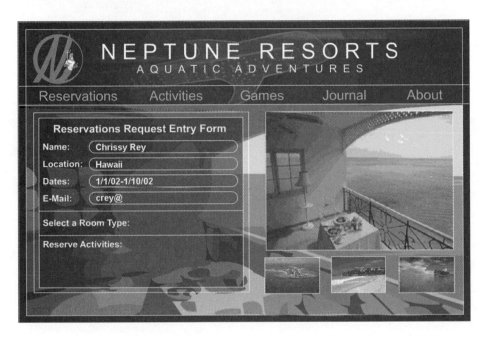

9) Close the test-movie window, and save your movie as neptune30.fla in the MyWork folder.

Don't close the file; you're not done with the form yet. In the next exercise, you will add some SmartClips to make the form even better.

USING SMART CLIPS

Smart Clips are reusable elements, such as pop-up menus, navigational menus, and multiple-choice forms. These elements can be shared across the site, with other members of your development team, or with others in the Flash community.

You create Smart Clips the same way that you do other symbols, but you use associated parameters that allow users to customize the clips. You can even create a SWF file to use as an easy interface for the Smart Clip you created.

In this exercise, you won't create a Smart Clip, but you will use one of the Smart Clips that comes with Flash as you continue to build the reservations form in frame 20. Adding the Smart Clip to the form lets you get some more data from your visitors.

1) Select frame 20 of the Form Elements layer in neptune30.fla. Drag an instance of the Menu symbol from the assets.fla library onto the stage, and position it at X: 152 and Y: 258.

This symbol isn't just a symbol; it's a Smart Clip. In the next step, you'll modify the parameters of the Smart Clip so that it contains the information you need.

2) Choose Window > Panels > Clip Parameters.

The Clip Parameters panel opens. This panel contains all the settings for a SmartClip that you can modify. When you opened the Clip Parameters panel, the Menu Smart Clip should still have been selected, so you can see that it has only one setting to be modified: items. The items setting lists the items in the pop-up menu that is created by the Menu Smart Clip. The setting currently has a value of (Array[]), which means that it can have a list of values.

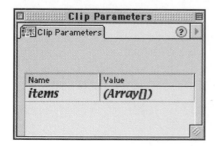

144

3) Double-click the (Array[]) value in the Clip Parameters panel.

The Values dialog box opens. You can use this dialog box to list the values associated with the items setting.

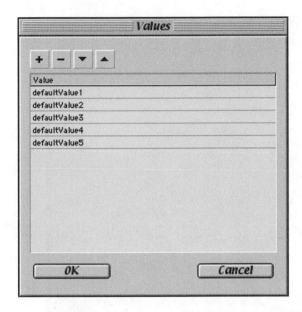

4) Double-click the line that contains the value defaultValue1. Type *Luxury*, and press Enter or Return. Change the next three values (defaultValue2, defaultValue3, and defaultValue4) to *Vacationer*, *Business*, and *Economy*, respectively. Delete defaultValue5, and click OK.

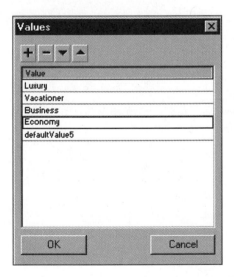

The dialog box closes and the Smart Clip now has your values applied to it.

5) Chose Control > Test Movie. When the test movie opens, click the Reservations button, and try your pop-up menu.

The menu should contain the text that you entered in the Values dialog box.

6) Close the test-movie window, and save your movie as neptune31.fla in the MyWork folder.

You're done with the form for now, but you still have some more changes to make in the movie, so keep it open.

USING THE GET URL ACTION

The Neptune Resorts site is for a resort hotel in Hawaii. What if your visitors wanted more information about Hawaii? Wouldn't it be nice if they could just click a button and load a Web site about Hawaii? You can make that possible by linking other Web sites to your buttons. You can use the Get URL action to launch a browser and load a new Web site.

In this exercise, you'll give credit where credit is due by linking the Neptune Resorts site to Fig Leaf Software, the designer of the site. You should still have neptune31.fla open as you begin.

1) In the Background Graphics layer, select frame 15. Drag an instance of the Made By symbol from the assets.fla library onto the stage, and position it at X: 10 and Y: 345.

The Made By symbol has the Fig Leaf Software logo in it. You're going to let users visit Fig Leaf's Web site to see what else the company can do.

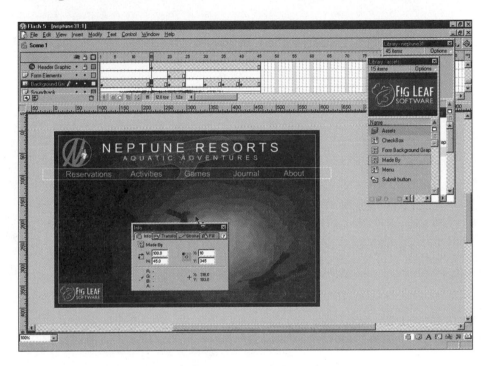

The instance of the Made By symbol should still be selected.

2) Open the Instance panel. From the Behavior pop-up menu, choose Button.

Even if a symbol was created as a movie clip, you can give an instance of the symbol a different behavior. In this case, changing the Made By symbol to a button lets you apply an action that will occur when the symbol is clicked.

147

3) Open the Actions panel. Select Get URL in the toolbox list, and add it to the actions list.

TIP *Again, the Made By symbol should still be selected. If it wasn't, and if you have trouble selecting it, chose Control > Enable Simple Buttons to turn off that option. When Enable Simple Buttons is turned on, the buttons are clickable, so they can be difficult to select.*

The following ActionScript is added to the actions list:

```
on (release) {
  getURL ("");
}
```

Right now, this bit of ActionScript can be translated to read, "When the user releases the mouse button, go to the URL contained in the quotes." Nothing appears inside the quotes, so you need to add that next.

4) In the parameters pane, type *http://www.figleaf.com* in the URL text box. From the Window pop-up menu, choose _blank.

The ActionScript changes to read:

```
on (release) {
  getURL ("http://www.figleaf.com", "_blank");
}
```

This script means that when the user clicks the Made By symbol is releases the mouse button, Flash will open a new browser window (_blank) and go to the URL http://www.figleaf.com.

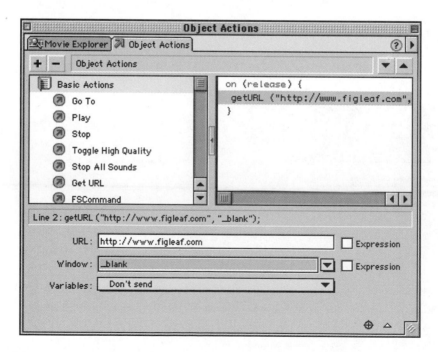

The URL parameter can be any URL, including an e-mail URL (mailto:). The Window parameter can be one of the windows listed in the pop-up menu (_self, _blank, _parent, or _top) or any other window named by JavaScript, VBScript, or a frameset.

5) Choose Control > Test Movie. When the movie gets to the frame labeled Home, click the button you just made.

A browser window should open, taking you to the Fig Leaf Software Web site at http://www.figleaf.com, if you're connected to the Internet.

6) Close the test-movie window, and save your movie as neptune32.fla in the MyWork folder.

You're done with the movie for now.

WHAT YOU HAVE LEARNED

In this lesson, you have:

- Explored the Actions panel, learning the functions of the toolbox list, the actions list, and the parameters panel (pages 130–132)
- Used the Stop action to control the timeline (pages 133–134)
- Created an invisible button (pages 135–136)
- Labeled sections of your movie (pages 137–138)
- Used the Go To action to create working buttons (pages 137–140)
- Created text boxes that accept user input (pages 140–143)
- Used and modified a Smart Clip (pages 143–146)
- Added a link to a button by using the Get URL action (pages 146–148)

programming with ActionScript

At this point, you should be feeling comfortable with the Flash basics. You've gotten to know the panels and tools, worked in the timeline and on the stage, used layers and simple actions, and created everything from simple graphics to working buttons. But Flash can do much more. This lesson will give you a taste of just how powerful Flash truly is.

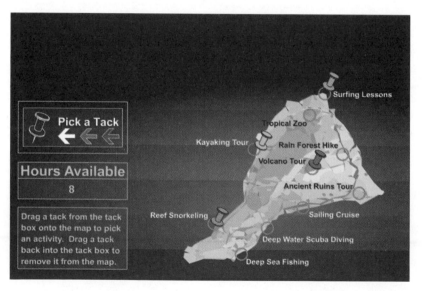

Users can drag and drop the colorful tacks shown on this map.

In the tasks in this lesson, you will build an interactive map to be used in the Neptune Resorts Web site. The map will have draggable tacks that your users can use to pinpoint activities. As you build this map, you will start to learn the underlying concepts required for programming in ActionScript.

WHAT YOU WILL LEARN

In this lesson, you will:

- Use a variable with a dynamic text box

- Add drag-and-drop interactivity to a movie

- Attach and remove movie clips with ActionScript

- Apply a random color to a movie clip

APPROXIMATE TIME

It usually takes about one hour to complete this lesson.

LESSON FILES

Media Files:

None

Starting Files:

Lesson07/Assets/map1.fla

Completed Project:

map9.fla

USING VARIABLES WITH DYNAMIC TEXT BOXES

A *variable* is a placeholder for information. Think of it as a container. The container (variable) itself is always the same, but the contents (value) can change. You can change the contents of a variable to record information about what a user has done, record values that change as the movie plays, or evaluate whether a condition is true or false. You can use variables to make updating your movie easy; every place where the variable is used, Flash fills in its value.

One place to which you can pass the value of a variable is a *dynamic text box*, which displays dynamically updating text such as scores and stock quotes. To pass the value of a variable to a dynamic text box, you give the variable and the dynamic text box the same name.

In Lesson 6, you learned how to make text boxes, complete with variable names, and making a dynamic text box is very similar. In the next exercise, you'll create a dynamic text box to show the amount of time visitors have for their activities.

1) Open map1.fla in the Lesson07/Assets folder.

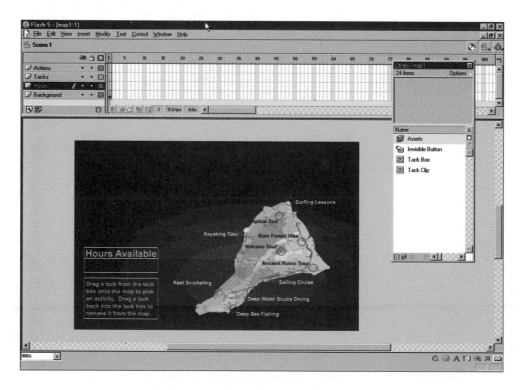

You are going to create your interactive map in this movie, which already contains all the symbols you need.

2) Click the text tool. In the Character panel, set the font to Arial or Helvetica, the font height to 16, and the font color to gold (#FFCC00).

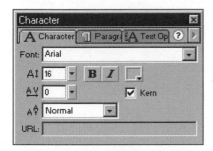

Make sure that the other settings are at their defaults: tracking at 0, character position at normal, and bold and italic deselected.

NOTE *If you can't the change character position or tracking in the Character panel, the text type is probably set to Dynamic Text or Input Text in the Text Options panel. Open the Text Options panel and change the text type to Static Text. Then make your changes in the Character panel.*

Now that you have the look of your text box set up, you'll make the text box dynamic.

3) Open the Text Options panel. Choose Dynamic Text from the text-type pop-up menu, and choose Single Line from the line-type pop-up menu.

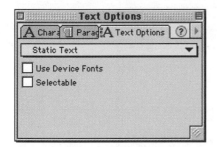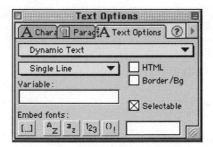

Notice that choosing Dynamic Text causes some radically different options to appear in the Text Options panel. The left half of the figure shows the Text Options panel before you choose Dynamic Text; the right half shows the panel after you choose Dynamic Text.

4) Select frame 1 of the Hours layer, and draw a text box on the stage in the space below Hours Available.

The text box should be wide enough to contain at least two characters.

TIP *If you'd like the text always to appear in the center of the text box, use the Paragraph panel to set the alignment to center.*

5) Select the text box. In the Text Options panel, type *Hours* in the Variable text box. Uncheck the Selectable checkbox.

Also make sure that the HTML and Border/Bg checkboxes are deselected.

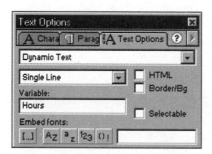

You just defined the variable name for this text box. Now if you use a little ActionScript to give the variable a value, the dynamic text box will display that value.

6) Select frame 1 of the Actions layer. Open the Actions panel, and click the actions category to expand it. Choose the `set variable` action, and add it to the actions list.

Remember that you can either drag or double-click an action to add it to the actions list.

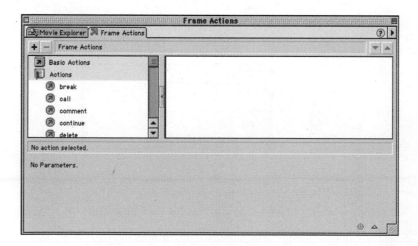

7) In the Parameters pane, type *Hours* in the Variable text box and *8* in the Value text box. Check the Expression checkbox next to the Value text box.

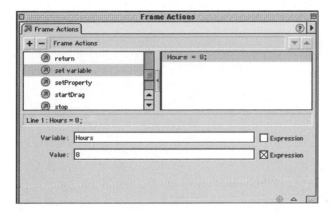

The ActionScript now looks like this:

```
Hours = 8;
```

This ActionScript sets the "container" to Hours, which is the name that you gave the variable in the dynamic text box. It also sets the contents to a value of 8.

8) Choose Control > Test Movie.

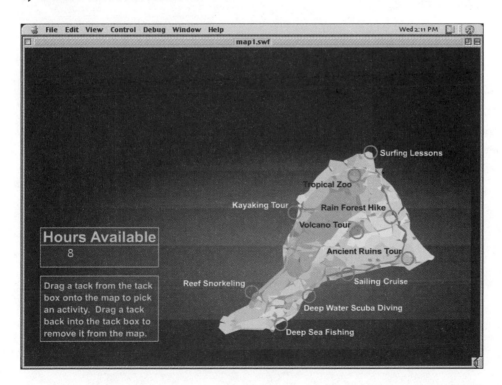

155

When the test movie opens, you should see the number 8 where you placed your dynamic text box. Flash is applying the value that you specified for the hours variable in your ActionScript to the text box with the same name.

8) Close the test movie, and save your movie in the MyWork folder as map2.fla.

You still have a lot of work to do with this map, so keep it open for the next exercise.

MAKING A DRAGGABLE MOVIE CLIP

Drag-and-drop interactivity is easy in Flash 5, and it can be very useful for shopping carts, navigational elements, games, and interactive maps. You can use the startDrag action to make a movie clip draggable while a movie is playing. The movie clip to which the startDrag action or method is applied remains draggable until it is explicitly stopped by the stopDrag action or until another movie clip is targeted with startDrag. Only one movie clip can be dragged at a time.

If the map2.fla symbol library isn't open, you'll need to open it before beginning this exercise. Either click the library icon in the launcher bar (the book icon) or choose Window > Library.

Also, you should still have the map2.fla file open from the preceding exercise.

1) Select frame 1 of the Tacks layer, and drag an instance of the Tack Clip symbol onto the stage.

It doesn't matter where you place this movie clip, so long as it's visible on the stage.

2) Double-click the instance of the Tack Clip symbol.

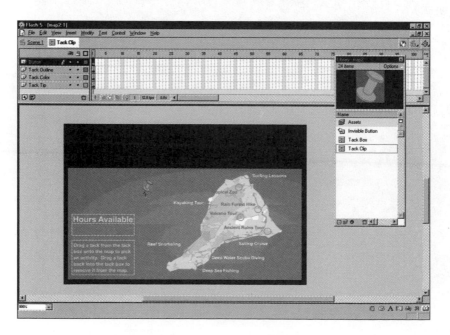

Flash goes into symbol-editing mode. The Tack Clip symbol consists of four layers: Button, Tack Outline, Tack Color, and Tack Clip. The Button layer contains an invisible button symbol, to which you are going to apply some ActionScript. You will work with the layers of the Tack Color and Tack Clip symbols later in this lesson.

3) Select the Button layer; then select the instance of the Invisible Button symbol. Open the Actions panel. Add the `startDrag` **action to the actions list.**

You'll find the `startDrag` action in the Actions category of the toolbox list.

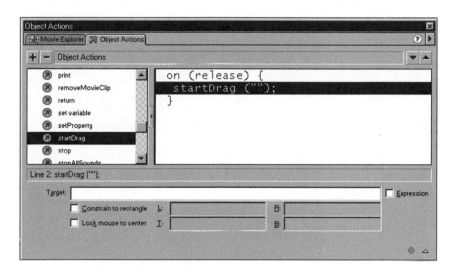

The following ActionScript is added to the button:

```
on (release) {
  startDrag ("");
}
```

The translation of this bit of ActionScript is, "When you release the mouse button, start dragging." The ActionScript doesn't specify what should be dragged, yet.

4) Select the first line of the ActionScript. In the Parameters pane, uncheck the Release checkbox, and check the Press checkbox.

The first line of the ActionScript now reads on (press) {.

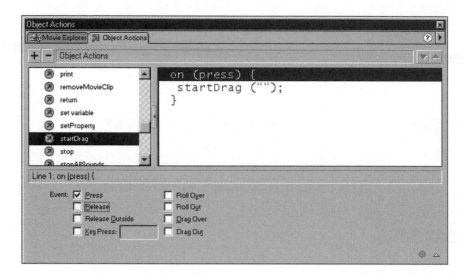

You want the dragging to occur when you press the mouse button, not when you release it.

5) Select the second line of the ActionScript.

The second line of the ActionScript reads startDrag ("");.

Several options are available for the startDrag action in the Parameters pane: Target, Constrain to rectangle, and Lock mouse to center.

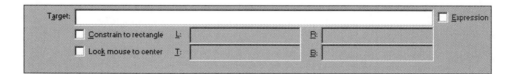

The Target option specifies what to drag—usually, an instance of a movie-clip symbol that's on the stage. The symbol is referred to by its instance name, which is set in the Instance panel. You don't have to specify a target if you want to drag the target to which the action is applied, because the startDrag action refers to the current timeline if no target is specified. You'll learn more about using targets later in this lesson.

The Constrain to rectangle option, when selected, allows you to specify the left, top, right, and bottom sides of a rectangle to constrain the dragging action. If you move the mouse outside the rectangle, the item that you are dragging stays at the edge of the rectangle.

The Lock mouse to center option, when selected, places the mouse pointer on the center of the item being dragged when the drag is initiated. The center of a symbol is indicated by a small crosshair on the stage. In the case of the Tack Clip symbol, the center point is located below all the items in the symbol, so if this option were selected, the tack clip would appear to jump off the mouse. You will use this option later in this lesson.

6) Select the last line of the ActionScript in the actions list. In the toolbox list, double-click the stopDrag **action.**

The following ActionScript is added to the actions list:

```
on (release) {
  stopDrag ();
}
```

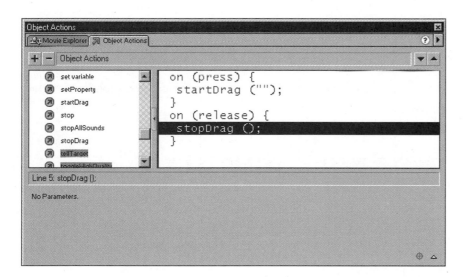

Flash translates this code to mean "When the mouse button is released, the drag action stops." This ActionScript drops the item that you started dragging around with the startDrag action, setting up drag-and-drop interactivity.

7) Choose Control > Test Movie. In the test-movie window, click the Activities button, and test the drag-and-drop interactivity of your tack clip.

You should be able to start dragging the tack clip around when you click it and drop it when you release the mouse button.

8) Close the test movie, and save your movie as map3.fla in the MyWork folder.

In Lesson 8, you'll learn how to take the ActionScript that you just added and modify it so that it uses the preferred method of creating interactivity in Flash: object-oriented programming.

USING METHODS INSTEAD OF ACTIONS

You've used basic ActionScript to create interactivity. Now you're going to take the ActionScript to the next level by using methods. A *method* is a bit of reusable code that can be applied to a target. The target can be several things, but in this exercise, you'll use a movie clip as the target. In ActionScript, this target is known as the *object* to which a method is applied.

In the preceding exercise, you used an action to control an instance of the tack clip's timeline. The action (startDrag) required a parameter: the target you wanted to start dragging. You could rewrite this line of ActionScript, using a method, and the functionality would remain the same.

1) In map3.fla, select the instance of the Invisible Button in the Button layer of the Tack Clip movie clip. Click the Options button in the top-right corner of the Actions panel, and choose Expert Mode from the pop-up menu.

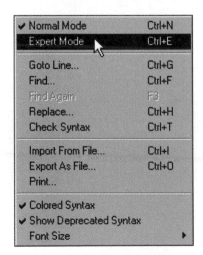

✔ Normal Mode	Ctrl+N
Expert Mode	Ctrl+E
Goto Line...	Ctrl+G
Find...	Ctrl+F
Find Again	F3
Replace...	Ctrl+H
Check Syntax	Ctrl+T
Import From File...	Ctrl+I
Export As File...	Ctrl+O
Print...	
✔ Colored Syntax	
✔ Show Deprecated Syntax	
Font Size	▶

The Options button is a small arrow in the top-right corner of the Actions panel. When you switch the Actions panel to expert mode, you still have the toolbox list on the left side of the panel, but the Basic Actions category no longer appears.

In expert mode, you can also type in the actions list, which makes modifying your ActionScript a little easier, especially if you already have experience writing code in other programming languages, such as JavaScript and C++.

2) In the Actions panel, click the Objects category in the toolbox list to expand it. Below the Objects category, click MovieClip to expand that subcategory.

A long list of actions appears in the toolbox list.

3) Select the second line of the ActionScript. Double-click the startDrag **method listed in the MovieClip category to add it to the actions list.**

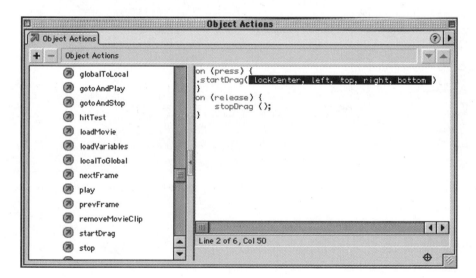

The following ActionScript replaces the second line in the actions list:

```
.startDrag( lockCenter, left, top, right, bottom )
```

This code is the startDrag method. To work, the method needs to have a target, or object. The object should be listed to the left of the method, before the dot (.).

4) Click to the left of the line of ActionScript that you just added, and type the word *this*.

Here's how the ActionScript should look:

```
on (press) {
  this.startDrag( lockCenter, left, top, right, bottom )
}
on (release) {
  stopDrag ();
}
```

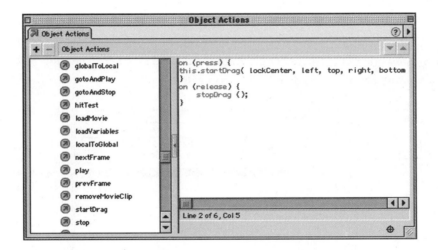

The this object refers to the current timeline, so the startDrag method is applied to the current movie clip.

5) Replace the contents of the parentheses following the startDrag **method with** true, 10, 110, 590, 390.

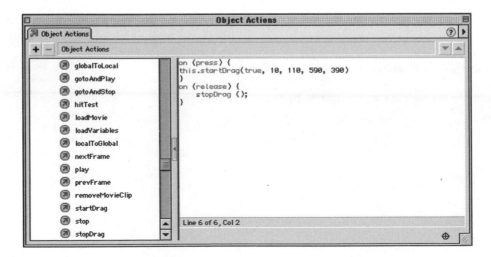

The startDrag method has several parameters, each of which is contained in the parentheses. The first parameter is lockCenter, which corresponds to the Lock mouse to center option for the startDrag action. The second through fifth parameters allow you to specify a bounding box for the draggable item, in this order: left, top, right, and bottom. This method is the same as selecting the Constrain to rectangle option for the startDrag action and then specifying the bounding box.

The settings that you specified make the movie clip's center lock to the mouse as you drag it, as well as constrain it to a rectangle with the left side starting at 10, the top starting at 110, right side at 590, and the bottom at 390.

6) In the fourth line of the actions list, type releaseOutside **before the end parentheses.**

The line of code should look like this:

```
on (release, releaseOutside) {
```

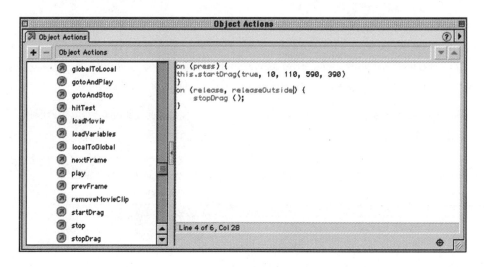

This change modifies the ActionScript so that the stopDrag function occurs when you release the mouse button outside the button symbol. This change is necessary because the movie clip's center will be locked to the mouse when you start to drag it, moving the button symbol away from the mouse.

7) Select the fifth line of the ActionScript. In the toolbox list, double-click `stopDrag`.
Type the word *this* **at the beginning of the fifth line.**

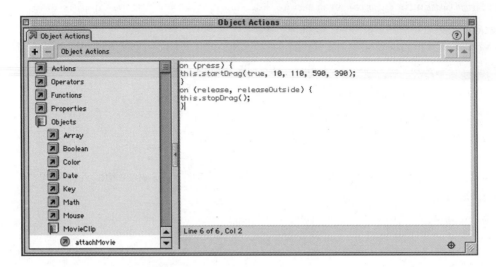

The fifth line of the ActionScript initially reads `stopDrag ();`. Double-clicking
`stopDrag` in the toolbox list replaces the `stopDrag` action with the `stopDrag` method.
The functionality is the same; it's simply achieved by different means.

By typing the word `this` at the beginning of the line, you set the object for the method
to the current timeline. (Think of the `this` object as meaning *this* timeline.)

8) Click the Options button, and from the pop-up menu, choose Normal Mode.

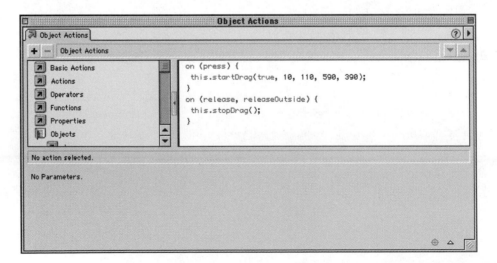

When you switch to normal mode, if your ActionScript is free of errors, Flash adds all the indentation and punctuation that makes your ActionScript easier to read. Notice that Flash indented the lines containing the methods, because these lines of code occur as part of the on (press) and on (release) events. Flash also adds a semicolon to the end of each line that contains a method, which is one way that ActionScript ends a line of code.

TIP *If Flash tells you that your script has errors, and you cannot switch to normal mode, don't despair. Click OK, and then check the Output window to see which line of your script has a problem. (The Output window opens automatically behind the initial error message.)*

9) Switch back to expert mode.

You switch to this mode by choosing Expert Mode from the Options pop-up menu.

10) Choose Control > Test Movie, and test your drag-and-drop interactivity.

The interactivity should be much like it was before, but the center point of the Tack Clip movie clip should lock to the mouse when you start dragging.

11) Close the test movie, and save the movie as map4.fla in the MyWork folder.

You still have quite a bit to do in this movie, so keep it open for the following exercise.

MODIFYING MOVIE-CLIP PROPERTIES

Movie clips have several properties, including alpha, x, y, xscale, and yscale. You can use ActionScript to retrieve the value of these properties. You can also use ActionScript to change those values dynamically.

When you use a movie-clip property in ActionScript, you must first reference the target path of the movie clip with the property you want to retrieve or control. You used a target path in the preceding exercise, when you referenced the target this for the startDrag and stopDrag methods. You'll learn more about how to use target paths in this exercise.

You should have the Actions panel and the map4.fla file open before you begin this exercise.

1) In the Tack Tip layer of the Tack Clip movie clip, select the instance of the Tack Tip symbol. Open the Instance panel, and type *tackTip* in the Name text box.

You can open the Instance panel by choosing Window > Panels > Instance or clicking the Instance icon in the launcher bar.

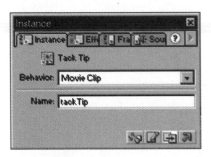

By typing *tackTip* in the Name box, you change the name of the instance of the symbol so that you can target the movie clip with ActionScript. The instance name provides a label that ActionScript can understand.

TIP *If you have any trouble selecting the instance of the Tack Tip movie clip, lock all the other layers in the symbol and then choose Edit > Select All. Just remember to unlock all the other layers when you're done setting the instance name.*

2) In the Button layer, select the instance of the Invisible Button. Add a new line after line 2 of the actions list, and add the ActionScript tackTip._visible = true; **to the new line.**

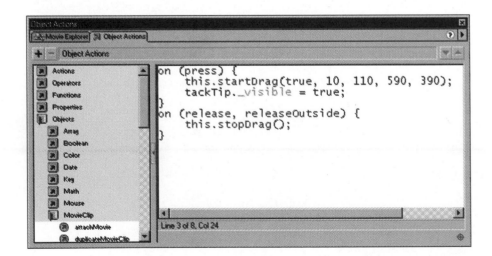

The ActionScript for your button should look like the following:

```
on (press) {
  this.startDrag(true, 10, 110, 590, 390);
  tackTip._visible = true;
}
on (release, releaseOutside) {
  this.stopDrag();
}
```

The line that you just added sets the _visible property of the instance named tackClip to true. That means that when this ActionScript is executed, just after you start dragging the tack, the instance of the Tack Tip movie clip inside the Tack Clip movie clip is visible. You can find a list of all the properties that you can modify in such a manner in the Properties category of the toolbox list.

Remember that you can have Flash indent lines and add punctuation for you by switching to normal mode and then back to expert mode.

TIP *If you're having trouble figuring out which line is which, look at the bottom of the Actions panel, which displays the current line, total lines, and current column.*

3) Add another new line after line 6 of the actions list and add the ActionScript tackTip._visible = false; **to the new line.**

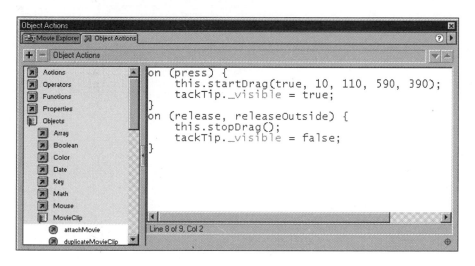

This ActionScript sets the _visible property of the instance named tackClip to false when it's executed.

4) Add the ActionScript `this._y = this._y + 11;` **in a new line following line 7.**

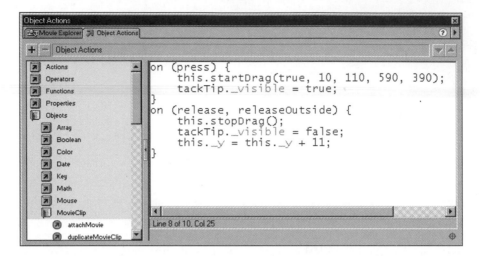

When this ActionScript is executed, the _y property of the object (this) will be set to the current _y property plus 11. The _y property is the current Y position of the object. You can not only set the value of a property, but also retrieve that value of a property. In this case, you're doing both.

Your ActionScript should now look like this:

```
on (press) {
  this.startDrag(true, 10, 110, 590, 390);
  tackTip._visible = true;
}
on (release, releaseOutside) {
  this.stopDrag();
  tackTip._visible = false;
  this._y = this._y + 11;
}
```

5) Choose Control > Test Movie, and test the drag-and-drop interactivity.

When you drag the tack around, it should appear as it did before. When you drop it, the instance named tackTip disappears, because its _visible property has been set to false. Also, the entire tack moves down 11 pixels, so the tack appears to be pushed into the map when you stop dragging it.

6) Close the test movie, and save the movie as map5.fla in the MyWork folder.

You still have work to do with this movie, so keep it open for the following exercise.

ATTACHING A MOVIE CLIP TO THE MOVIE

You can retrieve a copy of a movie clip from a library and play it as part of your movie by using the attachMovie method. The attached movie clip does not have to be on the stage or in the work area, but it does have to be exported with the movie. The way you retrieve the clip and play it is by modifying the linkage properties of the movie clip in the Library window.

After you use the attachMovie method to attach a movie clip to the movie, you can use the clip just as you would any other clip, so you can refer to and modify its properties dynamically. You can also remove an attached movie clip by using the removeMovieClip method, which you will learn about later in this lesson.

In this exercise, you will use the attachMovie method to add the tack directly from the library instead of placing it on the stage.

You should still have map5.fla open from the preceding exercise.

1) In the map5.fla library, right-click (Windows) or Control-click (Macintosh) the Tack Clip movie clip. From the contextual menu, choose Linkage.

The Symbol Linkage Properties dialog box opens. You worked with this dialog box in Lesson 3, so it should be somewhat familiar.

Before you can attach the movie clip directly from the library, you need to give it an identifier and set it to export with the movie.

2) Click the Export this symbol radio button. In the Identifier text box, type *tackClip*. Click OK to close the Symbol Linkage Properties dialog box.

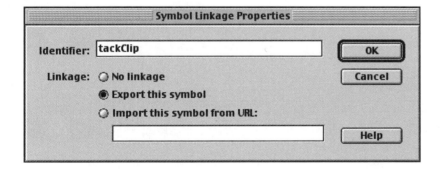

By default, symbols that are not on the stage are not exported with the movie, but you've modified the linkage properties of the Tack Clip symbol so that it will be exported with the movie. (You did the same thing when you created a shared library in Lesson 3.)

3) In the library, double-click the Tack Box icon.

Double-clicking the icon opens the symbol in symbol-editing mode. (Remember that double-clicking the name lets you edit the name.)

You are going to modify this symbol so that it can attach the Tack Clip movie clip to the movie. In the following steps, you will add this functionality to the button in the Tack Box symbol.

4) Select the instance of the Invisible Button symbol, and add the following ActionScript to the actions list:

```
on (press) {
  _root.attachMovie("tackClip", "tack", 1);
  _root.tack.startDrag(true, 10, 110, 590, 390);
}
```

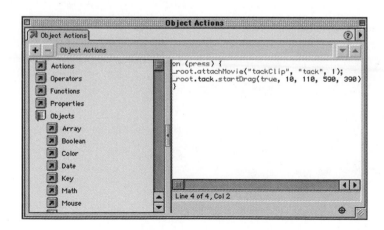

The easiest way to add this ActionScript is to switch to expert mode and just type it. If you prefer working in normal mode, you can find all the methods and properties required for this ActionScript in the toolbox list. You can create new lines by adding the Evaluate action (listed in the Actions category).

What does this ActionScript do? It begins by attaching a movie clip, using the attachMovie method. As you already know, a method needs an object—in this case, _root, which refers to the main timeline of the movie (the main movie itself). When you target _root with the attachMovie method, the movie clip is attached to the main movie, rather than nested inside another movie clip on the stage.

The arguments for the attachMovie method are idName (the identifier for the attached movie clip), newName (the new instance name of the attached movie clip), and depth (the depth of the attached movie clip). You use the Symbol Linkage Properties dialog box to set the identifier for the movie clip, which in this case is tackClip. You set the new instance name in the Instance panel in the preceding exercise; that name is tack. Finally, the depth is the z-index, or stacking order, of the attached movie clip. Attached movie clips are always higher in the stacking order than anything else in the movie.

Make sure that you put the values for the idName and newName arguments in quotation marks. You want the string "tackClip" to be used for the idName argument and the string "tack" to be used for the newName argument. If you forget the quotation marks, Flash tries to use the values of variables called tackClip and tack for those arguments. Because no such variables exist, your ActionScript won't work. The value for the depth argument doesn't need quotation marks, because it's a number. Flash uses that number for the argument.

After the movie clip is attached, it snaps to the mouse via the attachMovie method. Notice that the target for this method is _root.tack, which refers to the instance of the tack movie clip in the main timeline.

At this point, you might wonder why you need to add an action to drag an instance of the Tack Clip movie clip (the tack). The original symbol already includes such an action. However, in the original symbol, the press event is captured by the instance of the Invisible Button inside the Tack Box movie clip. You need an action to initiate the dragging of the Tack Clip movie clip.

5) Following the ActionScript you added in step 4, enter this ActionScript:

```
on (release, releaseOutside) {
  _root.tack.stopDrag();
  _root.tack.tackTip._visible = false;
  _root.tack._y = _root.tack._y + 11;
}
```

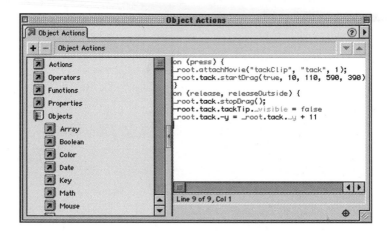

This section of ActionScript is contained in an on (release, releaseOutside) event, so these actions will occur when the button in the Tack Box movie clip is released. First, the _root.tack movie clip stops dragging. Then the instance named tackTip, which is inside the instance named tack in the main timeline (the attached movie clip), has its _visible property set to false. Finally, the instance named tack in the main timeline (_root.tack) has its _y property modified. These actions are almost identical to those used for the invisible button inside of the Tack Clip movie clip, but the targets for these methods are written differently.

You might be thinking, "But I already set up my movie clip to drop earlier in this lesson!" That's right; you did. But when you clicked the instance of the Invisible Button symbol in the Tack Box movie clip, that movie clip started to capture your mouse events. That means when you release the mouse button, the Tack Box movie clip has to catch the release. In the following exercise, you'll add some ActionScript to check whether the instance of the Invisible Button symbol inside the Tack Box movie clip has been released.

6) Choose Edit > Edit Movie. Delete the instance of the Tack Clip movie clip from the Tacks layer.

You don't need this tack anymore, because you're going to use ActionScript to attach a copy of it.

172

7) With frame 1 of the Tacks layer selected, drag an instance of the Tack Box movie clip onto the stage. Use the Info panel to position the clip at X: 20 and Y: 140.

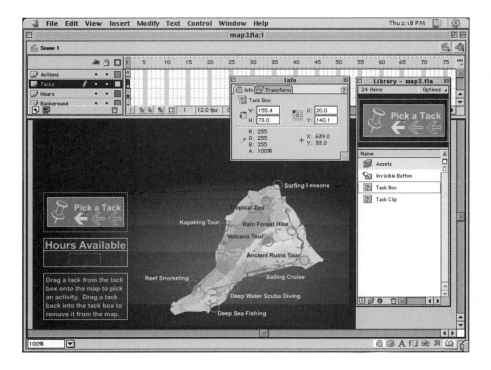

The Tack Box movie clip contains the button that will attach the tacks.

8) Choose Control > Test Movie, and test the tack box.

When you click the invisible button inside the tack box, a copy of the Tack Clip movie clip is added to the movie. If you drag the invisible button, the instance of the tack clip follows the mouse.

9) Close the test movie, and save the movie as map6.fla in the MyWork folder.

Now that you've managed to attach the tack clip with ActionScript, you have to attach multiple copies of it.

USING OPERATORS TO INCREMENT AND DECREMENT VALUES

An *expression* is any statement Flash can evaluate that returns a value. *Operators* specify how to combine, compare, or modify the values of expressions.

In this exercise, you use an operator to increment the values of some variables, which allows you to add multiple instances of the Tack Clip movie clip to the stage.

You should still have the map6.fla file open.

1) Double-click the instance of the Tack Box movie clip on the stage in map6.fla.

You need to make some more modifications in this movie clip.

2) Select frame 1 of the Actions layer, and add the ActionScript `tackID = 0;`.

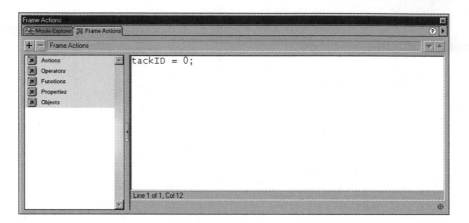

This bit of ActionScript creates a variable, `tackID`, that has a value of 0. Type this ActionScript in the actions list in expert mode.

> **TIP** *If you want the Actions panel always to open in expert mode, choose Edit > Preferences and set the Actions Panel Mode setting to Expert Mode.*

It's good practice to assign a known value the first time you define a variable in your ActionScript. This practice is known as *initializing* a variable, which makes the variable's value easier to track and compare as the movie plays.

3) Select the instance of the Invisible Button on the stage. In the Actions panel, add a new line before the line of ActionScript that attaches the movie clip. In this new line, type `++tackID;`.

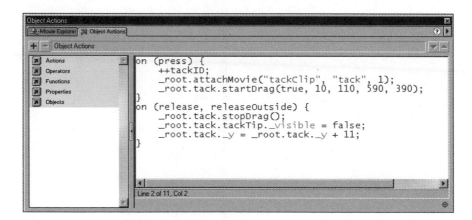

The ActionScript for the on (press) event should look like this:

```
on (press) {
  ++tackID;
  _root.attachMovie("tackClip", "tack", 1);
  _root.tack.startDrag(true, 10, 110, 590, 390);
  _root.tack.tackTip._visible = true;
}
```

When the ActionScript is executed, the value of tackID has 1 added to it. You initialized this variable to start at 0, so the first time the ActionScript is triggered (the first time you click the button), the new value is 1. The next time the ActionScript is triggered, the value is 2, and so on.

4) Modify the line of ActionScript that attaches the movie clip so that it reads _root.attachMovie("tackClip", "tack" + tackID, tackID);.

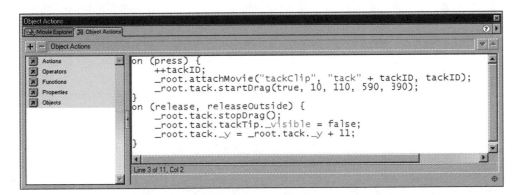

This minor change sets the instance name of the attached movie clip to the string "tack", plus the value of the variable tackID. The first time the code in the on (press) event is triggered, the value of tackID is incremented by 1, setting its value to 1. That value is passed to the next line of ActionScript, setting the instance name of the attached movie clip to tack1 and its depth to 1. The second time this ActionScript is triggered, the instance name is tack2, and the depth is 2.

5) Click the Options button in the Actions panel, and choose Replace from the menu. Type `_root.tack` **in the Find what text box and** `_root["tack" + tackID]` **in the Replace with text box. Click Replace All. After all the replacements have been made, close the window.**

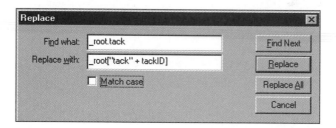

Flash replaces every instance of "`_root.tack`" with "`_root["tack" + tackID]`" in the actions list. This step sets up your ActionScript to use the dynamically generated instance name for the attached Tack Clip movie clip. Notice that no dot (.) follows the word `_root` in the code that replaces the original target path. Flash understands the value inside the brackets (`["tack" + tackID]`) as though the dot were used. This syntax is known as *associative array syntax*, which is the preferred method of placing expressions in the target path of an object.

6) Choose Control > Test Movie, and test the new and improved tack box.

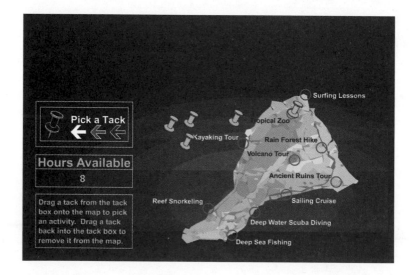

You should now be able to drag several instances of the Tack Clip movie clip from the tack box.

7) Close the test movie. Choose Edit > Edit Movie to return to the main timeline, and save your movie as map7.fla in the MyWork folder.

REMOVING A MOVIE CLIP FROM THE MOVIE

You can use the removeMovieClip method to remove a movie clip that has been attached. This method removes any movie clip that was created with the attachMovieClip or duplicateMovieClip method. The removeMovieClip method does not require any arguments, because it simply gets rid of an instance of a movie clip.

What happens if you decide to use only four tacks, but you've already dragged out five? In this exercise, you use the removeMovieClip method to remove copies of the attached Tack Clip movie clip.

1) Select the instance of the Tack Box symbol on the stage in map7.fla, and use the Instance panel to set its name to tackBox.

You are going to add some ActionScript that removes an instance of the Tack Clip movie clip from the movie if it is dropped on the instance of the Tack Box movie clip named tackBox.

2) Double-click the instance of the Tack Box movie clip that's on the stage to open it in symbol-editing mode. Select the Invisible Button, and add the following ActionScript to the on (release, releaseOutside) **event:**

```
if (eval(_root["tack" + tackID]._droptarget) == _root.tackBox) {
  _root["tack" + tackID].removeMovieClip();
}
```

You can add this ActionScript before or after the existing ActionScript in the on (release, releaseOutside) event.

The conditional statement if (eval(_root["tack" + tackID]._droptarget) == _root.tackBox) determines whether the instance of the movie clip you just added is dropped on the instance of the Tack Box movie clip in the main timeline named tackBox. If that condition is true, the ActionScript contained in the if statement (_root["tack" + tackID].removeMovieClip();) is executed.

You still have to add similar ActionScript to the Tack Clip movie clip, because you may want to remove movie clips that you've already dropped on the map.

3) Open the library for this movie (by choosing Window > Library), and locate the Tack Clip movie clip. Right-click or Control-click this symbol in the library, and choose Edit from the contextual menu.

Flash switches to symbol-editing mode for the Tack Clip movie clip.

4) Select the instance of the Invisible Button on the stage, and add the following ActionScript to the on (release, releaseOutside) **event:**

```
if (eval(this._droptarget) == _root.tackBox) {
  this.removeMovieClip();
}
```

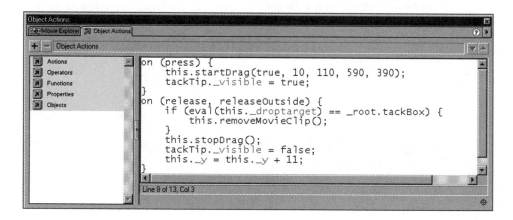

This ActionScript does the same thing as the ActionScript you added to the button in the Tack Box movie clip. The only difference is that the object that is being checked and removed is this instead of _root["tack" + tackID].removeMovieClip();.

5) Choose Control > Test Movie to test the interactivity.

When you drag a tack out of the tack box, everything works as did before. Now you can remove a tack from the movie by dragging it back into the tack box.

6) Close the test movie, and save the movie as map8.fla in the MyWork folder.

You are almost done with this movie. The final thing to do is modify the Tack Clip symbol so that each instance of it that's added to the stage has a different color.

USING THE COLOR OBJECT TO CREATE RANDOM COLORS

The color object lets you set and retrieve the RGB color value and transform settings of a movie clip. You can actually modify the color of any instance of a movie clip on the stage. In this exercise, you create a new color object to control the color of each instance of the Tack Clip movie clip. You won't actually modify the color of the Tack Clip movie clip, but you will use the setRGB method of the color object to modify the Tack Color movie clip that it contains. (You'll learn more about just what an object is later in this exercise.)

Before you begin, make sure that you have the Tack Clip movie clip from map8.fla open.

1) Select the instance of the Tack Color movie clip in the Tack Color layer, and use the Instance panel to set its name to tackColor.

You might have to lock all the other layers to perform this step.

2) Add a layer named Actions, and place it at the top of the layer stacking order.
You are going to add some ActionScript to this movie clip.

3) Select frame 1 of the Actions layer, and add the ActionScript myColor = new Color(tackColor);.
Before you can completely understand this ActionScript, you must know a little more about objects in ActionScript. In ActionScript, related functions and data structures (variables, properties, and so on) are grouped in classes defined by constructor functions. A *constructor function* (or constructor) is a set of instructions that defines the properties and methods of a class. You can create multiple instances of a class, each of which is called an object, to reuse throughout your code.

The ActionScript that you just added creates a new instance of the Color constructor. This constructor defines all the properties and methods for the Color class. The instance of the Color constructor that you create in this step is named myColor, and its target is tackColor. So the new myColor object will be applied to the tackColor instance.

179

4) Add a new line to the actions list, and add the following ActionScript:

```
myColor.setRGB(random(256)<<16|random(256)<<8|random(256));
```

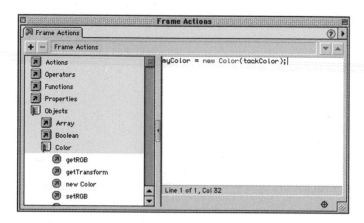

This expression allows you to generate a random RGB value.

◎ POWER TIP   *What exactly does the random function do? The random function picks a number up to, but not including, the number specified as its argument. The << (bitwise left shift operator) shifts all the bits in that random number 16 places to the left. Shifting a value left by one position is the equivalent of multiplying it by 2, so the ActionScript multiplies the random number by 2 16 times. The | (bitwise OR) operator converts the number on each side of it to a 32-bit integer and returns a 1 in each bit position where the corresponding bits of the number on either side of the operator is 1.*

In plain English, suppose that the random number chosen for each portion of the expression is 15. The result of the first portion of the expression (random(256)<<16) would be 983040 (15<<16, or 15*2^{16}). The result of the second portion of the expression (random(256)<<8) would be 3840 (15<<8, or 15*2^{8}). The result of the third portion of the expression would be 15. The | operators convert each of these numbers to 32-bit integers. After the numbers are converted to 32-bit integers, the operator returns a 1 in each bit position where the corresponding bits of the number on either side of the operator is 1. The resulting decimal is 986895, which the setRGB method can use as the value for the 0xRRGGBB argument. The following table illustrates the decimal and binary values used in the expressions:

DECIMAL	BINARY
983040	11110000000000000000
3840	111100000000
15	1111
(983040|3840|15), or 986895	11110000111100001111

5) Choose Control > Test Movie, and test the interactivity.

Each instance of the Tack Clip movie clip that is added to the movie has a randomly set color.

6) Close the test movie, and save the movie as map9.fla.

You're done with the map for now. You'll add it to the rest of the Neptune Resorts site in Lesson 12.

WHAT YOU HAVE LEARNED

In this lesson, you have:

- Used a dynamic text box to set a changing caption (pages 152–156)

- Used actions and methods in ActionScript to create a draggable movie clip (pages 156–165)

- Modified the properties of a movie clip with ActionScript (pages 165–168)

- Attached a movie clip to a movie (pages 169–173)

- Used operators to change values (pages 173–176)

- Removed a movie clip from a movie (pages 177–178)

- Used the color object to create random colors in a movie clip (pages 179–181)

adding complex
interactivity

LESSON 8

Your next project is a jigsaw puzzle, which you will add to the Neptune Resorts Web site in Lesson 12. This jigsaw puzzle is composed of nine draggable puzzle pieces. When you drag a piece to the correct spot, it will snap into place and can no longer be dragged. This puzzle also uses the swapDepths method, which you can use to set the depth, or *stacking order*, of movie clips dynamically.

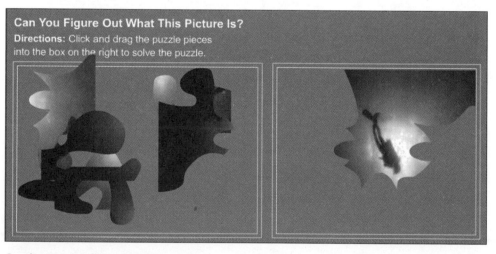

Creating your own jigsaw puzzle is a snap.

WHAT YOU WILL LEARN

In this lesson, you will:

- Reuse an ActionScript by using the `include` action

- Modify symbols quickly by using the Movie Explorer

- Make a draggable movie clip snap into place

- Use conditions to turn an action off

- Make a dragged movie clip appear above all other clips

APPROXIMATE TIME

It usually takes about one hour to complete this lesson.

LESSON FILES

Media Files:

None

Starting File:

Lesson08/Assets/jigsaw1.fla

Completed Project:

jigsaw3.fla

USING THE INCLUDE ACTION

You can use the `include` action to include the contents of an external file in your ActionScript. This procedure is great for complicated ActionScript or for ActionScript you want to reuse many times throughout your movie.

The `include` action has the following syntax: `#include "filename.as"`. This action requires a filename argument, which refers to the name of an external file containing the ActionScript you want to include. The recommended extension for the external file is .as.

In the next exercise, you will add the `startDrag` and `stopDrag` methods to one of the buttons in the Puzzle Pieces layer. Because all the puzzle pieces can use the same action, you will export those actions to an external ActionScript (AS) file and then include that file in every button on the Puzzle Pieces layer.

1) Open jigsaw1.fla in the Lesson08/Assets folder.

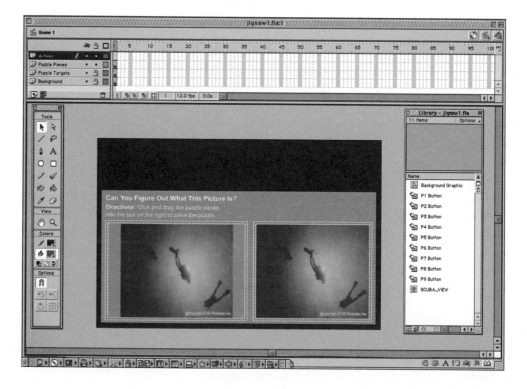

This movie has four layers: Actions, Puzzle Pieces, Puzzle Targets, and Background. The Background layer contains the Background Graphic symbol. The Puzzle Pieces and Puzzle Targets layers contain nine buttons each: P1 Button, P2 Button, P3 Button, P4 Button, P5 Button, P6 Button, P7 Button, P8 Button, and P9 Button.

2) Open the Movie Explorer, and click the customize button to open the Movie Explorer Settings dialog box. Select the Buttons and Layers options, deselect all the other options, and click OK.

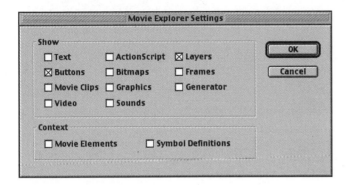

You can open the Movie Explorer by choosing Window > Movie Explorer or by clicking the Movie Explorer button in the launcher bar.

The Movie Explorer displays all the layers in the movie. If you expand the Puzzle Pieces layer, you'll see all the buttons contained in that layer. No other symbols are displayed.

3) Select the P1 Button in the Puzzle Pieces layer in the Movie Explorer. In the Actions panel, add the following ActionScript:

```
on (press) {
  this.startDrag();
}
on (release, releaseOutside) {
  this.stopDrag();
}
```

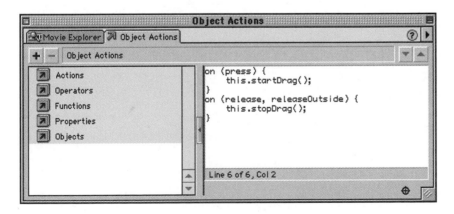

Use expert mode to type the ActionScript directly in the Actions panel.

The ActionScript should look familiar; you used it in Lesson 7 to add some drag-and-drop interactivity.

NOTE *Make sure that you add this ActionScript to the P1 Button symbol in the Puzzle Pieces layer, not the Puzzle Targets layer.*

You are going to add this ActionScript to all the other buttons in the Puzzle Pieces layer. But you are going to be making quite a few changes in the ActionScript. It would be easier to make those changes in one place, rather than change the ActionScript for each button. Therefore, you'll export the ActionScript to an external file. Then you can use the include action to include the contents of that file when it's tested, published, or exported.

4) Click the Options button in the Actions panel, and choose Export As File from the Options menu. When the Save As dialog box opens, save the file as jigsaw.as in the MyWork folder.

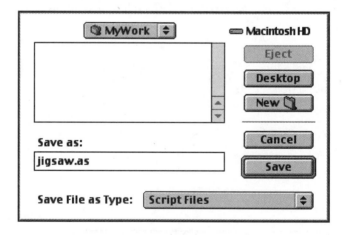

You can export this file with any extension, but it's best to get into the habit of using .as for consistency and easy recognition.

TIP *Make sure that you save the file in the correct location, because the movie must be able to find the .as file to use its ActionScript.*

5) Select the contents of the Actions list in the Actions panel, and replace them with the following ActionScript:

```
#include "jigsaw.as"
```

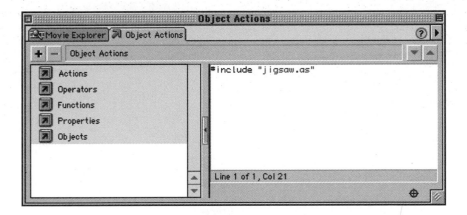

This ActionScript is the `include` action. Don't put a semicolon (;) at the end of this line.

The script in the Actions panel now refers to the file you just created by exporting the ActionScript.

Before you do anything else, you should save the movie. You must save it in the same folder in which you saved jigsaw.as so that Flash can find the ActionScript for the `include` action.

6) Save the movie in the MyWork folder as jigsaw2.fla.

You could test the movie now, but it's not yet ready to work correctly. The ActionScript is on a button that's sitting on the main timeline, so the `startDrag` and `stopDrag` methods, which use `this` as the object, would drag the main timeline, rather than the individual button.

USING THE MOVIE EXPLORER TO STREAMLINE WORKFLOW

As you learned in Lesson 3, the Movie Explorer is a useful feature new to Flash 5. In the Movie Explorer, you can view your movie as a tree structure. You can apply filters to the tree structure so that only certain parts of the movie appear in the Movie Explorer. In the following exercise, you will use the Movie Explorer to modify symbols easily.

You should be in the file jigsaw2.fla to begin this exercise.

1) In the Movie Explorer, select the P2 button in the Puzzle Pieces layer. In the Actions list of the Actions panel, type `#include "jigsaw.as"`. **Do the same for each of the other buttons.**

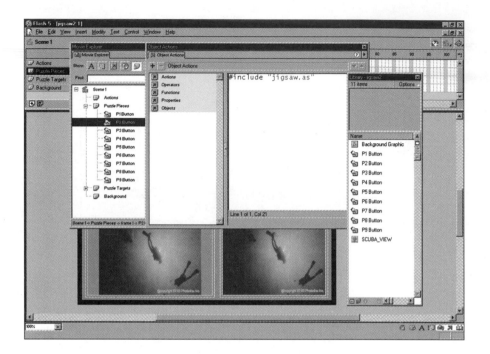

You want all the buttons to use the same ActionScript as the P1 Button. Using the `include` action means that if you need to revise the buttons' script, a single revision will affect all the buttons.

2) Select the P1 Button in the Puzzle Pieces layer, and choose Insert > Convert to Symbol. In the Symbol Properties dialog box, type *P1 MC* **in the Name text box, click the Movie Clip radio button, and click OK.**

To make the drag-and-drop interactivity work, you must nest the button inside a movie clip. If you don't, the `this` target in the ActionScript refers to the main timeline, and your user will end up dragging the whole movie around.

3) In the Movie Explorer, select each of the other buttons in the Puzzle Pieces layer, and nest each one in a movie clip as you did with the P1 Button.

NOTE *The name of the movie clip inside which you nest the button should correspond to the name of the button itself. The P2 Button should be nested in P2 MC, the P3 Button in P3 MC, and so on.*

When you create a new symbol, the new symbol becomes selected on the stage, regardless of what is selected in the Movie Explorer. Make sure that you actually select the next button that you want to embed in a movie clip before you choose Insert > Convert to Symbol; otherwise, the last movie clip that you created will be embedded in the new symbol.

Notice that as you nest each button in a movie clip, it disappears from the Movie Explorer, because you set the Movie Explorer to display only buttons. In the next step, you'll set the Movie Explorer to display movie clips as well. That setting will make it easier for you to work with the instances now that they are movie clips.

4) In the Movie Explorer, click the customize button. In the Movie Explorer Settings dialog box, check the Movie Clips checkbox.
The movie clips appear in the Movie Explorer.

5) Select the instance of P1 MC in the Puzzle Pieces layer, and use the Instance panel to set its name to P1. Do the same with each of the other movie clips in the Puzzle Pieces layer.

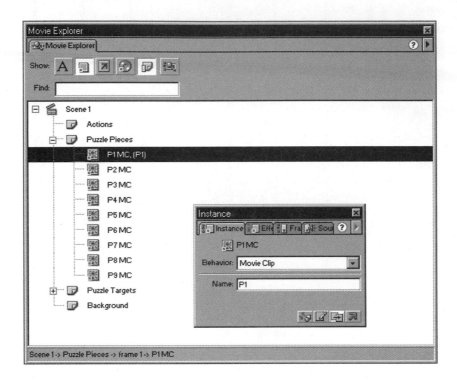

Again, the name of the instance of P2 MC should be P2; for the instance of P3 MC, it should be P3; and so on.

After you type the instance name in the Instance panel and press Enter or Return, the name should appear next to the symbol in the Movie Explorer.

6) Lock the Puzzle Pieces layer, and unlock the Puzzle Targets layer. Choose Edit > Select All. Then, in the Instance panel, choose Movie Clip from the Behavior drop-down menu.

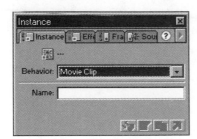

You are going to use these instances as the droptargets for the movie clips in the Puzzle Pieces layer. When you drag a movie clip, the movie clip that you drop it on is known as its **droptarget**. The droptarget for a dragged movie clip is captured in the _droptarget property. But before you can use a symbol instance as a droptarget, the instance must have an instance name, so you must make it a movie clip.

7) Select the instance of the P1 Button symbol in the Puzzle Targets layer, and use the Instance panel to set its name to P1target. Select each of the other symbol instances in this layer, and change their names accordingly.

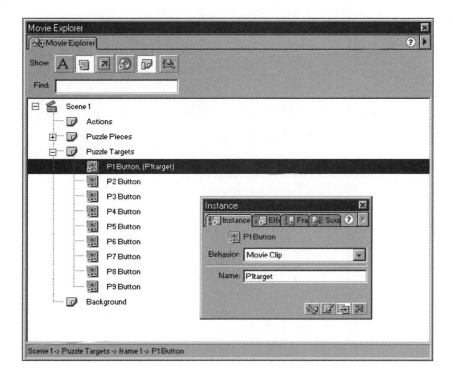

You can test the movie if you want to, but all that you have set up right now is basic drag-and-drop interactivity in the Puzzle Pieces layer.

8) Save the movie in the MyWork folder as jigsaw3.fla.

MAKING A DRAGGABLE MOVIE CLIP SNAP INTO PLACE

In Lesson 7, you learned how to make a drag-and-drop movie clip. In this lesson, you'll take that interactivity to the next level. You will learn how to make your draggable movie clip snap into place if it's dropped in a particular location.

The first thing you need to do is determine what the movie clip is being dropped over. You did this in Lesson 7 by using the _droptarget property, which you'll use in this lesson. The _droptarget property returns the absolute path of the movie-clip instance on which a draggable movie clip was dropped.

After you determine the _droptarget of the movie clip, decide whether it's the one to which you want the movie clip to snap. Then you need to provide some additional information: the X and Y coordinates to which the movie clip should snap. You can do this by using the x and y properties of the movie clip.

In the next exercise, you will add some ActionScript that checks whether a movie clip from the Puzzle Pieces layer has been dropped over the corresponding movie clip in the Target Pieces layer. When the movie clip is dropped over the correct target, you will make it snap into place by setting the x and y properties of the draggable puzzle piece to those of the target movie clip. Also, you will modify jigsaw.as in such a way that the puzzle pieces will snap to the location of their targets when they are dropped.

1) Open jigsaw.as (in the MyWork folder) in a text editor such as Notepad (Windows) or SimpleText (Macintosh).

```
on (press) {
    this.startDrag();
}
on (release, releaseOutside) {
    this.stopDrag();
}
```

You should see the following text:

```
on (press) {
  this.startDrag();
}
on (release, releaseOutside) {
  this.stopDrag();
}
```

192

2) After the fifth line—the one that says `this.stopDrag();` **—type the following:**

```
if (eval(this._droptarget) == eval("_root."+this._name+"target")) {
}
```

```
┌──────────────────────────── jigsaw.as ────────────────────────────┐
on (press) {
   this.startDrag();
}
on (release, releaseOutside) {
   this.stopDrag();
   if (eval(this._droptarget) == eval("_root." + this._name + "target")) {

   }
}
```

You already used the _droptarget property in Lesson 7. This time, you are checking to see whether the droptarget of the movie clip of which the action is a part (a movie clip in the Puzzle Pieces layer) is equivalent to the value of the expression `eval("_root."+this._name+"target")`. This expression checks the instance name of the movie clip you're dragging, and then adds the string "target" to the end. If you're dragging the movie clip with the instance name P1, for example, the ActionScript checks to see whether the droptarget is "P1target". Remember that you gave instance names to all those movie clips in the Puzzle Targets layer; P1target was one of them.

NOTE *You should indent the text you just added so that it's aligned with the* `this.stopDrag();` *line.*

The ActionScript in jigsaw.as should now look like this:

```
on (press) {
  this.startDrag();
}
on (release, releaseOutside) {
  this.stopDrag();
  if (eval(this._droptarget) == eval("_root."+this._name+"target")) {
  }
}
```

Now you need to tell Flash what to do if the condition you just added is true.

3) Add a new line after the line containing `if (eval(this._droptarget) ==` `eval("_root."+this._name+"target")) {.` **On that new line, type the following:**

```
this._x = eval(this._droptarget)._x;
this._y = eval(this._droptarget)._y;
```

```
================ jigsaw.as ================
on (press) {
   this.startDrag();
}
on (release, releaseOutside) {
   this.stopDrag();
   if (eval(this._droptarget) == eval("_root." + this._name + "target")) {
      this._x = eval(this._droptarget)._x;
      this._y = eval(this._droptarget)._y;
   }
}
```

Once again, you are working with movie-clip properties. In this case, you are setting the x and y properties of the movie clip that contains the ActionScript to be equal to the x and y properties of the movie clip's droptarget. In other words, if you're dragging the movie clip with an instance name of P1, and you drop it over the movie clip that has an instance name of P1target, the x and y properties of the P1 movie clip will be the same as for the P1target movie clip. This situation happens only if the condition you added in the step 2 is true, however.

As before, you should indent this text. This time, it should be indented so that it looks like the following ActionScript:

```
on (press) {
  this.startDrag();
}
on (release, releaseOutside) {
  this.stopDrag();
  if (eval(this._droptarget) == eval("_root."+this._name+"target")) {
    this._x = eval(this._droptarget)._x;
    this._y = eval(this._droptarget)._y;
  }
}
```

4) Save jigsaw.as, and return to Flash. Make sure that jigsaw3.fla is still open. Choose Control > Test Movie.

When you drag one of the puzzle pieces from the left to the corresponding target on the right, the puzzle piece should snap into place. If you try to drop the movie clip on the wrong target, it will not snap into place. The targets on the right are completely visible, so it might be hard to see the pieces snap. In that case, just set the Alpha of all the movie clips in the Puzzle Pieces layer to 0%, and test again.

194

5) Close the test movie.

You don't need to save the movie, because you didn't make any changes in it. You changed only the jigsaw.as file.

TURNING ACTIONS OFF

When your visitors have dragged the puzzle pieces to the correct targets, you don't want them to mess things up by dragging the pieces off again, so you need to find a way to turn off the drag action in each of the puzzle pieces. You can do this by using conditions. You can use conditions to limit the number of times a piece of ActionScript is performed.

In the next exercise, you will use a condition to turn off the drag action for a puzzle piece when it has been dropped on the correct target.

1) Open jigsaw.as (in the MyWork folder) in a text editor.

The ActionScript you're building should look like the following at this point:

```
on (press) {
  this.startDrag();
}
on (release, releaseOutside) {
  this.stopDrag();
  if (eval(this._droptarget) == eval("_root."+this._name+"target")) {
    this._x = eval(this._droptarget)._x;
    this._y = eval(this._droptarget)._y;
  }
}
```

2) Add a new line after the `this._y = eval(this._droptarget)._y;` **line. On the new line, add the following text:**

```
done = true;
```

```
jigsaw - Notepad
File  Edit  Search  Help
on (press) {
    this.startDrag();
}
on (release, releaseOutside) {
    this.stopDrag();
    if (eval(this._droptarget) == eval("_root."+this._name+"target")) {
        this._x = eval(this._droptarget)._x;
        this._y = eval(this._droptarget)._y;
        done = true;
    }
}
```

The line you just added sets the done variable equal to the Boolean value true. As with the x and y properties, the change in the variable occurs only if you drop the movie clip over the appropriate target. Your ActionScript should now look like this:

```
on (press) {
  this.startDrag();
}
on (release, releaseOutside) {
  this.stopDrag();
  if (eval(this._droptarget) == eval("_root."+this._name+"target")) {
    this._x = eval(this._droptarget)._x;
    this._y = eval(this._droptarget)._y;
    done = true;
  }
}
```

What are you going to do with the done variable? You're going to use it to keep the puzzle pieces from being dragged when they've been dropped over their targets. To do so, you need to add a condition to the on (press) portion of the ActionScript.

3) Add a new line after the on (press) **line. On the new line, type the following:**

```
if (done != true) {
```

```
on (press) {
  if (done != true) {
  this.startDrag();
}
on (release, releaseOutside) {
  this.stopDrag();
  if (eval(this._droptarget) == eval("_root."+this._name+"target")) {
    this._x = eval(this._droptarget)._x;
    this._y = eval(this._droptarget)._y;
    done = true;
  }
```

This line starts an if statement that checks to see whether done is *not* equal to true.

In the next step, you'll finish the if statement.

4) Add a new line after `this.startDrag();`. **On the new line, type a curly bracket (}).**

```
on (press) {
    if (done != true) {
        this.startDrag();
    }|
}
on (release, releaseOutside) {
    this.stopDrag();
    if (eval(this._droptarget) == eval("_root."+this._name+"target")) {
        this._x = eval(this._droptarget)._x;
        this._y = eval(this._droptarget)._y;
        done = true;
```

With the `if` statement completed, you can see that the drag interactivity indicated by `this.startDrag();` occurs only if done is not equal to true. In step 2, you set up the ActionScript to make done equal to true when you drop the puzzle piece on the appropriate target. In steps 3 and 4, you disabled the drag action of the puzzle piece when it has been dropped on its target. Your ActionScript in jigsaw.as should now look like the following:

```
on (press) {
  if (done != true) {
    this.startDrag();
  }
}
on (release, releaseOutside) {
  this.stopDrag();
  if (eval(this._droptarget) == eval("_root."+this._name+"target")) {
    this._x = eval(this._droptarget)._x;
    this._y = eval(this._droptarget)._y;
    done = true;
  }
}
```

5) Save jigsaw.as in the MyWork folder, and return to jigsaw3.fla in Flash. Test the movie (Control > Test Movie).

When you drag one of the puzzle pieces to the correct target, it will snap into place, and you will no longer be able to drag it. Close the test movie when you have finished.

CHANGING MOVIE-CLIP DEPTH BY
USING THE SWAPDEPTHS METHOD

Your puzzle is nearly finished, but you can make a few improvements. As you drag the pieces around, you might notice that you seem to lose them as they go behind other puzzle pieces. You can fix this situation by forcing the puzzle piece you are currently dragging to go to the top of the stacking order. To do so, you use the swapDepths method, as follows:

```
movieClipPath.swapDepths(depth or target);
```

The swapDepths method is one of many methods built into Flash 5 for use with movie clips. It swaps the stacking, or z, order (depth level) of the specified instance with the movie specified by the target argument or with the movie that currently occupies the depth level specified in the argument. Both movies must have the same parent movie clip. Swapping the depth level of movie clips has the effect of moving one movie in front of or behind the other. If a movie is tweening when this method is called, the tweening is stopped.

In the next exercise, you will use the swapDepths method to change the depth of each puzzle piece as it's dragged.

1) Select frame 1 of the Actions layer in jigsaw3.fla (in the MyWork folder). In the Actions panel, add the following ActionScript:

```
currentTop = 100;
```

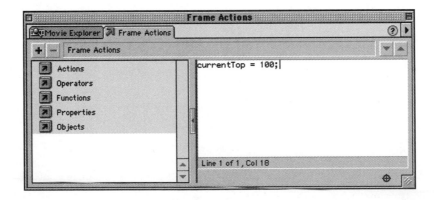

You just created a variable, named currentTop, with an initial value of 100.

2) Choose Edit > Select All to select everything in the Puzzle Targets layer. In the Effect panel, set the Alpha of everything you selected to 0%.

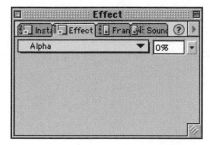

This setting makes the puzzle targets appear to be invisible. You still need to add some ActionScript to the jigsaw.as file to use the currentTop variable.

3) Open jigsaw.as in a text editor.

The ActionScript you're building should look like the following at this point:

```
on (press) {
  if (done != true) {
    this.startDrag();
  }
}
on (release, releaseOutside) {
  this.stopDrag();
  if (eval(this._droptarget) == eval("_root."+this._name+"target")) {
    this._x = eval(this._droptarget)._x;
    this._y = eval(this._droptarget)._y;
    done = true;
  }
}
```

4) Add a new line after the `if (done != true) {` **line. On this new line, add the following ActionScript:**

```
this.swapDepths(_root.currentTop);
++_root.currentTop;
```

```
                          jigsaw.as
on (press) {
   if (done != true) {
      this.swapDepths(_root.currentTop);
      ++_root.currentTop;
      this.startDrag();
   }
}
on (release, releaseOutside) {
   this.stopDrag();
   if (eval(this._droptarget) == eval("_root." + this._name + "target")) {
      this._x = eval(this._droptarget)._x;
      this._y = eval(this._droptarget)._y;
      done = true;
   }
}
```

This ActionScript applies the swapDepths method to this, which is the movie clip being dragged. The swapDepths method swaps the stacking, or z, order (depth level) of the specified instance with the movie specified by the target argument or with the movie that currently occupies the depth level specified in the argument. You specified _root.currentTop in the argument, so Flash will put the movie clip in the main timeline at a depth equal to the value of the currentTop variable. The second line of the ActionScript simply increments the value of the currentTop variable, so the depth increases by 1 each time the ActionScript is processed, making sure that the movie clip you click is sent to the top.

Your finished ActionScript should look like the following:

```
on (press) {
  if (done != true) {
    this.swapDepths(_root.currentTop);
    ++_root.currentTop;
    this.startDrag();
  }
}
on (release, releaseOutside) {
  this.stopDrag();
  if (eval(this._droptarget) == eval("_root."+this._name+"target")) {
    this._x = eval(this._droptarget)._x;
    this._y = eval(this._droptarget)._y;
    done = true;
  }
}
```

5) Save jigsaw.as in the MyWork folder, and return to jigsaw3.fla in Flash. Unlock the Puzzle Pieces layer, and shuffle the pieces around on the stage.

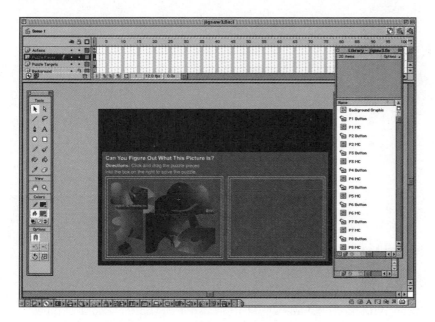

You have to give users a little bit of a challenge when they attempt to put the puzzle together.

6) Test your movie (Control > Test Movie).

Now whenever you drag a puzzle piece, it will jump to the top of the stacking order. Close the test movie when you finish. You'll add this jigsaw puzzle to the Neptune Resorts Web site in Lesson 12.

WHAT YOU HAVE LEARNED

In this lesson, you have

- Exported ActionScript to a file called jigsaw.as and used the include action to re-use that file (pages 184–187)

- Used the Movie Explorer to select symbols in the Puzzle Pieces and Puzzle Targets layers and to apply changes to each symbol (pages 187–191)

- Set the x and y properties of a movie clip to those of the corresponding droptarget movie clip (pages 191–194)

- Used an if statement to turn off the drag action for each puzzle piece when it has been dropped on the appropriate target (pages 195–197)

- Used the swapDepths method to set the depth of the currently selected puzzle piece to the value of the currentTop variable (pages 198–201)

using the sound object

In this lesson, you will learn how to work with sound, and you will make a music toggle and the merfolk choir, an interactive sound-mixing activity for children. Both of these items use the new Macromedia Flash Sound object, which you will learn about in this lesson. The merfolk-choir application also uses sliders to control the volume of the sounds.

The members of the Musical Merfolk choir are able to sing at different volumes after you create volume sliders.

WHAT YOU WILL LEARN

In this lesson, you will:

- Use ActionScript to create a slider

- Use the Sound object

- Control sound volume through the slider

- Create a sound toggle

APPROXIMATE TIME

It usually takes about one hour to complete this lesson.

LESSON FILES

Media Files:

Lesson09/Assets/assets.fla

Starting File:

Lesson09/Assets/neptune33.fla

Lesson09/Assets/merfolk1.fla

Completed Project:

neptune34.fla

merfolk4.fla

MAKING A SLIDER

You've already learned most of the ActionScript necessary to create a slider. A **slider** is simply a movie clip that is dragged up and down, or left and right, within a constrained area. Think back to when you first used the startDrag method. This method has several arguments: lockCenter, Left, Right, Top, and Bottom. You can use the Left, Right, Top, and Bottom arguments to constrain the movement of a draggable movie clip, and that's exactly what you need to do to make a slider.

In the following exercise, you will use the startDrag method to create a simple slider. You will constrain the slider to a rectangle defined by the slider's x and y properties.

1) Open merfolk1.fla in the Lesson09/Assets folder.

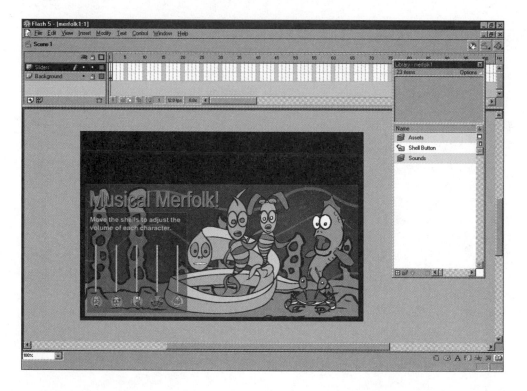

This file is the movie you're going to use to make the merfolk choir.

2) Open the library for merfolk1.fla, if it's not already open. Locate the Shell Button symbol in the library, and drag an instance of it onto the stage in the Sliders layer.

You are going to embed the Shell Button in a movie clip, but before you do, you have to add some ActionScript to it.

3) With the instance of the Shell Button symbol selected, open the Actions panel, and add the following ActionScript to the Actions list:

```
on (press) {
  this.startDrag(false, left, top, right, bottom);
}
on (release, releaseOutside) {
  this.stopDrag();
}
```

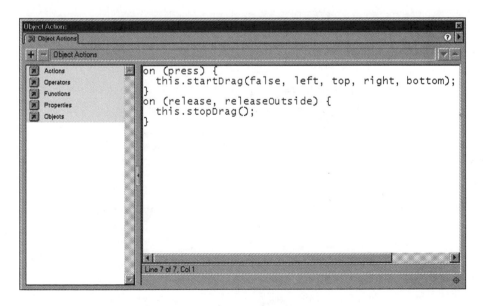

The ActionScript sets up a simple drag-and-drop action. In this case, you are passing several arguments along with the startDrag method: lockCenter, left, top, right, and bottom. The lockCenter argument is set to false in the ActionScript you added, so the movie clip will not be locked to the center of the pointer as you drag it around. The left, top, right, and bottom arguments are placeholders for now. These arguments specify the boundaries of the rectangle that constrains the movie clip being dragged. You'll set the variables that hold the places of these arguments later in this exercise.

4) With the instance of the Shell Button still selected, press F8 on your keyboard. The Symbol Properties dialog box opens. Type *Volume Slider* in the Name text box, set the Behavior option to Movie Clip, and click OK.

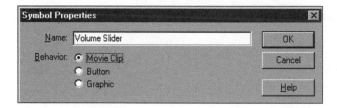

You have embedded the instance of the Shell Button symbol in the Volume Control movie clip. Now you need to edit that movie clip a bit to make this thing a slider.

5) Double-click the instance of the Volume Slider that's on the stage to open it in symbol-editing mode. Name the existing layer Shell Button, and add a new layer named Actions.

206

You have to add some actions to this movie clip to make it a slider. As always, it's a good idea to place the Actions layer at the top of the layer stacking order.

6) Select frame 1 of the Actions layer, and use the Actions panel to add the following ActionScript to this frame:

```
top = this._y;
left = this._x;
right = this._x;
bottom = this._y + 100;
```

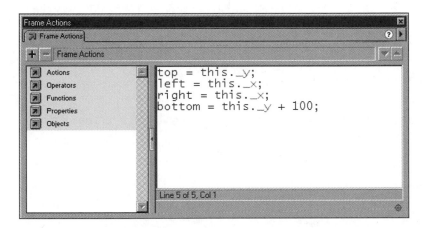

Once again, you're initializing some variables. These variables will be initialized every time this movie clip is loaded on the stage. When the movie clip is loaded, it has x and y positions. These variables will use those positions to set values for the top, left, right, and bottom variables, which you use in the arguments for the startDrag method applied to the instance of the Shell Button.

7) Choose Control > Test Movie, and test the slider.
You should be able to drag the slider up and down over a 100-pixel area, but you cannot move it to the left or right.

8) Close the test movie, and save the movie as merfolk2.fla in the MyWork folder.
Keep this movie open, because you will use it in the following exercises.

USING THE SOUND OBJECT

Macromedia Flash 5 comes with a built-in (predefined) Sound object. You can use the Sound object to set and control sounds in a particular movie-clip instance or the main timeline. To use the methods of the Sound object, you must first create a new Sound object, as follows:

```
mySound = new Sound(target);
```

This little bit of ActionScript uses the new operator to create a new instance of the Sound object called mySound. This object has an optional argument called target, which refers to the timeline to which the Sound object applies. If you do not specify a target for the Sound object, the object will control all sounds in the movie.

For the following exercise, merfolk2.fla should be open, and the Volume Slider symbol should be in symbol-editing mode.

1) Add the following ActionScript to frame 1 of the Actions layer, after the existing ActionScript:

```
//Create a new sound object
mySound = new Sound(this);
```

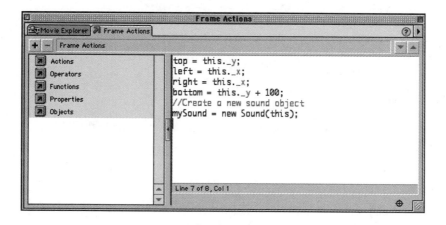

The first line of this ActionScript is a comment. When you add it to the Actions panel, the comment is highlighted in pink. The comment reminds you what a particular piece of ActionScript does, and it's helpful for other programmers who might need to use your code.

The second line creates a new instance, or object, based on the sound constructor. This constructor defines all the properties and methods for the sound class. The instance of the sound constructor that you are creating in this exercise is named mySound, and its target is this. This ActionScript means that the new mySound object will be applied to each instance of the Volume Slider movie clip.

2) Add the following ActionScript in the Actions panel, after the existing ActionScript:

```
//Attach the sound
mySound.attachSound(this._name + "Sound");
```

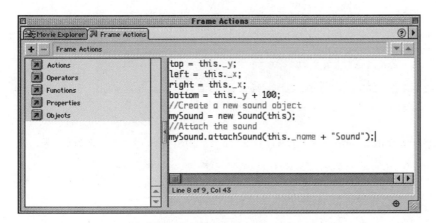

After you create an instance of the Sound object, you can use the attachSound method to insert a sound from the library into a movie while the movie is running, as follows:

```
mySound.attachSound("idName");
```

This ActionScript applies the attachSound method to the mySound object. The idName argument is the name of the new instance of the sound. This name is displayed in the Symbol Linkage Properties dialog box as the identifier for the sound you want to attach. You are going to use the _name (instance name) property of each instance of the movie clip to control the idName. The idName of the sound you attach to an instance of the Volume Slider will be the instance name of that slider, plus the string "Sound". In this movie, the sounds already have identifiers applied to them: char1Sound, char2Sound, char3Sound, char4Sound, and char5Sound. You'll be using instance names that use the expression for the idName to create these identifiers and attach the appropriate sounds.

3) Add the following ActionScript in the Actions panel:

```
//Start the sound
mySound.start(0, 9999);
```

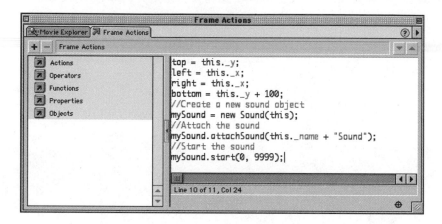

After you attach a sound, you need to use the Start method to make it start playing, as follows:

```
mySound.start(secondOffset, loop);
```

This ActionScript applies the Start method to the mySound object. The secondOffset argument, which is optional, enables you to start playing the sound at a specific point. If you have a 10-second sound, for example, and you specify a secondOffset of 5, the sound starts playing at the 5-second mark. The second argument, loop, is also optional and specifies the number of times the attached sound will loop. If you do not specify a loop argument, the sound plays only once. So mySound.start(5, 2); starts the sound at the 5-second mark and loops twice.

In this case, the secondOffset is 0, so the sound starts at its beginning. The loop is set to 9999, so the sound will play 9,999 times.

4) Choose Edit > Edit Movie to return to the main movie. Delete the instance of the Volume Slider that's on the stage.

You're going to use a little ActionScript to attach several instances of the Volume Slider to the stage.

5) Locate the Volume Slider movie clip in the library. Right+click (Windows) or Control+click (Macintosh) the symbol, and choose Linkage from the contextual menu. The Symbol Linkage Properties dialog box opens. Set the Linkage option to Export This Symbol, type *volumeSlider* in the Identifier text box, and click OK.

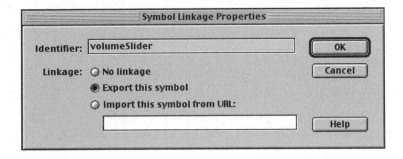

Now you can attach this movie clip to the movie by using the attachMovie method.

6) Change the name of the Sliders layer to Actions. Select frame 1 of the Actions layer, and add the following ActionScript:

```
//Initialize the variables
maxSliders = 5;
topSide = 235;
startLeft = 33;
spacing = 43;
count = 0;
//Add the sliders
while (count < maxSliders) {
  _root.attachMovie("volumeSlider", "char", count);
  _root.char._y = topSide;
  _root.char._x = startLeft + (spacing*count)
  ++count;
  _root.char._name = "char" + count;
}
```

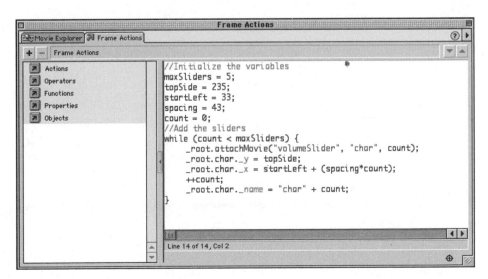

211

That's an awful lot of ActionScript. Let's break it down piece by piece to explain what it does. The first line is a comment, telling you what you're doing in that part of the code—in this case, initializing some variables. The variables that you're initializing are maxSliders (the maximum number of sliders you want to have), topSide (the starting y position of each slider), startLeft (the x position of the first slider, which will be the one on the left side of the movie), spacing (the number of pixels between sliders), and count (a placeholder, which you'll use to give each slider a different name and different properties).

After you initialized the variables, you added a while loop. The while loop is similar to an if statement; it performs the actions contained in it until its condition is true. In this case, the while loop is testing whether count is less than maxSliders. The first several times through the loop, this condition is false, so the ActionScript executes. When the condition becomes true, Flash stops running the ActionScript inside the while loop.

What is going on in the while loop? Some of it should already look familiar. First, you are attaching the movie clip that has an identifier of "volumeSlider", setting its new instance name to "char", and giving it a depth equal to the current value of count. Then you are setting that new instance's _y and _x properties to be equal to topSide and startLeft + (spacing*count), respectively. This ActionScript sets the y position of each slider to the value of topSide (235). The first attached instance of the slider has an x position of 19 + (43*0), which equals 19. The second instance will have an x position of 19 + (43*1), which equals 62. Each subsequent instance is positioned in the same way. After you position the instance, you increment the count variable (++count) and use the new value to set the name (_name) for the instance to "char" + count. So the first time through this loop, the instance that's added will have a _name property of char1, and the second time through the loop, the instance will have a _name property of char2.

7) Choose Control > Test Movie, and test the sliders.
When the movie plays, a cacophony of sounds should accompany it. It'll sound pretty horrible, but you'll know that the sounds are being attached to the movie. You can slide the sliders up and down, but they don't control anything yet.

8) Close the test movie, and save the movie as merfolk3.fla in the MyWork folder.
In the following section, you'll add the functionality that will control the sound, so keep this file open.

MAKING THE SLIDER CONTROL THE VOLUME

Now that the sound is attached and started, you need to control the volume. In this section, you turn the slider into a control. To control the attached sound, you need to use another method of the Sound object, setVolume, as follows:

```
mySound.setVolume(volume);
```

The setVolume method has a single argument, volume, which can be a number from 0 (no volume) to 100 (full volume). The default setting is 100.

You should still have merfolk3.fla open.

1) Locate the Volume Slider symbol in the library, and open this symbol in symbol-editing mode.

You are going to add some more ActionScript to this movie clip so that when you move the slider to a new position, the volume of the sound will change based on that position.

2) Select the instance of the Shell Button symbol on the stage, and add the following ActionScript to the on (release, releaseOutside) **event:**

```
mySound.setVolume(100-(_y-top));
```

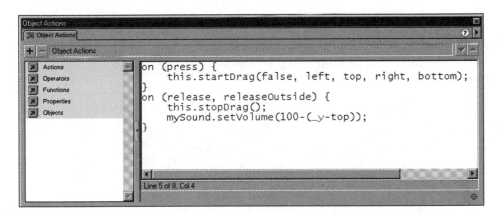

It doesn't matter whether you add this line before or after the line that contains the stopDrag method.

This ActionScript sets the volume of the mySound object attached to the instance of the Shell Clip movie clip. The volume argument is the expression 100–(_y-top). First, the difference between the current y property of the movie clip and the value of the top variable is calculated. Then that difference is subtracted from the number 100.

Because you're adding this line to the on (release, releaseOutside) event, it occurs after you release the mouse button.

3) Choose Control > Test Movie, and test the sliders.

When you move a slider and release it, the volume of that sound changes.

4) Close the test movie, save the movie as merfolk4.fla in the MyWork folder, and close it.

You're done with this movie for now, but you will add it to the Neptune Resorts Web site later.

MAKING A SOUND TOGGLE

If you add a music loop to your movie, you probably should give visitors a **sound toggle**—an option that turns off the sound. Although the music loop might sound great the first few times through, it could get annoying after a while. You don't want visitors to leave your site because the music gets on their nerves, so give them a sound toggle.

In the following exercise, you'll add a sound toggle to the Neptune Resorts site.

1) Open neptune33.fla in the MyWork folder.

This file is much like the one you completed in Lesson 6, but with the library cleaned up a bit, the Soundtrack layer removed, and a couple of symbols—which you'll use in this lesson—added.

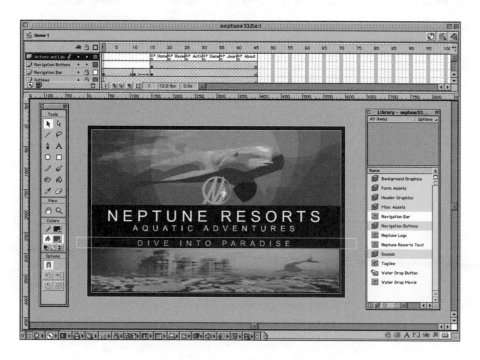

2) Select frame 1 of the Actions and Labels layer, and use the Actions panel to add the following ActionScript:

```
mySound = new Sound();
mySound.attachSound("loop");
mySound.start(0, 9999);
soundOff = false;
```

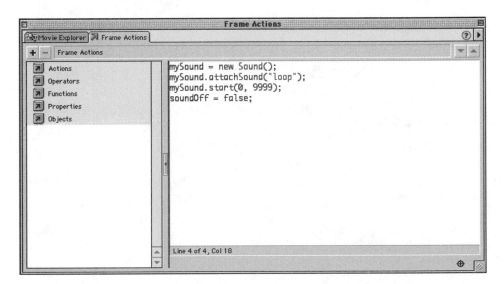

This ActionScript is much like the code you used for the merfolk choir. In this case, you didn't specify a target for the new Sound object, so mySound will control all sounds in the timeline. The last line of this ActionScript initializes a variable (soundOff) with a value of false.

3) Select frame 15 of the Navigation Buttons layer. Locate the Water Drop Button symbol in the library, and drag an instance of it onto the stage. Use the Info panel to position it at X: 530 and Y: 38.

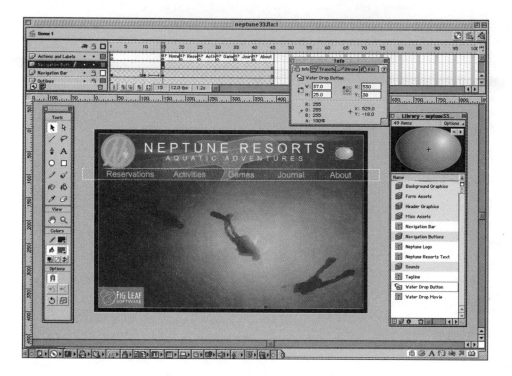

You are going to make your sound toggle with this button.

4) Select the instance of the Water Drop Button symbol on the stage, and use the Actions panel to add the following ActionScript to the button:

```
on (release) {
  if (soundOff == true) {
    soundOff = false;
    mySound.setVolume(100)
  } else {
    soundOff = true;
    mySound.setVolume(0)
  }
}
```

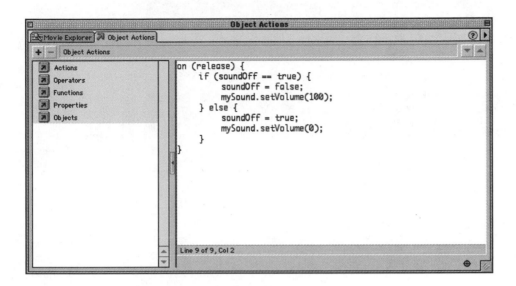

```
on (release) {
    if (soundOff == true) {
        soundOff = false;
        mySound.setVolume(100);
    } else {
        soundOff = true;
        mySound.setVolume(0);
    }
}
```

This ActionScript uses a bit of logic to figure out what to do. First, it checks whether the value of the soundOff variable is true. If it is, the code sets that variable equal to false and then sets the volume of the mySound object to 100 (on). If soundOff is not true, the ActionScript sets it to true and then sets the volume of the mySound object to 0 (off). This code toggles the sound on and off.

5) Choose Control > Test Movie, and test out your sound toggle.

When you click the button the first time, the sound should turn off. When you click the button again, the sound comes back on. The sound does not start and stop; it continues to play. But the volume is either 0 or 100.

6) Close the test movie, and save the movie as neptune34.fla in the MyWork folder.

WHAT YOU HAVE LEARNED

In this lesson, you have:

- Created a slider using ActionScript (pages 204–207)
- Used the Sound object to attach sounds to a Flash movie (pages 208–212)
- Controlled the volume of the sounds using a slider (pages 213–214)
- Created a sound toggle to turn the sound on and off (pages 214–217)

processing data using middleware

LESSON 10

The next project you're going to work on for the Neptune Resorts Web site is the Neptune Resorts Guest Journal—a fancy name for a relatively simple guestbook. The journal loads content from a dynamically generated text file. The journal also lets users add their own comments.

The Neptune Resorts Guest Journal: See what others had to say about their Neptune Resorts experiences. You can even add your own comments to the Neptune Resorts Guest Journal.

Submit	Cancel
Name:	Jane Doe
Email:	
Entry:	Neptune Resorts is lovely.

You'll create a journal that visitors to your site can use.

WHAT YOU WILL LEARN

In this lesson, you will:

- Load variables from an external file

- Use the scroll property to control the scrolling of a dynamic text box

- Use ColdFusion to send information to the server

- Use the onClipEvent movie event

APPROXIMATE TIME

It usually takes about one hour
to complete this lesson.

LESSON FILES

Media Files:

Lesson10/Assets/submit.txt

Lesson10/Assets/readwrite.cfm

Starting File:

Lesson10/Assets/journal1.fla

Completed Project:

journal6.fla

LOADING VARIABLES FROM AN EXTERNAL FILE

The loadVariables method reads data from an external file, such as a text file or text generated by middleware (ColdFusion, Active Server Pages, and so on), and sets the values for variables in a movie or movie clip. The syntax of this method is as follows:

```
myPath.loadVariables(url, variables);
```

In this ActionScript, myPath refers to the target path of the loadVariables method. This path can be the main timeline (_root), a relative reference to the current timeline (this), or any other target path. The loadVariables method has two arguments: url and variables. Url is the absolute or relative URL of the external file. The host for the URL must be in the same subdomain as the movie clip when the movie is to be viewed with the Macromedia Flash Web Player. This is not the case when the movie is viewed in the stand-alone Flash Player or in the test-movie window. The Variables argument specifies the process of retrieving the variables. This method can be GET or POST. GET appends the variables to the end of the URL; POST sends the variables in a separate HTTP header.

1) Open journal1.fla in the Lesson10/Assets folder.

This file is partially built for you. It consists of seven layers (Actions, Scrollers, Add Entry, Cancel Entry, Input Text, Dynamic Text, and Background) in two frames. The frames in the Actions layer each contain a Stop action and are labeled *read* and *write*. The Add Entry layer contains a button (in frame 1) that takes the movie to the frame labeled write, and the Cancel Entry layer contains a button (in frame 2) that takes the movie to the frame labeled read. The Input Text layer contains a movie clip called Input Text, which you will work with later in this lesson.

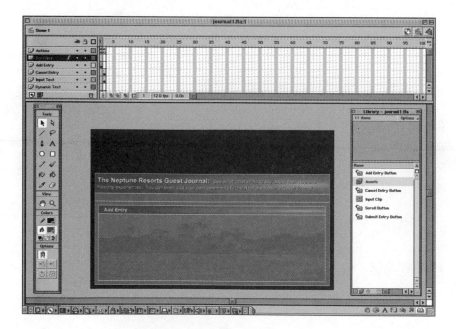

2) Select frame 1 of the Dynamic Text, and select the Text tool in the toolbox. In the Character panel, set the font to Arial or Helvetica and the font height to 12. Make sure that the Bold and Italic options are deselected, and set the text color to White (#FFFFFF).

Before you draw your text box, you have to make some changes in the Text Options panel.

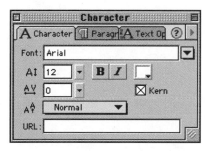

3) In the Text Options panel, set the text type to Dynamic Text and the line type to Multiline. Check the HTML, Word Wrap, and Selectable checkboxes, and draw a text box that takes up the space available in the background.

Make sure that you leave some space on the right side of the text box; you're going to add some scroll buttons later.

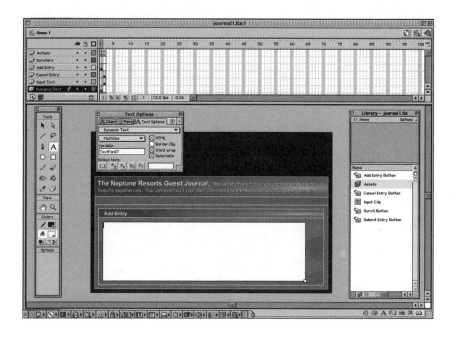

221

4) Switch to the arrow tool, and select the text box that you just drew. In the Text Options panel, type *text* in the Variable text box, and deselect the Selectable option.

You are going to supply a value for this variable from an external text file.

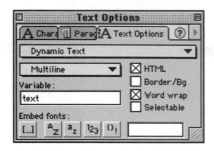

5) Select frame 1 of the Actions layer. In the Actions panel, add the following ActionScript after the stop **action:**

```
text = "Loading Data…";
_root.loadVariables("http://www.neptuneresortsinc.com/readwrite.cfm?action=
read");
```

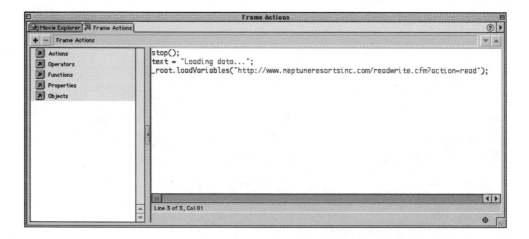

The first line of this ActionScript initializes a value for the text variable. The second line uses the loadVariables method to read data from a URL. This method is applied to the _root object, because that is where you want to load the variables.

This URL refers to a ColdFusion file on the Neptune Resorts Web site. A copy of this ColdFusion file (readwrite.cfm) is located in the Lesson10/Assets file, if you want to look at it. The important thing to know about this ColdFusion file is that using the URL causes the ColdFusion file to return text in a format that Flash can understand. The processed ColdFusion file might look like the following:

```
&text=<br><font size="14" color="#990000">Tue Oct 3 19:28:48 GMT-0400
2000</font><br>This is a great site!<br><br><font size="14"
color="#990000">Tue Oct 3 19:28:53 GMT-0400 2000</font><br>I'd like more
information about Hawaii.<br><br>
```

The ColdFusion file generates text that sets the text variable equal to a long string of HTML. That format is just how you set up a variable in Flash, so Flash understands the text from the ColdFusion file as though it were an internal variable. That internal variable fills the dynamic text box named text with the value of text in the ColdFusion file.

6) Choose Control > Test Movie.

If you are connected to the Internet, and if there are any journal entries on the server, some text should appear in the dynamic text box. If you are not connected to the Internet, you should just see the message *Loading data…*. If there are no journal entries on the server, the *Loading data…* text should disappear, and the text box will be empty. You can test it again after you add an entry later in this lesson, or you can change the variable name for the text box to testData and test the movie again. When the variable is set to testData and you're connected to the Internet, *OK* should appear in the text box.

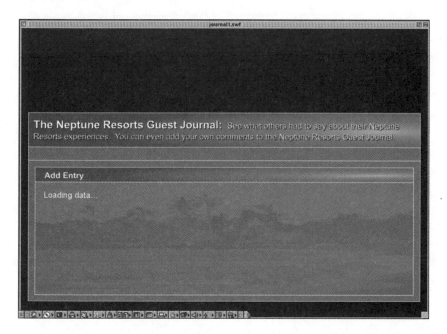

A window might appear, telling you that Flash was unable to connect to the ColdFusion file. If that's the case, you did everything right, but Flash can't reach the ColdFusion file that contains all the variables. If you have ColdFusion Server installed on your computer, you can place the readwrite.cfm file on your Web server and try to connect to it locally.

7) Close the test movie, and save the movie as journal2.fla in the MyWork folder.
You still have a great deal of work to do with this file. In the following section, you'll add some scroll buttons so that you can read the large amounts of text in the dynamic text box easily.

USING THE *SCROLL* PROPERTY

The scroll property controls the display of information in a text box associated with a variable, defining where the text box begins displaying content. This property has the following syntax:

```
variableName.scroll = x;
```

In this ActionScript, variableName refers to the target path of the variable whose scroll property you want to control. The number of the topmost visible line in the text box is represented by x.

In the following exercise, you will use a little ActionScript to increment and decrement the scroll property for the text box named text in the main timeline (_root.text), effectively scrolling the contents of the text box up and down.

1) Select frame 1 of the Scrollers layer in journal2.fla, and drag an instance of the Scroll Button symbol from the library onto the stage. Position the button to the top and right of the dynamic text box.
You are going to use this button to scroll through the text box. You can position this button at X: *545* and Y: *225*, if you want to be precise.

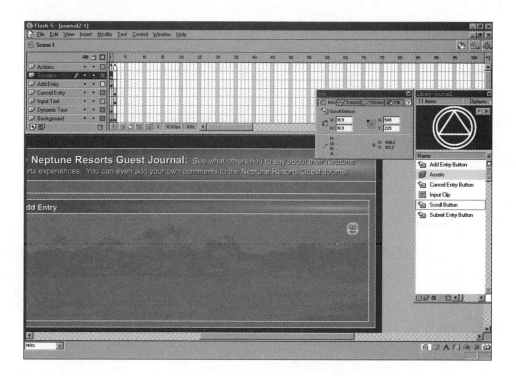

2) Select the instance of the Scroll Button symbol on the stage, and add the following ActionScript to the button:

```
on (press) {
  scrolling = true;
}
on (release, releaseOutside) {
  scrolling = false;
}
```

This ActionScript simply sets a variable named scrolling to have a value of true when the button is clicked. It also sets the scrolling variable to false when the mouse button is released or when the mouse button is clicked and then released outside the button.

225

3) Make sure that you have selected only the instance of the Scroll Button symbol on the stage; then choose Insert > Convert to Symbol. The Symbol Properties dialog box opens. Name the new symbol *Scroll Clip*, set the Behavior option to Movie Clip, and click OK.

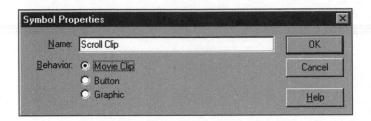

You're not quite done with this button. Now that it's nested in a movie clip, you are going to add some ActionScript to that movie clip.

4) Select the instance of the Scroll Clip movie clip. In the Actions panel, add the following ActionScript:

```
onClipEvent (enterFrame) {
  if (scrolling == true) {
    --_root.text.scroll;
  }
}
```

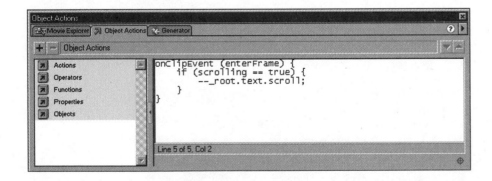

Some of this ActionScript should look familiar, but the onClipEvent section is new. The onClipEvent handler is similar to the on handler used for buttons, but it is used exclusively for movie clips. The handler follows this syntax:

```
onClipEvent(movieEvent) {
  statement;
}
```

The movieEvent argument can be load, unload, enterFrame, mouseMove, mouseDown, mouseUp, keyDown, keyUp, or data. Load executes the statement as soon as the instance of the movie clip is loaded and appears in the timeline. Unload executes the action in the first frame after the movie clip is removed from the timeline. When you use the enterFrame event, the action is executed as each frame of the movie clip is played, even if the movie clip has only one frame. This event can be useful for attaching actions that you want to execute repeatedly. The mouseMove, mouseDown, and mouseUp events execute the statement every time the pointer is moved, when the left mouse button is clicked, or when the left mouse button is released. The keyDown and keyUp events execute the statement when a key is pressed or released. The data event executes the statement when data is received in a loadVariables or loadMovie action. When specified with a loadVariables action, the data event occurs only once: when the last variable is loaded. When specified with a loadMovie action, the data event occurs repeatedly as each section of data is retrieved.

5) With the instance of the Scroll Clip movie clip selected on the stage, choose Edit > Duplicate to create a duplicate instance of the symbol.

A second instance of the Scroll Clip symbol appears on the stage. Attached to this duplicate instance is all the ActionScript you added to the first instance.

6) Select the duplicate instance of the Scroll Clip symbol, and choose Modify > Transform > Flip Vertical. Then use the Info panel to position this instance of the symbol at X: *545* and Y: *350*.

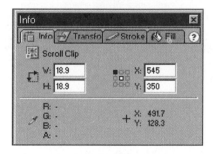

You are going to use this instance of the Scroll Clip symbol to scroll the text in the opposite direction, so you have to modify the ActionScript.

7) With the second instance of the Scroll Clip symbol still selected, modify line 3 of the ActionScript so that it increments the `scroll` **property of the** `_root.text` **text box instead of decrementing it (** `++_root.text.scroll;` **).**

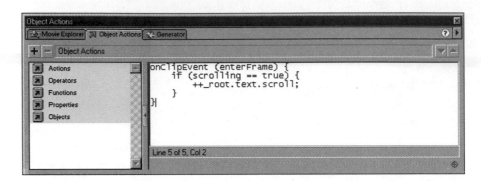

The ActionScript should look like this when you're done:

```
onClipEvent (enterFrame) {
  if (scrolling == true) {
    ++_root.text.scroll;
  }
}
```

8) Choose Control > Test Movie.

When you click the instances of the Scroll Clip movie clip, the dynamic text in the _root.text text box should scroll in the appropriate direction. If the text box doesn't contain enough text, you won't see any scrolling. In that case, come back and test this functionality after you complete the rest of this lesson, open the completed file (journal6.fla) and add several entries.

9) Close the test movie, and save the file as journal3.fla in the MyWork folder.

You have more to do with this movie, so keep it open. You're going to work on the write section of the movie in the following section.

USING THE SELECTION OBJECT

You can use the selection object to set and control the focus on a text box. The text box that has the focus is the one where the user's mouse pointer is placed. One method of the selection object is setFocus, which enables you to set the focus to a specified text box, as follows:

```
Selection.setFocus(variableName);
```

The variableName argument refers to the relative or absolute path of the variable name assigned to the text box to which you want to assign the focus. This path must be contained in quotes, as follows:

```
Selection.setFocus("userName");
```

In the following exercise, you will use the setFocus method of the selection object to set the focus on the Name text box in the Input Clip symbol. When you finish, your visitors will not have to click the text box to enter their information.

1) Select frame 2 of the Input Text layer in journal3.fla. Double-click the instance of the Input Clip movie clip on the stage.

The Input Clip movie clip looks like a form; it has a background and several text boxes. The text boxes have the variable names userName, userEmail, and userEntry.

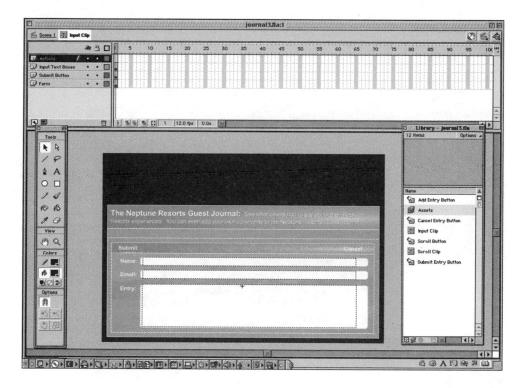

2) Select frame 1 of the Input Clip movie clip. In the Actions panel, add the following ActionScript:

```
Selection.setFocus("userName");
```

This ActionScript uses the selection object, with which you can set and control the focus on a text box. In this case, you are using the selection object with the setFocus method to set the focus on the text box for which the variable name is specified in the argument variableName. In this case, the variableName argument is "userName".

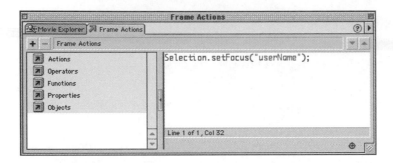

3) Choose Control > Test Movie. Click the Add Entry button when the test window opens.

When you click the Add Entry button, the journal jumps to the write frame. When the movie enters this frame, the insertion point enters the Name text box automatically. You can type in each text box in the form.

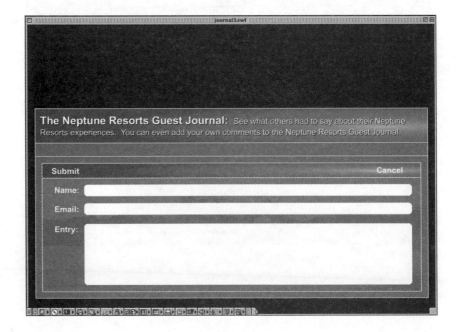

4) Close the test movie, and save the file as journal4.fla in the MyWork folder.

You're almost done. In the following section, you add some more ActionScript to handle the text users enter in the Input Clip form.

230

PROCESSING DATA AND SENDING IT TO THE SERVER

You already know how to get external data into your Flash movie by using the loadVariables method. As you will see in the following exercise, you can use the same method to send data to the server. Before the data is sent to the server, you must apply a little bit of ActionScript to format it properly for inclusion in the external data source.

You should still have the Input Clip symbol in journal4.fla open in symbol-editing mode.

1) Select the instance of the Submit Entry Button symbol that's in the Submit Button layer. In the Actions panel, add the following ActionScript:

```
on (press) {
  entry = "<b>On "+new Date().toString()+", <font color=\"#0000FF\"><a
href=\"mailto:"+userEmail+"\">"+userName+"</a></font> entered the
following:</b><br>"+userEntry+"<br><br>";
  action="write";
  this.loadVariables("http://www.neptuneresortsinc.com/readwrite.cfm",
"GET");
}
```

That's a lot of ActionScript. To minimize the chance of typos, you can copy this ActionScript from submit.as in the Lesson10/Assets folder, or you can import this ActionScript by choosing Options > Import from File in the Actions panel,

The ActionScript that you added is contained in an on (press) handler, which lets Flash know that everything should happen when the mouse button is clicked. The first line of the handler contains a variable, entry, that has a long value. The value contains some HTML, some strings of text, and several variables. When the ActionScript is translated, you end up with the following value for entry:

```
<b>On CurrentDateAndTime, <font color="#0000FF"><a
href="mailto:userEmail">userName</a></font> entered the
following:</b><br>userEntry<br><br>
```

The expression new Date().toString() outputs the value of the current date and time as a string. Then the values of the userEmail, userName, and userEntry variables are inserted into the string.

After it provides a value for the entry variable, the ActionScript provides a value of write for the action variable. The next line is similar to the loadVariables method that you used earlier in this lesson. This time, you specify the target of the method as this, which refers to the timeline where the action occurs. The loaded variables, therefore, apply to the Input Clip timeline. The URL argument

231

is http://www.neptuneresortsinc.com/readwrite.cfm—similar to what you specified earlier in this lesson. In this case, however, you are also adding the loadVariables argument, which has the value "GET". This argument appends the variables that exist in the target (this) to the URL string. The argument is useful for a small number of variables, which is fine for the purposes of your guest journal. The values of the entry and action variables are sent to the ColdFusion file when you use "GET" as the loadVariables argument.

2) Choose Control > Test Movie. Click the Add Entry button when the test movie opens.

The form opens as it did before, and the insertion point should appear in the Name text box.

3) Type some text in the form, and click the Submit button.

When you click the Submit button, it looks like nothing is happening, but all the ActionScript that you added to the button is being triggered, setting up the required variables and sending the information to the readwrite.cfm file.

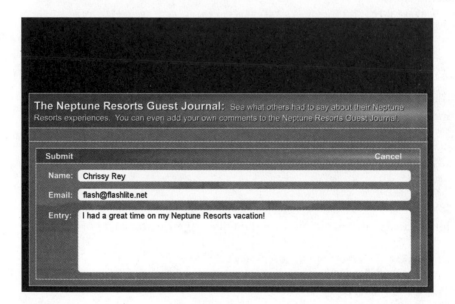

4) Click the Cancel button to switch back to the frame labeled read.

The Cancel button contains some ActionScript to make the movie jump back to the frame labeled read. When you click this button, the movie switches back to the first frame, and you should be able to see the text that you entered when you clicked the Submit button. If the text box contains enough text, you should be able to scroll through it.

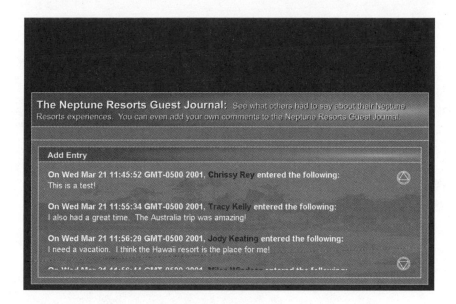

The Neptune Resorts Guest Journal: See what others had to say about their Neptune Resorts experiences. You can even add your own comments to the Neptune Resorts Guest Journal.

Add Entry

On Wed Mar 21 11:45:52 GMT-0500 2001, Chrissy Rey entered the following:
This is a test!

On Wed Mar 21 11:55:34 GMT-0500 2001, Tracy Kelly entered the following:
I also had a great time. The Australia trip was amazing!

On Wed Mar 21 11:56:29 GMT-0500 2001, Jody Keating entered the following:
I need a vacation. I think the Hawaii resort is the place for me!

5) Close the test movie, and save the movie as journal5.fla in the myfiles folder.

You have one more thing left to do: add some ActionScript that verifies that your entry was sent and then takes the journal back to the frame labeled read.

USING THE *ONCLIPEVENT* HANDLER

Handlers are special actions that "handle," or manage, events such as press or release. You have used handlers to attach ActionScript to buttons (on (press)), and you can use the onClipEvent handler to attach ActionScript to a movie clip in a similar fashion. The onClipEvent handler has a single arguement: movieEvent. When Data is specified as the MovieEvent arguement, the action contained in the onClipEvent handler is initiated when data is received in a loadVariables or loadMovie action. When it is specified with a loadVariables action, the Data event occurs only once: when the last variable is loaded. When it is specified with a loadMovie action, the Data event occurs repeatedly as each section of data is retrieved.

In the following exercise, you will assign an onClipEvent handler to the instance of the Input Clip movie clip on the stage. Then you will set the value of the handler's movieEvent to Data so that the ActionScript in the handler executes only when data is received in the movie clip. The data will be received only when the information sent to the ColdFusion file has been processed, so this code works as an error-checker to ensure that the movie doesn't proceed until the data has been processed.

You should still have journal5.fla open. If the Input Clip symbol is still in symbol-editing mode, choose Edit > Edit Movie. You want to be on the main timeline, not inside a symbol.

1) Select the instance of the Input Clip movie clip in frame 2 of the Input Text layer. In the Actions panel, apply the following ActionScript to this movie clip:

```
onClipEvent (data) {
  if (written == "true") {
    _root.gotoAndStop(1);
  }
}
```

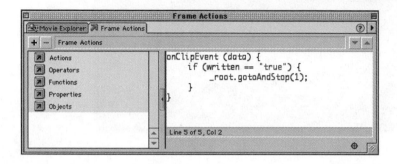

The onClipEvent handler waits until the last variable is loaded by the loadVariables method, which is triggered when the user clicks the Submit button. When the last variable is loaded, the ActionScript checks whether a variable called written has a value of true. The written variable is in the ColdFusion file. When all the information sent to it has been processed, the ColdFusion file sets the value of the written variable to true, so the condition is true when the information has been processed. When the condition is true, the main timeline (_root) jumps to frame 1.

2) Choose Control > Test Movie, and test the movie.

When you add an entry, the journal should jump back to the read frame after the data has been processed.

3) Close the test movie, and save the file as journal6.fla in the myfiles folder.

You're done with the journal. Remember that the host for the URL specified in the loadVariables method must be in the same subdomain as the movie clip when the movie is to be viewed with the Macromedia Flash Web Player. So this journal works only when you test it in Flash or play it in the stand-alone Flash Player.

If you want to make a journal for your own Web page, you must install the appropriate middleware server (ColdFusion, ASP, PHP, and so on) in your domain, and create a file similar to readwrite.cfm to process the information.

WHAT YOU HAVE LEARNED

In this lesson, you have:

- Loaded variables from an external file (pages 220–224)

- Controlled the display of information in a text box (pages 225–228)

- Controlled the selection of a text box (pages 228–230)

- Processed data and sent it to a server (pages 231–233)

- Created an error checker to test data (pages 233–234)

adding generator content

In this lesson, you will learn how to add some basic Generator content to your Flash movie. Then you will use the `print` action to create a printable version of that content. Generator is the first Web-server production application that lets you combine text, graphics, and sound dynamically to build rich media content and deliver the final product in a variety of animated or static forms. With Generator, designers can create templates within Flash containing variable elements (graphics, text, and sound) to be replaced with content later. This generated content can be played back in the client's browser as a Flash Player movie or a JPEG, PNG, GIF, or QuickTime movie.

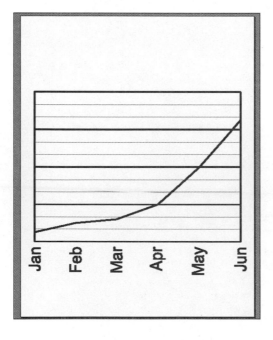

With Generator, you can create templates containing variable data that update automatically.

WHAT YOU WILL LEARN

In this lesson, you will:

- Add dynamic text with Generator

- Add a Generator object

- Add a print action

- Specify a print area

APPROXIMATE TIME

It usually takes about one hour to complete this lesson.

LESSON FILES

Media Files:

none

Starting File:

Lesson11/Assets/about1.fla

Completed Project:

about6.fla

DEFINING A GENERATOR VARIABLE

By using variables and data sources, you can have Generator insert text dynamically into a Generator template. A **variable** is a placeholder for a value supplied by a data source. Generator variables are among the basic building blocks of Generator templates. Variables hold positions where you want to insert any string literal (text string). You aren't limited to visible text; you can use variables in ActionScript and even inside other Generator objects.

You use the following syntax to define text variables:

```
{VariableName}
```

The braces ({}) indicate a variable definition. You specify the name of the variable between the braces. The variable name can consist of any alphanumeric characters but cannot contain spaces, and it is not case-sensitive.

In the following exercise, you will add some Generator content to your movie.

1) Open about1.fla in the Lesson11/Assets folder on the CD-ROM.

The movie has four layers (Chart, Text, Print Button, and Background), each of which has a single frame.

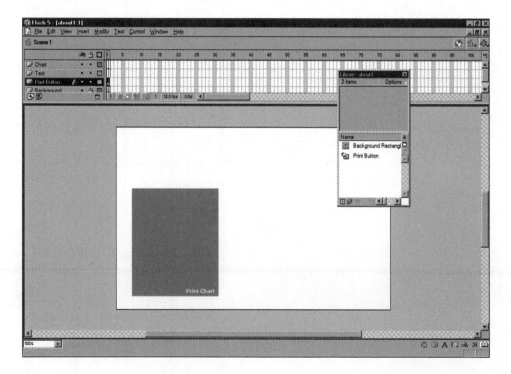

238

2) Select the text tool. In the Character panel, set the font to Arial or Helvetica, the font height to 12, and the text (fill) color to black (#000000). In the Text Options panel, set the text type to Static Text.

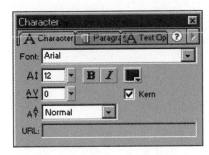

Make sure that the Bold and Italic options are deselected in the Character panel and that the Use Device Fonts and Selectable options are not selected in the Text Options panel.

Now that you have your text settings ready, you have to add a text box to the stage.

3) Select frame 1 of the Text layer, and use the text tool to add the following text to the stage, in the area defined by the blue rectangle in the Background layer:

{heading}

{caption}

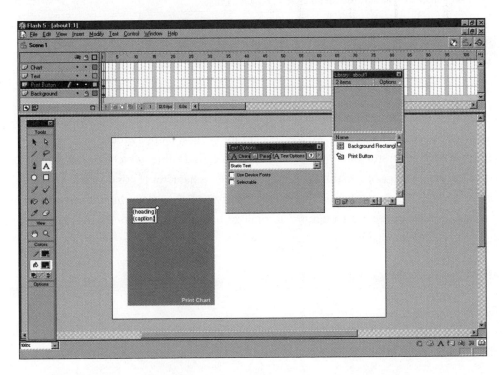

You just added two Generator variables. The first variable is called heading, and the second one is called caption. In the source files for this lesson, the first line of the text box is bold. You can do the same thing or leave both lines as they are.

4) Click the Generator Environment Variable button, near the top-right corner of the Flash window. When the Set Environment dialog box opens, type the following, and click OK:

#name, value

heading, "Business is Booming!"

caption, "Visitors are coming to our resorts in record numbers."

The Generator Environment Variable button opens the Set Environment dialog box, where you can set your template's environment data source.

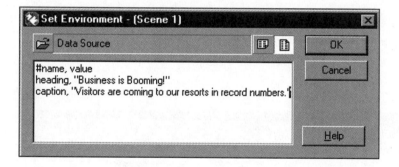

This text is one example of a Generator data source. The first row determines the format of the data. In this case, you have a column called name, which contains the names of the Generator variable(s), and a column called value, which contains the values of the Generator variable(s). The pound-sign character (#) that starts the data source lets Generator know that this data is a native data source, which means that it is typed directly in the Set Environment dialog box. You'll use a non-native data source in the following exercise.

5) Choose File > Publish Settings to open the Publish Settings dialog box. Check the Generator Template checkbox in the Formats tab, and click OK.

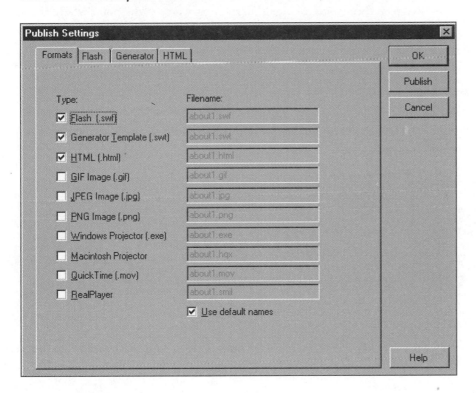

Before you can preview your movie, you have to let Flash know that the movie is a Generator template.

6) Choose Control > Test Movie.

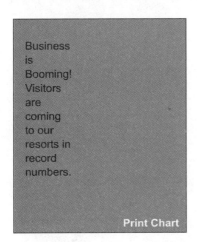

The Flash movie, which is now a Generator template, opens in the test-movie window. You should see the text *Business is Booming!* and *Visitors are coming to our resorts in record numbers* wrap on the screen. Notice that the text wraps at the point where the text box containing the Generator variables ends. You can fix that situation by extending the text box, as you will do in the next step.

7) Close the test movie. Select the arrow tool, and double-click the text box on the stage. When a small square appears in the top-right corner of the text box, drag it to the right until the text box is approximately the same width as the blue rectangle in the Background layer.

This step lengthens the text box, giving the text more space before it wraps.

8) Test the movie again.

This time, the text should wrap at the point that you defined as the right side of the text box.

9) Close the test movie, and save the file as about2.fla in the MyWork folder.
You need to continue working with this file, so leave it open.

ADDING A DATA SOURCE

Generator can use several data-source formats: a comma-delimited text file, a URL that references a comma-delimited text file, a result set from an SQL query passed through a JDBC/ODBC connection, a native data source, or a Java class. You can also use ASP, ColdFusion, PHP, Perl, and other programs to dynamically generate a comma-delimited text file that Generator can use. In the preceding exercise, you used a native data source to fill in the value of the {heading} and {caption} Generator variables. In this exercise, you will use an external text file to do the same thing.

1) Click the Generator Environment Variable button in about2.fla. When the Set Environment dialog box opens, replace the existing text with *mydata.txt*, and click OK:

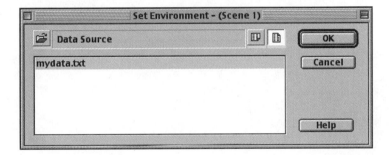

You can refer to an external text file in the Set Environment dialog box. Generator will use the external text file as the data source for the movie. In the next step, you'll create that data source.

2) Open your favorite text editor (Notepad or SimpleText will do), and type the following in a new text document:

name, value
heading, "Business is Booming!"
caption, "Visitors are coming to our resorts in record numbers."

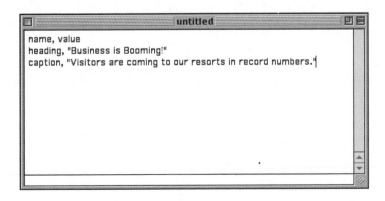

243

This text should look almost exactly like the text that you entered in the Set Environment dialog box in the preceding exercise. The only difference is that it does not contain the pound-sign character (#).

3) Save the text file as mydata.txt in the MyWork folder.

You have to save the text file in the same folder as the Generator template in this case, because you typed a relative path to the data source in the Set Environment dialog box.

4) Return to about2.fla, and test the movie.

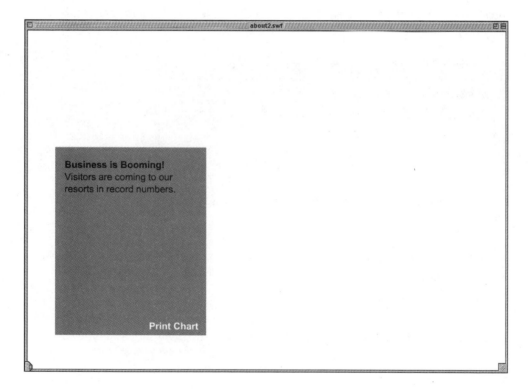

The movie should be identical to that which you saw the last time you tested it. The only difference is that the values for the Generator variables in the text box are being drawn from an external data source instead of a native one.

5) Close the test movie, and save the file as about3.fla in the MyWork folder.

Inserting dynamic text is one of the awesome things that Generator can do. In the following exercise, you will add some more Generator content.

ADDING A GENERATOR OBJECT

Text replacement might be enough for some projects, but you can do so much more with Generator. You can also insert objects such as charts, lists, tickers, and tables. You can use ActionScript to do some of these things, but that method usually takes much more time. With Generator, all you have to do is insert the object, modify some settings, and connect the object to a data source.

Some Generator objects provide functionality that you just can't get with Flash alone. Generator's Basic Charts object, for example, allows you to insert a chart dynamically when the Web server requests the Generator template. In the following exercise, you will learn how to use the Basic Charts object.

1) Select frame 1 of the Chart layer in about3.fla. Choose Window > Generator Objects to open the Generator Objects panel.

The Generator Objects panel contains all the Generator objects that you can add to a movie. You can drag any object from the panel onto the stage.

2) Locate the Basic Charts object in the Generator Objects panel, and drag it onto the stage. Use the Info panel to set W to 150, H to 110, X to 55, and Y to 205.

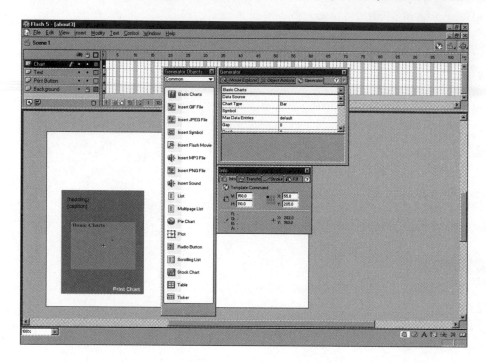

When you drag the Basic Charts object onto the stage, the Generator panel opens. You'll use the Generator panel to modify some of the chart's settings in the next step.

3) Open your favorite text editor (Notepad or SimpleText will do), and type the following in a new text document:

value, hlabel

50, Jan

100, Feb

120, Mar

200, Apr

400, May

650, Jun

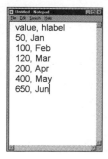

The Basic Charts object requires its own data source. This data source must contain certain named columns. For this chart, you are going to create a line chart, so you need at least a value column. The hlabel column will define the horizontal label for each value. The first row of the data source defines the format, and the subsequent rows contain the data.

4) Save the text file as chartdata.txt in the MyWork folder.

You need to save the file so that the Generator template can access it.

5) Return to about3.fla. Select the Basic Charts object placeholder that's in frame 1 of the Chart layer. In the Generator panel, set Data Source to chartdata.txt, Chart Type to Line, and Labels to off.

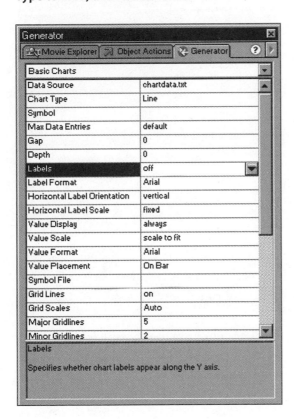

If the Generator panel is not still open from when you added the object, open it by choosing Window > Panels > Generator.

TIP *You can also open the Generator panel by double-clicking any Generator object that's been added to the movie.*

The Data Source setting lets you specify the properly formatted data source for this chart. You want to make a line chart, so you have to set Chart Type to Line. Notice that the Chart Type pop-up menu lists several other types of charts including Bar and Area. The Labels setting specifies whether labels will appear on the Y axis of the Basic Charts object.

6) Choose Control > Test Movie.

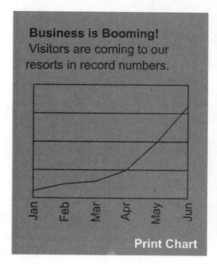
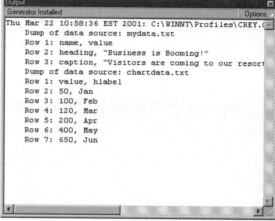

TIP *You can open the Output window by choosing Window > Output.*

When you test your movie, a line chart should appear in the space occupied by the Basic Charts object placeholder. This line chart will display the data in chartdata.txt, using the settings you specified in the Generator panel.

7) Close the test movie, and save the file as about4.fla in the MyWork folder.
Now that you have a little content, you need to give your users a way to print it. That's what you'll do in the following exercise.

PRINTING FLASH CONTENT

If your site contains important information, your visitors might want to print some of it. They can try to use the Print command in their browsers, but that command often isn't adequate for printing Flash content. You can use Flash's built-in print capabilities to control the look of the printed content. In this exercise, you will create a movie clip containing only the dynamically generated chart. Then you will add some ActionScript that allows you to print just that chart.

1) Select the Basic Charts object placeholder in frame 1 of the Chart layer in about4.fla. Choose Insert > Convert to Symbol. When the Symbol Properties dialog box opens, name the symbol Chart Clip, and set its behavior to Movie Clip.

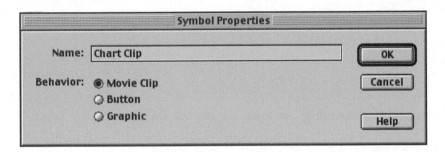

You are going to use the Print action to print only the chart. To do that, you must place it inside a movie clip.

2) Make sure you have the instance of the Chart Clip in frame 1 of the Chart layer. In the Instance panel, type *chart* in the Name text box.

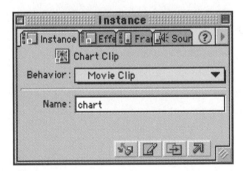

The movie clip needs an instance name so that you can target it for printing.

3) Select the instance of the Print Button in frame 1 of the Print Button layer, and apply the following ActionScript:

```
on (release) {
  print ("chart", "bframe");
}
```

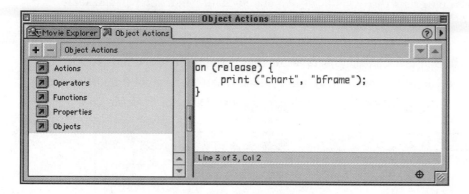

This ActionScript triggers a print action when the user releases the mouse button.

The print action has two arguments: target and type. The target argument specifies the path of the timeline that should be printed. If you want to print the main movie, you can set this argument to _root. If you want to print the contents of a movie clip, you should set this argument to the path of that movie clip. In this example, the movie clip that you want to print is the one with an instance name of chart.

The type argument specifies the bounding area for the print action. This argument can have one of three settings: bmovie, bframe, and bmax. Using bmovie makes the print action use the dimensions of the movie as the bounding area. The bframe option sets the bounding area for the printed content to the bounding area of each individual frame. You can use bmax to specify a bounding area set by the composite bounding area of all frames in the targeted movie clip. In this case, you are using bframe, so the printed content will scale to the bounding area of each individual frame. The targeted movie clip has only one frame, so the printed content will scale to that frame.

4) Choose Control > Test Movie. When the test movie opens, click the Print button to print your chart.

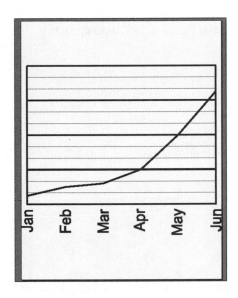

Look at the printed chart. Notice that only the chart is printed, not the text or background. It should take up most of the page, which isn't exactly the result you want. The printed chart should have some margins so that it looks better.

5) Close the test movie, and save the file as about5.fla in the MyWork folder.

You need to specify a bounding area, which is what you'll do in the following exercise.

SPECIFYING A PRINT AREA

You can exercise a great deal of control of the appearance of printed content in Flash. One thing you can do is specify a print area to provide precise page layout. In the following exercise, you'll do just that.

1) Double-click the Chart Clip movie clip in frame 1 of the Chart layer in about5.fla to open it in symbol-editing mode. Name the layer in the Chart Clip movie clip Chart. Add two more layers, named Actions/Labels and Print Area.

You're going to modify the movie clip just a bit to provide a better print area for the printed content.

2) Select frame 1 of the Actions/Labels layer. In the Frame panel, type *#p* in the Label text box. Add the ActionScript stop(); **.**

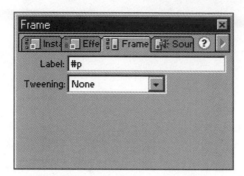

If you want to print only the contents of a specific frame in the targeted timeline, you have to label that frame #p. The bounding area will be in a new frame, which you'll add in the following step, but you don't ever want the movie clip to play that frame. That's why you need to add a stop action in this step.

3) Insert a keyframe at frame 2 of the Actions/Labels layer. In the Frame panel, type *#b* in the Label text box.

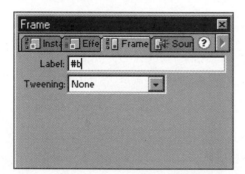

If you want to specify the bounding area of a single frame as the print area for the printed content, you must label that frame #b.

4) Insert a keyframe at frame 2 of the Print Area layer. Select this new keyframe, and add an instance of the Background Rectangle. In the Info panel, set W to 170, H to 130, X to –85, and Y to –65.

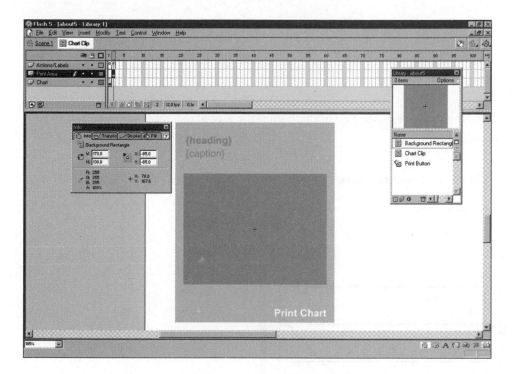

This instance of the Background Rectangle will act as the print area for the printed content.

5) Choose Edit > Edit Movie. Select the instance of the Print Button symbol in the Print Button layer. In the Action panel, change the ActionScript so that the type is bmovie.

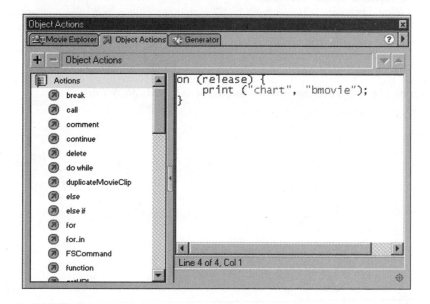

The ActionScript should look like this:

```
on (release) {
 print ("chart", "bmovie");
}
```

To use the print area specified in the frame labeled #b, the type argument has to be set to bmovie.

6) Choose Control > Test Movie. When the test movie opens, click the Print button.

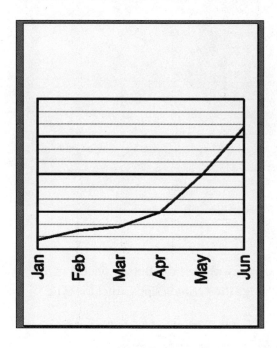

The chart should now have a nice margin when it's printed.

7) Close the test movie, and save the file as about6.fla in the MyWork folder.
You're done with this movie, so you can close it.

WHAT YOU HAVE LEARNED

In this lesson, you have:

- Used a native data source to add dynamic text (pages 238–242)
- Used an external text file to add dynamic text (pages 243–244)
- Added a chart by using a Generator object (pages 245–248)
- Printed Flash content (pages 249–251)
- Specified a print area (pages 251–256)

publishing and exporting

LESSON 12

You have spent all this time creating the amazing Neptune Resorts Web site, but now you need to prepare it for distribution. First, you need to make sure that the movie is optimized. Then you need to publish or export the movie in the appropriate format. Flash allows you to output your work in a variety of formats, including Flash (.swf), Generator Template (.swt), GIF, JPEG, PNG, Windows Projector (.exe), Macintosh Projector, QuickTime movie, HTLML, and RealPlayer.

At last, you put everything you've created together and export your site to the Web.

WHAT YOU WILL LEARN

In this lesson, you will:

- Use the Bandwidth Profiler
- View a movie as it would appear over the Internet
- Optimize a graphic
- Reduce the file size of a sound
- Create a preloader
- Export a movie
- Load external movies
- Create an HTML file to embed a movie
- Create a stand-alone projector containing the Flash movie

APPROXIMATE TIME

It usually takes about one hour to complete this lesson.

LESSON FILES

Media Files:

Lesson12/Assets/map9.fla
Lesson12/Assets/merfolk4.fla
Lesson12/Assets/music.fla
Lesson12/Assets/jigsaw3.fla
Lesson12/Assets/journal6.fla

Starting File:

Lesson12/Assets/neptune35.fla

Completed Project:

neptune39.fla
neptune39.swf
map.swf
music.swf
merfolk.swf
jigsaw.swf
journal.swf
neptune39.html
neptune39.exe
neptune39.hqx (Windows) or neptune39 Projector (Macintosh)
neptune39 Report.txt (Windows) or neptune39.swf Report (Macintosh)

USING THE BANDWIDTH PROFILER

Before you publish your movie for the first time, you should check to see how your users might view it on the Web. You can do this in Flash by using the Bandwidth Profiler in test-movie mode.

The Bandwidth Profiler provides a graphical representation of your movie's size by frame. You can use the Debug menu to choose a modem speed for the Bandwidth Profiler to emulate. Any item above the red line will cause some download-performance issues at the modem speed you choose from the Debug menu.

**1) Open neptune35.fla in the Lesson12/Assets folder, and choose Control ›
Test Movie.**

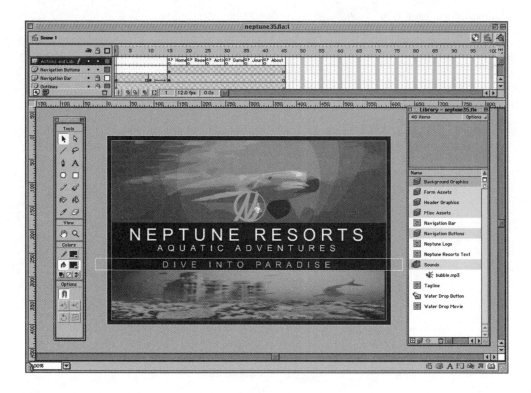

This movie is almost identical to neptune34.fla, which you worked with in Lesson 9. A few changes make the finished file a bit larger. (These changes were added so that you'd have something to optimize.) And the music toggle has been removed so that you can load it in a separate movie on top of the site later.

The movie opens in test-movie mode. Every time you test the movie in this way, Flash creates a .swf file in the directory in which you last saved the .fla file. The new file has the same name as your .fla file, and overwrites any file created from a previous test.

2) Choose View > Bandwidth Profiler to open the Bandwidth Profiler.

RED LINE

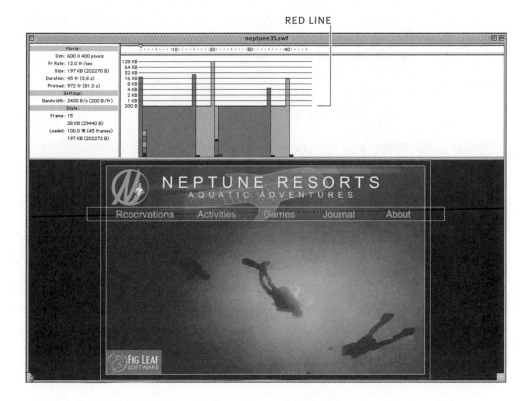

If a check appears next to this menu option, the Bandwidth Profiler is already open. The left side of the Bandwidth Profiler contains basic movie information: dimensions, file size, length, and frame rate. The right side of the Bandwidth Profiler contains a graph, showing the size of the file in each frame. The red line in the graph indicates whether a given frame streams in real time at the current modem speed set in the Control menu. If a bar extends above the red line, the movie must wait for that frame to load.

Notice that right now, the bar extends above the red line in several places. Those bars mean that Flash will have to pause to load the content for those frames before the movie can play. You should also take note of the file size, which is listed in the area to the left of the graph. Right now, the movie should be approximately 197 KB. Later in this lesson you will optimize the movie to bring that file size down.

TIP *Now that you have set up the test movie to show the Bandwidth Profiler, each movie you test will include this feature. To toggle the profiler on and off, choose View > Bandwidth Profiler.*

3) Choose Debug > 56k (4.7 KB/s); then choose View > Show Streaming.

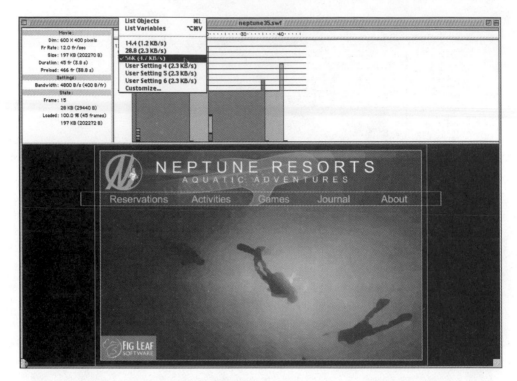

A green bar appears at the top of the Bandwidth Profiler to indicate how much of the movie has been loaded. When you turn on the Show Streaming option, the movie plays as though you're looking at it over the Web on a modem that's the same speed as the one you chose from the Debug menu. You should see that the green bar stops moving at places where the bars extend above the red line.

Don't rely solely on the Bandwidth Profiler to test the performance of your movie. You should always test it over a variety of Internet connections and on different computers and operating systems. You should also generate a size report when you publish your movie, as you will see later in this lesson.

4) Close the test movie.

You haven't made any changes, so you don't need to save the movie at this point.

OPTIMIZING A MOVIE

The larger the movie file, the longer the download time. When you identify frames that are too large to stream efficiently, as indicated by the Bandwidth Profiler, you might want to optimize your movie. You can take several steps to prepare your movie for optimal playback. As part of the publishing process, Flash automatically performs some optimizing on movies, including detecting duplicate shapes on export and placing these shapes in the file only once and converting nested groups to single groups. In the following exercise, you will do a couple of things to optimize your movie and reduce the size of the file, making the download time much less.

1) Open the library for neptune35.fla, and locate the Dolphin Graphic movie clip in the Background Graphics folder. Open this clip in symbol-editing mode.

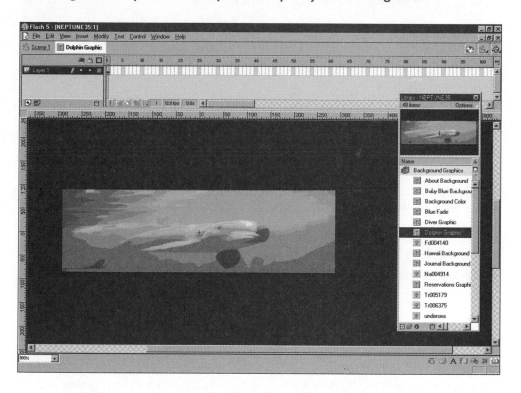

The Dolphin Graphic symbol contains a somewhat complex vector graphic. You are going to optimize this symbol to reduce the size of your movie.

2) Choose Edit > Select All; then choose Modify > Optimize.

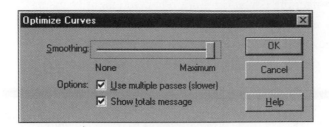

The Optimize Curves dialog box opens. This dialog box lets you optimize the selected strokes and fills by reducing the number of curves. These changes often result in a smaller file size for the finished movie.

3) In the Optimize Curves dialog box, drag the Smoothing slider all the way to the right. Check both the Use multiple passes (slower) and Show totals message checkboxes, and click OK.

The Smoothing slider lets you select the amount of smoothing, or curve reduction. Dragging it all the way to the right (Maximum) results in a more optimized curve. Be careful when you use this slider, though The optimized curve, with fewer curves, might not resemble the original outline. When you optimize your graphics in this way, you have to start deciding between quality and file size. You usually can find a happy medium that will keep your graphics visually appealing but smaller.

The Use multiple passes option forces Flash to optimize the curves repeatedly. This setting usually results in the maximum optimization possible, although you might find that optimizing the curves again results in a further, though less significant, reduction in file size.

The Show totals message option causes a dialog box to appear when Flash is done optimizing the curves. This dialog box shows the original number of curves, the optimized number of curves, and the percentage of curve reduction. The optimization that you just performed should result in a significant reduction in the number of curves. Click OK to close this dialog box.

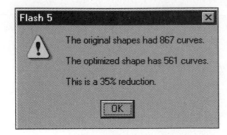

4) Perform the optimization procedure again.

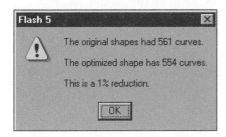

Note that this time the original shapes had far fewer curves.

Even though the Use multiple passes option forces Flash to run the optimization multiple times, you can optimize the shapes a bit more sometimes. Make sure that you look at the graphic each time you optimize it to make sure that it still looks good.

5) Choose Control > Test Movie to see how your change affected the size of the movie.

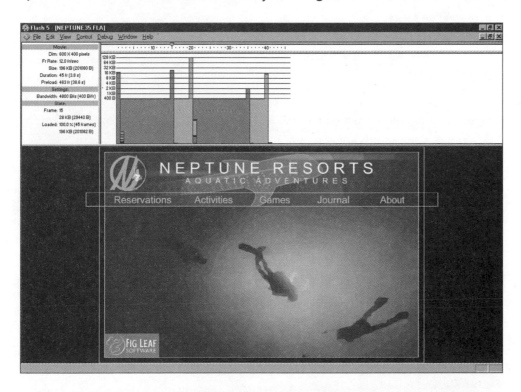

The size of the file might not have changed dramatically, but with Flash and the Web, every kilobyte counts. If you can pare a bit of file size by optimizing a single symbol, think how much you can shave off by optimizing every symbol.

6) Close the test movie. Locate the bubble.mp3 sound in the Sounds folder in the library. Double-click the icon to the left of the sound to open the Sound Properties dialog box.

Graphic elements aren't the only thing to consider when it comes to optimization. Many times, your sounds add a significant amount of file size.

7) In the Sound Properties dialog box, set the compression to MP3 and the bit rate to 8 kbps. Click OK to close the dialog box.

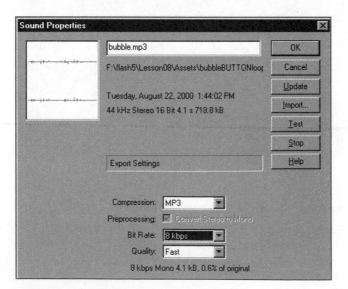

264

The bubble.mp3 sound plays whenever you move the mouse over one of the buttons in the navigation bar. You can apply the maximum compression to this sound, which normally sacrifices too much sound quality, because the distortion that occurs with the compression doesn't affect this sound adversely. Many times, a sound gets an underwater effect when the compression applied to it is significant. In this case, the sound is bubbles, so that underwater effect isn't necessarily a bad thing.

8) Choose Control › Test Movie.

```
        Movie:
     Dim:  600 X 400 pixels
  Fr Rate: 12.0 fr/sec
     Size: 192 KB (196764 B)
 Duration: 45 fr (3.8 s)
  Preload: 452 fr (37.7 s)
        Settings:
Bandwidth: 4800 B/s (400 B/fr)
        State:
    Frame: 15
           24 KB (25124 B)
   Loaded: 100.0 % (45 frames)
           192 KB (196766 B)
```

The file size should once again be reduced.

9) Close the test movie, and save the file as neptune36.fla in the MyWork folder.
The optimization that you just performed brought your file size down a bit, but think about ways that you might be able to reduce the size even more. You should limit the number of gradient fills and alpha transparencies when possible, for example. You can also optimize your movie by using bitmaps instead of complex (photographic-quality) vector graphics.

CREATING A PRELOADER

After you add graphics, sound, and content to your movie, the file can become rather large. Even after you optimize your movie, you might find that integral parts of the movie have frames that go above the red line in the Bandwidth Profiler. What happens if a user clicks a button to go to a particular frame, and that frame hasn't been downloaded yet? Flash will not go to frames that haven't been loaded, so you need to make sure that everything that needs to be loaded is loaded before you let Flash perform such actions. A solution to this problem is a preloader. A **preloader** is an animation that plays while the contents of the Flash movie download.

You'll make a preloader in this exercise. Before you begin, make sure that you have neptune36.fla open.

1) Open the Scene panel (by choosing Window > Panels > Scene), and double-click the name of the current scene (Scene 1). Change the name to Content.

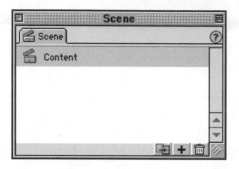

Scenes allow you to break your movie into segments. Segments are useful for adding content before or after your existing content, particularly when that content is markedly different from what you already have. In this case, you're going to add a scene that is empty except for a stop action. When you make your preloader, you want this movie to appear as a blank screen until all of it has been loaded. Adding an empty scene with a stop action lets you do just that.

TIP *You should always give your scenes meaningful names. Otherwise, you'll get lost in a sea of Scene 1, Scene 2, Scene 3, and so on.*

2) Click the Add Scene button in the Scene panel. When a new scene is added to your movie, change its name to Preloader. Select the Preloader scene in the Scene panel, and drag it to the top of the list.

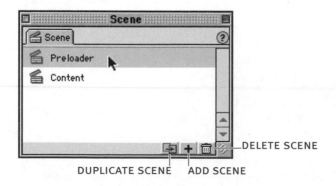

DELETE SCENE

DUPLICATE SCENE   ADD SCENE

By default, scenes play in the order in which they are listed in the Scene panel. So if the Preloader scene is listed first, that scene will be the first one to play.

3) Select the Preloader scene in the Scene panel. Name the layer in that scene Actions/Labels. Insert a keyframe at frame 2 of this layer. In the Frame panel, type *check* **in the Name text box.**

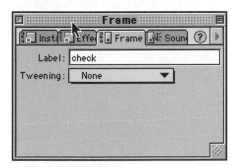

Notice when you select a scene in the Scene panel, Flash switches to that scene. The name of the scene appears in the top-left corner of the movie's timeline, so you always know where you are.

You are going to add the first part of your preloader in frame 2 of the Actions/Labels layer.

4) Select frame 2 of the Actions/Labels layer in the Preloader scene, and add the following ActionScript:

```
if (_root.getBytesLoaded() >= _root.getBytesTotal()) {
  _root.gotoAndPlay("loaded");
}
```

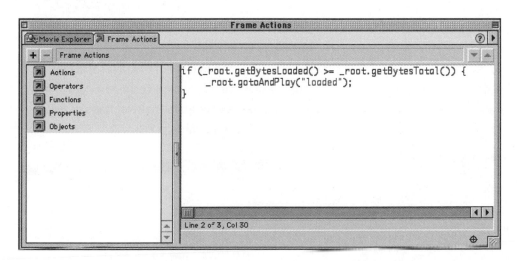

267

This ActionScript checks whether the value returned by the getBytesLoaded method of the main timeline is greater than or equal to the value returned by the getBytesTotal method of the same timeline. The getBytesLoaded method returns the number of bytes of a particular timeline that have been loaded, and getBytesTotal returns the total byte size of a timeline.

5) Insert another keyframe at frame 3 of the Actions/Labels layer. In the Actions panel, add the ActionScript _root.gotoAndPlay("check"); **to this keyframe.**

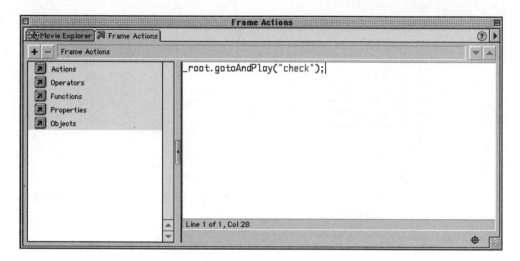

If the condition in frame 2 is not true, the Flash movie continues to play. The ActionScript in this frame sends the movie back to that frame to check the condition again.

Now that you have the basic interactivity set up, you have to give your users something to look at while the Flash movie loads. This content should have a very small file size. You'll add a little text to let users know how much of the movie has loaded.

6) Add a new layer named Text, and place it at the bottom of the layer stacking order. Insert a keyframe at frame 2 of the new Text layer. Select the text tool. Draw a dynamic text box on the stage, making it large enough for several lines of text. In the Text Options panel, type *loadingText* in the Variable text box.

TIP *If necessary, set the text type to Dynamic and the line type to Multiline in the Text Options panel before you draw the text box.*

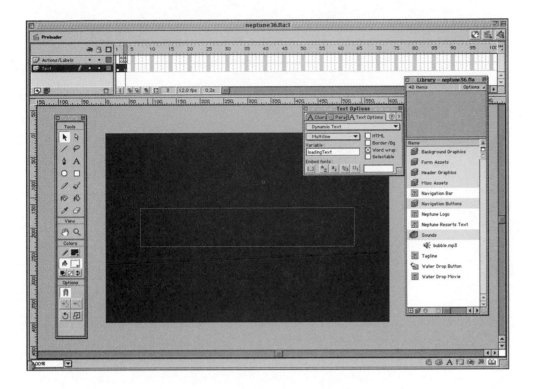

You are going to add some dynamic text that will keep track of the percentage of the movie that has loaded.

You can use the Character and Text Options panels to set up this text box. Set up the options in the Character panel to suit your own taste; just make sure that the fill color is not the same as the background color of the movie. In the Text Options panel, make sure that the text type is set to Dynamic, the line type is Multiline, the Word Wrap option is selected, and the Selectable option is deselected.

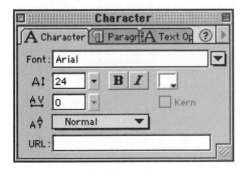

PUBLISHING AND EXPORTING

7) Select frame 2 of the Actions/Labels layer, and add the following ActionScript after the existing `if` **statement:**

```
percentLoaded = Math.round
((_root.getBytesLoaded()/_root.getBytesTotal())*100);
loadingText = "Loading content…" + percentLoaded + "% loaded so far.";
```

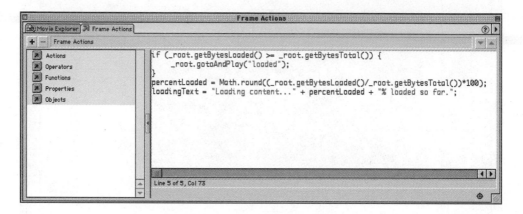

In the first line of the ActionScript you just added, you're setting the value of a variable called percentLoaded to be the amount loaded divided by the total size of the movie multiplied by 100, which is essentially the percentage of the movie loaded out of the total size. This number is rounded using the round method of the Math object. The next line of code sets the variable `loadingText`, which is the variable you gave the text box, to *"Loading content…" + percentLoaded + " loaded so far."* So if 10% of the movie has been loaded, the movie will display *Loading content… 10% loaded so far.*

The ActionScript for this frame should now look like this:

```
if (_root.getBytesLoaded() >= _root.getBytesTotal()) {
  _root.gotoAndPlay("loaded");
}
percentLoaded = Math.round
((_root.getBytesLoaded()/_root.getBytesTotal())*100);
loadingText = "Loading content…" + percentLoaded + "% loaded so far.";
```

Now you need to add a little more ActionScript to give the movie something to do when all of the movie has loaded. Otherwise, the movie will continue to loop, telling level 1 to play over and over.

8) Insert a blank keyframe at frame 10 of the Text layer. Insert a keyframe at frame 10 of the Actions/Labels layer. In the Frame panel, type *loaded* in the Label text box. In the Actions panel, apply the ActionScript play(); **to this frame.**

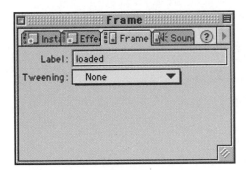

This frame is where the preloader movie will go when it's done checking to see whether the movie has loaded. The play action here makes the movie keep playing if some ActionScript tells the movie to go to this frame.

9) Choose Control > Test Movie. When the test movie opens, choose View > Show Streaming.

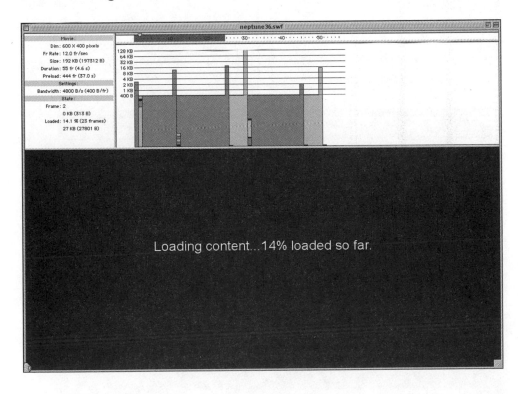

The movie plays as though it's being downloaded over the connection speed specified in the Debug menu. You should be able to watch the movie load. Pay special attention to the Loaded section in the bottom-right corner of the Bandwidth Profiler, which shows how many kilobytes have loaded. As you watch that number grow, the percentage displayed in the preloader should reflect the percentage of the total movie that has been loaded.

10) Close the test movie, and save the movie as neptune37.fla.

Now you have to load some external content into your movie, but first, you have to export that content.

EXPORTING A MOVIE

Every time you choose Control > Test Movie command, Flash creates a .swf file in the same directory as the .fla file. So if you were to look in your MyWork folder, you'd see several .swf files there, each of which was created when you tested a movie. This procedure is just one way to create a .swf file. Another way to create this type of file, as well as several other formats, is to export your movie by using the Export Movie command. You can use this command to give the .swf file a name other than of the name of the .fla file. That's what you'll do in this exercise. You'll also learn how to add content to an existing movie.

1) Select frame 30 of the Background Graphic layer in the Content scene of neptune37.fla, and choose Insert > Clear Keyframe. Do the same for frame 35 of the Background Graphic layer.

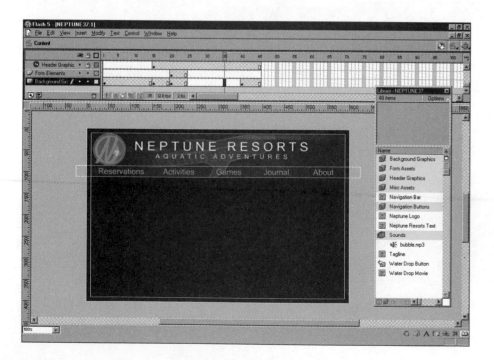

272

LESSON 12

If you do not have a copy of neptune37.fla in the MyWork folder, you can find a copy in the Lesson12/Assets folder. Just open that file and save it in the MyWork folder before you continue.

These two frames have content loaded into them, complete with a unique background graphic, so they don't need to have a background in this movie. By removing the contents of these two frames, you make the movie even smaller. You can test the movie to see how much the file size has decreased. Just remember that you have a new scene with a stop action at the beginning of the movie, so you'll see a black screen if you test the movie.

2) Open map9.fla in the MyWork folder. Choose File > Export Movie. When the Export Movie dialog box opens, choose Flash Player (*.swf) from the Save As Type drop-down menu, browse to the MyWork folder, type *map.swf* in the File Name text box, and click Save.

If you can't find map9.fla in the MyWork folder, you can find a copy of it in the Lesson12/Assets folder. You don't have to save the .fla file to the MyWork folder; just export the .swf file.

When you export the movie as a Flash Player movie, all the interactivity and sound in the movie are preserved. Notice that you can save the movie as several file types, including QuickTime, Animated GIF, and JPEG sequence. These file types might not preserve the interactivity and sound of your movie.

Before the movie is exported, the Export Flash Player dialog box opens. You can leave all these settings at their defaults and click OK. You'll look at some of the export options later in this lesson.

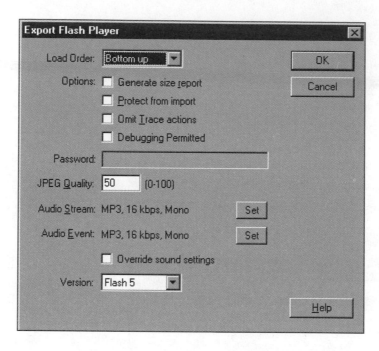

3) Repeat step 2 for merfolk4.fla, music.fla, jigsaw3.fla, and journal6.fla. Export these movies as merfolk.swf, music.swf, jigsaw.swf, and journal.swf, respectively.
If you don't find the correct .fla files in the MyWork folder, you can find copies of them in the Lesson12/Assets folder. The music.fla file contains the music toggle that was removed from the movie because it contains a linked sound. Linked sounds must be loaded completely during the beginning of a movie, before any actions occur. This toggle would make your preloader inoperable until the sound has been loaded.

When you export any movies that contain bitmaps (GIF, JPEG, and PNG files, for example), you should specify a JPEG Quality setting in the Export Flash Player dialog box. The default setting is 50, which produces a relatively small file with low-quality bitmaps. If you'd like to increase the quality of the bitmaps, increase the JPEG Quality setting to, say, 80. You can also specify lossless compression in the Bitmap Properties dialog box. To open this dialog box, double-click the icon to the left of a bitmap in the library.

4) Select frame 25 of the Actions Labels layer in neptune37.fla. Add the ActionScript loadMovieNum ("map.swf", 1);.

274

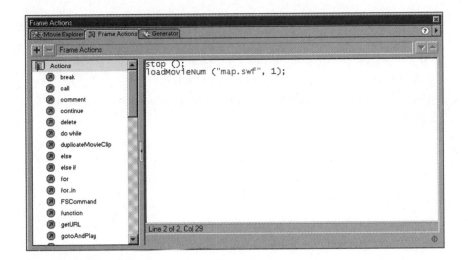

The `loadMovieNum` action has two arguments: `URL` and `level`. The `URL` argument contains the URL of the .swf file that you want to load. The level is much like a layer. Levels have a stacking order. The movie that Flash Player loads (the movie you're working with) is in level 0. In this case, you are loading map.swf into level 1, so it will be above the current movie in the level stacking order.

Now you need to load the rest of the .swf files that you exported in the appropriate frames.

5) Select frame 30 of the Actions/Labels layer. Add the following ActionScript:

```
myMovies = new Array();
myMovies[0] = "jigsaw.swf";
myMovies[1] = "merfolk.swf";
moviePick = random(myMovies.length);
loadMovieNum (myMovies[moviePick], 1);
```

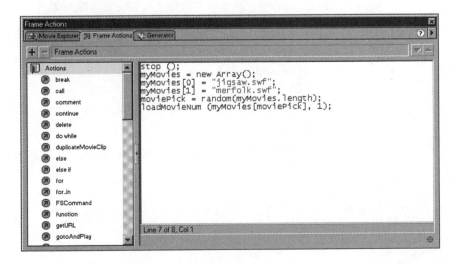

275

The ActionScript you just added first creates a new array containing the names of the .swf files that you want to load into this frame. Then it sets the value of a variable named moviePick to a random number based on the length of the array. Because the array has a length of 2, the value of moviePick is either 0 or 1. Finally, the loadMovieNum action loads a movie from the myMovies array, based on the moviePick variable, into level 1.

NOTE *An array is a list of variables. Each line of the list can contain a single variable, the value of which can be anything from a string to a number or an object or even another array. After you have created an array, you reference a line of the array by giving the name of your instance and then the line number inside square brackets like this:* myArray [2]. *The line number is called the index. It always starts at 0.*

6) Add some ActionScript to frame 35 of the Actions/Labels layer to load journal.swf into level 1. Add some more ActionScript to frame 1 of the Actions/Labels layer to load music.swf into level 10.

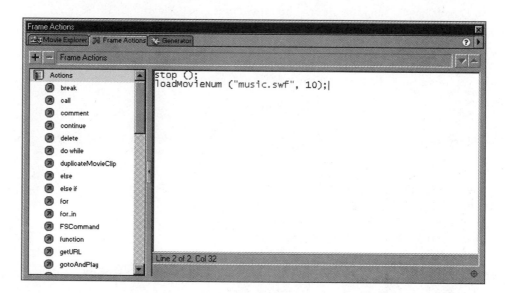

This ActionScript will be similar to the ActionScript that you added to frame 25. You just use a different URL argument for each frame. The URL argument for frame 35 will be journal.swf, and music.swf will be the argument for the ActionScript in frame 1. The loadMovieNum action in frame 1 also requires a new level argument, as follows, to reflect that you want to load the movie into level 10:

```
loadMovieNum ("music.swf", 10);
```

You can load a movie into any level, whether or not movies are loaded into all the levels below it.

276

7) Add the ActionScript `unloadMovieNum (1);` **to frames 15, 20, and 40 of the Actions/Labels layer:**

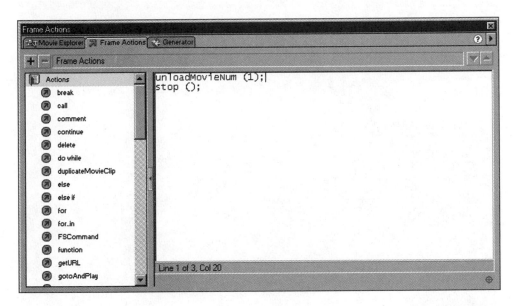

You should add this ActionScript to the top of the Actions list so that it occurs before the rest of the actions in each frame. This ActionScript unloads the movie in level 1, if a movie is already loaded there. This situation is important, because some of the frames contain content that is not loaded. Because the levels have a stacking order, and because you're loading content into level 1 in other frames, frames that don't have loaded content will have their contents hidden by the level-1 movies.

If a movie is already loaded into a level, and a `loadMovieNum` action attempts to load a movie into that level, the old movie is replaced by the new one. So you don't need to add any `unloadMovieNum` actions to the frames that load a new movie into level 1.

8) Choose Control > Test Movie, and test the movie.

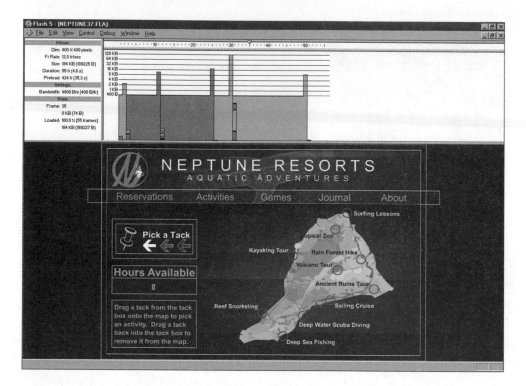

As you view each section of the movie, you should see the appropriate content when you click one of the buttons in the navigation bar. Some of the content is loaded, and some of it is part of the neptune37.fla movie.

9) Close the test movie, and save the movie as neptune38.fla.

You're almost done. After you complete one more exercise, your project will be ready for the Web.

PUBLISHING A MOVIE

You now have a working Flash site, complete with a preloader. All you have left to do is publish that content and upload it to your Web site so that other people can view it. When you publish a movie, you can create multiple formats for your Flash movie, along with the HTML required to embed it for viewing on the Web.

1) With neptune38.fla open, choose File > Publish Settings to open the Publish Settings dialog box.

When you're ready to publish your movie, you first have to check the Publish Settings dialog box to make sure that all the settings are correct.

The Publish command (File > Publish) creates all the files you need to deliver your Flash movie. By default, the Publish command creates a .swf file containing your movie and an HTML file containing the code to embed the .swf file. After Flash creates these files for you, you must upload both of them to your Web server. Visitors then just have to view the HTML file to see the .swf file. They do have to have the Flash Player installed for this file to work correctly, of course.

If you are concerned that your audience might not have the Flash Player, you can change the settings in the Publish Settings dialog box so that the Publish command also creates executable versions of the Flash movie for Windows and Macintosh computers. The executable version of the Flash movie is known as a **projector**. You can also make Flash publish a Generator template (.swt), GIF image, JPEG image, PNG image, QuickTime movie, or RealPlayer SMIL file.

2) In the Formats tab of the Publish Settings dialog box, make sure that the Flash and HTML checkboxes are checked. Also check the Windows Projector and Macintosh Projector checkboxes.

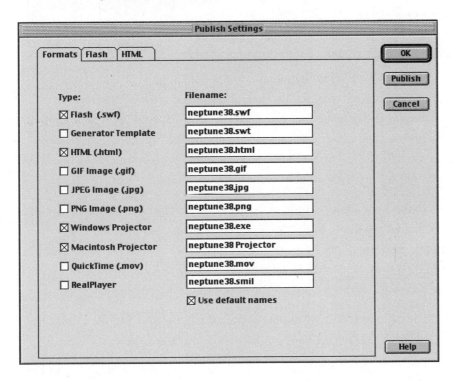

When you publish a movie, you can output several formats at the same time, including Flash Player movie (.swf), Generator template (.swt), GIF, JPEG, PNG, Windows Projector (.exe), Macintosh Projector, QuickTime movie, and RealPlayer. You can also create an HTML file that embeds the .swf file for playback over the Web.

3) Click the Flash tab in the Publish Settings dialog box, and choose the Generate Size Report option.

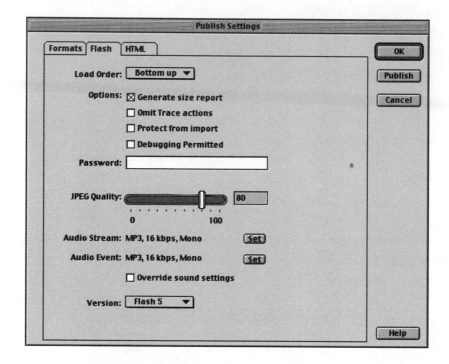

Many of the formats that you can publish from Flash have settings that you can modify to customize the finished file. When you publish a Flash Player movie (.swf), you have the option of generating a size report. This option, which is also available when you export a movie as .swf, creates a text file containing information about the movie. You'll look at a size report later in this exercise.

The settings in the Load Order drop-down menu determine the order in which the layers in each individual frame load—an important setting when files are being downloaded over slow modems. Flash shows each layer that appears as soon as it has downloaded. Top Down loads the top layer in each frame first and then loads each frame below it in order; Bottom Up does the opposite.

When you choose the Protect from Import option, the published .swf file cannot be imported into Flash. This setting keeps other people from stealing your movie.

The JPEG Quality, Audio Stream, and Audio Event settings are useful if you don't specify compression settings for each individual bitmap or sound file.

You have the option of choosing Flash versions other than 5 from the Version drop-down menu, but if you do, you will you lose some of the functionality of your movie. If you use anything that is Flash 5-specific and export it as an earlier version, you lose all the Flash 5-specific portions of the movie.

4) Click the HTML tab in the Publish Settings dialog box. Uncheck the Display Menu checkbox.

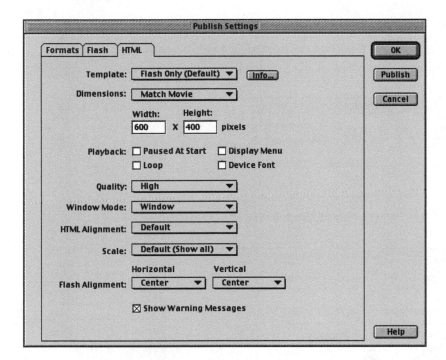

When you deselect the Display Menu option, you disable the shortcut menu that appears when users right+click (Windows) or Control+click (Macintosh) the movie while viewing it through the HTML file in the browser.

The Template drop-down menu specifies the HTML template that you want to publish. When you choose Flash Only (Default), Flash creates the HTML to embed your Flash file. Other templates that are available include Generator Only (Default) and Generator Image Output.

The Dimensions drop-down menu lets you specify the dimensions of the movie in percentage or pixels. If you choose Match Movie from this menu, you can't set the height and width of the movie. If you choose Pixels or Percent, you can modify the height and width settings.

You usually should set the Quality drop-down menu to High, which prioritizes appearance over playback. Low prioritizes playback over quality, turning off antialiasing. Auto Low is similar to Low but improves quality if possible. (If Flash determines that the computer can handle antialiasing, it turns on that feature) Auto High prioritizes playback and quality equally, reducing appearance first if playback problems occur; it turns off antialiasing if the frame rate continues to decrease. Medium produces better quality than Low. It does not antialias bitmaps but does apply some antialiasing. Best produces the best-quality appearance without considering speed; all images and bitmaps are antialiased.

5) Click OK to close the Publish Settings dialog box. Save the movie as neptune39.fla in the MyWork folder. Choose File > Publish to publish the movie.

The Publishing dialog box opens, indicating the progress of the publishing operation.

6) Open the size report in the MyWork folder.

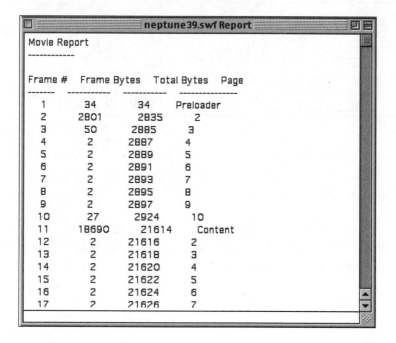

This file will be named neptune39 Report.txt (Windows) or neptune39.swf Report (Macintosh). You can open it in your favorite text editor.

The size report contains information about the movie, including how much size each frame takes up, how large each symbol is, which fonts and characters are used (and how much file size they take up), and which sounds are used (and how much file size they add to the finished movie). You can use the size report to optimize your movie better. If you notice that one symbol is very large, for example, you might want to concentrate on reducing that symbol's size.

7) Open neptune39.html (in the MyWork folder) in your browser.

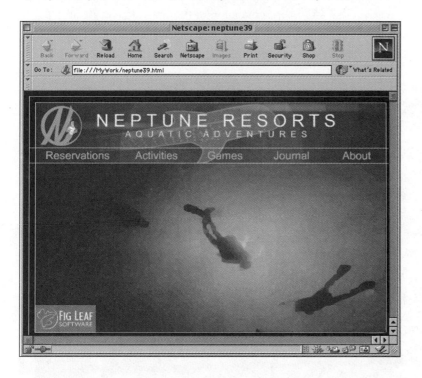

```
<HTML>
<HEAD>
<TITLE>neptune39</TITLE>
</HEAD>
<BODY bgcolor="#000000">
<!-- URL's used in the movie-->
<A HREF=http://www.figleaf.com></A> <!-- text used in the movie-->
<!--Reservations Request Entry Form Name: E-Mail: Reserve Activities: Location: Dates:
Select a Room Type: Reservations Request Entry Form Name: E-Mail: Reserve Activities:
Location: Dates: Select a Room Type: Reservations Request Entry Form Name: E-Mail:
Reserve Activities: Location: Dates: Select a Room Type: Reservations Request Entry
Form Name: E-Mail: Reserve Activities: Location: Dates: Select a Room Type: Reservations
Request Entry Form Name: E-Mail: Reserve Activities: Location: Dates: Select a Room
Type: --><OBJECT classid="clsid:D27CDB6E-AE6D-11cf-96B8-444553540000"

codebase="http://download.macromedia.com/pub/shockwave/cabs/flash/swflash.cab#ve
rsion=5,0,0,0"
 WIDTH=600 HEIGHT=400>
 <PARAM NAME=movie VALUE="neptune39.swf"> <PARAM NAME=loop VALUE=false>
<PARAM NAME=menu VALUE=false> <PARAM NAME=quality VALUE=high> <PARAM
NAME=bgcolor VALUE=#000000> <EMBED src="neptune39.swf" loop=false menu=false
quality=high bgcolor=#000000  WIDTH=600 HEIGHT=400
TYPE="application/x-shockwave-flash"
PLUGINSPAGE="http://www.macromedia.com/shockwave/download/index.cgi?P1_Prod_V
ersion=ShockwaveFlash"></EMBED>
</OBJECT>
</BODY>
</HTMI >
```

This file contains all the HTML that's needed to view neptune39swf in the browser properly, provided that you have the correct version of the Flash Player installed.

8) Open neptune39.exe (Windows) or neptune39 Projector (Macintosh).

This file is a stand-alone version of your movie. Flash wrapped the .swf file in a stand-alone projector. You can send this file to other people to view without requiring them to install the Flash Player. Just make sure that you send the right file; you published both Windows and Macintosh projectors.

9) Upload neptune39.html, neptune39.swf, jigsaw.swf, journal.swf, map.swf, merfolk.swf, and music.swf to your Web site, and browse to them.
You can't just upload the HTML file and expect to see the Flash content; you have to upload the .swf files too. The HTML file is set up so that the .swf files should be in the same directory. If you know a little HTML, you can easily change this setup.

If you try to use the journal in your uploaded version, it probably won't work, because the ColdFusion file that you're trying to connect to is on another domain. Because of security measures in the Flash Player, you won't be able to connect to that file.

You're done. You have just made your own Flash Web site.

WHAT YOU HAVE LEARNED

In this lesson, you have:

- Used the Bandwidth Profiler to assess your movie (pages 258–260)

- Viewed a Flash movie as it would appear over the Internet (page 260)

- Optimized a graphic and reduced the file size of a sound (pages 261–265)

- Created a preloader (pages 265–272)

- Exported a movie (pages 272–274)

- Loaded external movies (pages 274–277)

- Created an HTML file to embed a movie (pages 278–284)

- Created a stand-alone projector containing the Flash movie (pages 278–284)

windows shortcuts

TOOLBOX

Command	Shortcut
Arrow	V
Subselect	A
Line	N
Lasso	L
Pen	P
Text	T
Oval	O
Rectangle	R
Pencil	Y
Paint Brush	B
Ink Bottle	S
Paint Bucket	K
Eyeropper	I
Eraser	E
Hand	H
Magnifier	M, Z

FILE MENU

Command	Shortcut
New	Ctrl+N
Open	Ctrl+O
Open As Library	Ctrl+Shift+O
Close	Ctrl+W
Save	Ctrl+S
Save As	Ctrl+Shift+S
Import	Ctrl+R
Export Movie	Ctrl+Alt+Shift+S
Publish	Shift+F12
Print	Ctrl+P
Exit	Ctrl+Q

VIEW MENU

Command	Shortcut
Go to First	Home
Go to Previous	Page Up
Go to Next	Page Down
Go to Last	End
Zoom In	Ctrl+=
Zoom Out	Ctrl+−
100% Magnification	Ctrl+1
Show Frame	Ctrl+2
Show All	Ctrl+3
Outlines	Ctrl+Alt+Shift+O
Fast	Ctrl+Alt+Shift+F
Antialias	Ctrl+Alt+Shift+A
Antialias Text	Ctrl+Alt+Shift+T
Timeline	Ctrl+Alt+T
Work Area	Ctrl+Shift+W
Rulers	Ctrl+Alt+Shift+R
Show Grid	Ctrl+'
Snap to Grid	Ctrl+Shift+'
Edit Grid	Ctrl+Alt+G
Show Guides	Ctrl+;
Lock Guides	Ctrl+Alt+;
Snap to Guides	Ctrl+Shift+;
Edit Guides	Ctrl+Alt+Shift+G
Snap to Objects	Ctrl+Shift+/
Show Shape Hints	Ctrl+Alt+H
Hide Edges	Ctrl+H
Hide Panels	Tab

INSERT MENU

Command	Shortcut
Convert to Symbol	F8
New Symbol	Ctrl+F8
Frame	F5
Remove Frame	Shift+F5
Keyframe	F6
Blank Keyframe	F7
Clear Keyframe	Shift+F6

MODIFY MENU

Command	Shortcut
Instance	Ctrl+I
Frame	Ctrl+F
Movie	Ctrl+M
Optimize	Ctrl+Alt+Shift+C
Scale and Rotate	Ctrl+Alt+S
Remove Transform	Ctrl+Shift+Z
Add Shape Hint	Ctrl+Shift+H
Bring to Front	Ctrl+Shift+Up arrow
Bring Forward	Ctrl+Up arrow
Send Backward	Ctrl+Down arrow
Send to Back	Ctrl+Shift+Down arrow
Lock	Ctrl+Alt+l
Unlock All	Ctrl+Alt+Shift+L
Group	Ctrl+G
Ungroup	Ctrl+Shift+G
Break Apart	Ctrl+B

TEXT MENU

Command	Shortcut
Plain	Ctrl+Shift+P
Bold	Ctrl+Shift+B
Italic	Ctrl+Shift+I
Align Left	Ctrl+Shift+L
Align Center	Ctrl+Shift+C
Align Right	Ctrl+Shift+R
Justify	Ctrl+Shift+J
Increase Tracking	Ctrl+Alt+Right
Decrease Tracking	Ctrl+Alt+Left
Reset Tracking	Ctrl+Alt+Up
Character	Ctrl+T
Paragraph	Ctrl+Shift+T

CONTROL MENU

Command	Shortcut
Play	Enter
Rewind	Ctrl+Alt+R
Step Forward	.
Step Backward	,
Test Movie	Ctrl+Enter
Debug Movie	Ctrl+Shift+Enter
Test Scene	Ctrl+Alt+Enter
Enable Simple Buttons	Ctrl+Alt+B

WINDOW MENU

Command	Shortcut
New Window	Ctrl+Alt+N
Info Panel	Ctrl+Alt+I
Align Panel	Ctrl+K
Character Panel	Ctrl+T
Paragraph Panel	Ctrl+Shift+T
Instance Panel	Ctrl+I
Frame Panel	Ctrl+F
Actions Panel	Ctrl+Alt+A
Movie Explorer	Ctrl+Alt+M
Library	Ctrl+L

macintosh shortcuts

TOOLBOX

Command	Shortcut
Arrow	V
Subselect	A
Line	N
Lasso	L
Pen	P
Text	T
Oval	O
Rectangle	R
Pencil	Y
Paint Brush	B
Ink Bottle	S
Paint Bucket	K
Eyedropper	I
Eraser	E
Hand	H
Magnifier	M, Z

FILE MENU

Command	Shortcut
New	Command+N
Open	Command+O
Open As Library	Command+Shift+O
Close	Command+W
Save	Command+S
Save As	Command+Shift+S
Import	Command+R
Export Movie	Command+Option+Shift+S
Publish	Shift+F12
Print	Command+P
Exit	Command+Q

VIEW MENU

Command	Shortcut
Go to First	Home
Go to Previous	Page Up
Go to Next	Page Down
Go to Last	End
Zoom In	Command+=
Zoom Out	Command+−
100% Magnification	Command+1
Show Frame	Command+2
Show All	Command+3
Outlines	Command+Option+Shift+O
Fast	Command+Option+Shift+F
Antialias	Command+Option+Shift+A
Antialias Text	Command+Option+Shift+T
Timeline	Command+Option+T
Work Area	Command+Shift+W
Rulers	Command+Option+Shift+R
Show Grid	Command+'
Snap to Grid	Command+Shift+'
Edit Grid	Command+Option+G
Show Guides	Command+;
Lock Guides	Command+Option+;
Snap to Guides	Command+Shift+;
Edit Guides	Command+Option+Shift+G
Snap to Objects	Command+Shift+/
Show Shape Hints	Command+Option+H
Hide Edges	Command+H
Hide Panels	Tab

INSERT MENU

Command	Shortcut
Convert to Symbol	F8
New Symbol	Command+F8
Frame	F5
Remove Frame	Shift+F5
Keyframe	F6
Blank Keyframe	F7
Clear Keyframe	Shift+F6

MODIFY MENU

Command	Shortcut
Instance	Command+I
Frame	Command+F
Movie	Command+M
Optimize	Command+Option+Shift+C
Scale and Rotate	Command+Option+S
Remove Transform	Command+Shift+Z
Add Shape Hint	Command+Shift+H
Bring to Front	Command+Shift+Up arrow
Bring Forward	Command+Up arrow
Send Backward	Command+Down arrow
Send to Back	Command+Shift+Down arrow
Lock	Command+Option+l
Unlock All	Command+Option+Shift+L
Group	Command+G
Ungroup	Command+Shift+G
Break Apart	Command+B

292

TEXT MENU

Command	Shortcut
Plain	Command+Shift+P
Bold	Command+Shift+B
Italic	Command+Shift+I
Align Left	Command+Shift+L
Align Center	Command+Shift+C
Align Right	Command+Shift+R
Justify	Command+Shift+J
Increase Tracking	Command+Option+Right
Decrease Tracking	Command+Option+Left
Reset Tracking	Command+Option+Up
Character	Command+T
Paragraph	Command+Shift+T

WINDOW MENU

Command	Shortcut
New Window	Command+Option+N
Info Panel	Command+Option+I
Align Panel	Command+K
Character Panel	Command+T
Paragraph Panel	Command+Shift+T
Instance Panel	Command+I
Frame Panel	Command+F
Actions Panel	Command+Option+A
Movie Explorer	Command+Option+M
Library	Command+L

CONTROL MENU

Command	Shortcut
Play	Enter
Rewind	Command+Option+R
Step Forward	.
Step Backward	,
Test Movie	Command+Enter
Debug Movie	Command+Shift+Enter
Test Scene	Command+Option+Enter
Enable Simple Buttons	Command+Option+B

additional resources

FLASH RESOURCES

Macromedia Flash Support and Developers Center:

www.macromedia.com/support/flash

FlashLite: www.flashlite.net

FlashPlanet: www.flashplanet.com

FlashKit: www.flashkit.com

Virtual-FX: www.virtual-fx.net

We're Here: www.were-here.com

Flashcoders mailing list: chattyfig.figleaf.com/mailman/listinfo/flashcoders

Flasher-L mailing list: mailto:list-manager@shocker.com (send message Subscribe)

Flashnewbie mailing list: chattyfig.figleaf.com/mailman/listinfo/flashnewbie

GENERATOR RESOURCES

Macromedia Generator Support and Developers Center:

www.macromedia.com/support/generator

FlashLite: www.flashlite.net

FlashGen: www.flashgen.com

Generator Developers Network: www.gendev.net

Powerhouse mailing list: chattyfig.figleaf.com/mailman/listinfo/powerhouse

XML RESOURCES

XML.com: www.xml.com

The XML Files: www.webdeveloper.com/xml

The O'Reilly XML Center: xml.oreilly.com

MIDDLEWARE INFORMATION

Active Server Pages (ASP): www.microsoft.com

ColdFusion: www.allaire.com

JSP: java.sun.com/products/jsp

PHP: www.php.net

ActionScript quick reference

This reference provides information about the various ActionScript terms used in this book, as well as some additional terms that you might find useful.

DELIMITERS AND KEYWORDS

Name	Syntax and Description	Examples

//
(comment delimiter)
	`// comment here`
	
	Inserts a comment into your code that is ignored by the ActionScript interpreter.
		`// set value of the variable`
		`// called name`
		`name = "Shark";`

" " **(string delimiter)**	`"text"` When used before and after a string, quotes indicate that the string is a literal, not a variable, numerical value or other ActionScript element.	`("_root."+this._name+"target")`

null	`null`
	
	A special keyword that can be assigned to variables. It will be returned by a function if no data was provided.
		`if (x == null) {`
		`  gotoAndStop(10);`
		`}`

this	`this`
	
	A keyword that is used to refer to the current movie clip—the clip that contains the script.
		`// sets the x position of the`
		`// current movie clip to 300`
		
		`this._x = 300;`

OPERATORS

Operator	Syntax and Description	Examples

. (dot operator)	`object.property`
	`object.method`
	`instancename.variable`
	`instancename.child.variable`
	
	Used to navigate movie-clip hierarchies to access nested movie clips, variables, or properties. The dot operator is also used to test or set the properties of an object, execute a method of an object, or create a data structure.
		The following identifies the pattern property of the seashell object:
		
		`seaShell.pattern`

++ (increment)	`++expression;`
	`expression++;`
	
	Adds 1 to the expression. The preincrement form (++expression) adds 1 to the expression and returns the result. The postincrement form adds 1 to the expression and returns the initial value of the expression.
		`+myVar;`

-- (decrement)	`--expression;`
	`expression--;`
	
	Subtracts 1 from the expression. The predecrement form (--expression) subtracts 1 from expression and returns the result. The postdecrement form subtracts 1 from the expression and returns the initial value of the expression.
		`--myVar;`

+ (addition)	`expression1 + expression2`
	
	Adds numeric expressions and concatenates strings. If one expression is a string, all other expressions are converted to strings and concatenated. If both expressions are integers, the sum is an integer; if either or both expressions are floating-point numbers, the sum is a floating-point number.
		Example 1:
		
		`trace(1+2);`
		
		The output window would display 3.
		
		Example 2:
		
		When `myVar = "shark"`, the following expression returns "Oh no! It's a shark!":
		
		`trace("Oh no! It's a " +myVar+ "!");`

OPERATORS (cont'd)

Operator	Syntax and Description	Examples

–
(subtraction and negation)
	`-expression1;`
	`expression1-expression2`
	
	Used for subtraction and negation. If used for negation, it reverses the sign of the expression. If used for subtraction, it finds the difference between the two numbers.
		`x=5;`
		`y=4;`
		`trace(-x);`
		`trace(x-y);`
		
		The output window would display –5, then 1.

* **(multiplication)**	`expression1*expression2` Multiplies two numbers.	`trace (2*4);` The output window would display 8.
/ **(division)**	`expression1/expression2` Divides expression1 by expression2.	`trace (21/3);` The output window would display 7.

+=
(addition and assignment)
	`expression1 += expression2`
	
	Assigns expression1 the value of expression1 + expression2.
	
	`x += y` is equivalent to `x = x+y`.
		Example 1:
		
		`x = 5;`
		`x += 10;`
		`trace (x);`
		
		The output window would display 15.
		
		Example 2:
		
		`x = "I am afraid of";`
		`x += "sharks!";`
		`trace(x);`
		
		The output window would display:
		
		`I am afraid of sharks!`

= (assignment)	`expression1 = expression2` Assigns the type expression2 to the variable, array element, or property in expression1.	`tackID = 0;`
== **(equality)**	`expression1 == expression2` Tests two expressions for equality. If expression1 is equal to expression2, the result is true.	When `myVar = "shark"`, the following expression returns true: `myVar == "shark"`

OPERATORS (cont'd)

Operator	Syntax and Description	Examples
!= (inequality)	expression1 != expression2 Tests for inequality. If expression1 is not equal to expression2, the result is true.	1 != 2 returns true
< (less than)	expression1 < expression2 Compares two expressions and determines whether expression1 is less than expression2.	1 < 2 returns true
> (greater than)	expression1 > expression2 Compares two expressions to determine whether expression1 is greater in value than expression2.	300 > 900 returns false
<= (less than or equal to)	expression1 <= expression2 Compares two expressions to determine whether expression1 is less than or equal to expression2 in value.	4 <= 4 returns true 5 <= 3 returns false
>= (greater than or equal to)	expression1 >= expression2 Compares two expressions to determine whether expression1 is greater than or equal to expression2.	8 >= 5 returns true 30 >= 30 returns true

&& (logical AND)	expression1 && expression2
	
	Performs a Boolean (true or false) operation on both expressions. Both expression1 and expression2 must be true for the operator to return a final result of true.
		x= 10;
		y= 20;
		if ((x == 10) && (y == 20)) {
		  trace ("The Neptune Resorts are great!");
		}
		
		The output window would display:
		
		The Neptune Resorts are great!

OPERATORS (cont'd)

Operator	Syntax and Description	Examples

‖ (logical OR)	`expression1 || expression2`
	
	Performs a Boolean (`true` or `false`) operation on both expressions. The operator will return a final result of `true` if either `expression1` or `expression2` is true.
		`x = 10;`
		`y = 30;`
		`if ((x == 10) || (y == 20)) {`
		`   trace ("The Neptune Resorts are great!");`
		`}`
		
		The output window would display:
		
		`The Neptune Resorts are great!`

delete	`delete (reference);`
	
	Deletes the object or variable specified in reference. Useful for removing no-longer-needed variables from your ActionScript.
		`x = 10;`
		`delete x;`
		`shark.teeth = "large";`
		`delete shark.teeth;`

new	`new constructor(arguments);` Creates a new object, calls the function identified by the constructor argument and passes additional optional arguments in the parentheses.	`tigerShark = new Shark (large, mean);` `hammerHeadShark = new Shark (medium, aggressive);`

PROPERTIES

Property	Syntax and Description	Example(s)

_alpha	`instancename._alpha`
	`instancename._alpha = value;`
	
	Sets or gets the alpha transparency (0 is fully transparent, 100 fully opaque).
		`seaShell._alpha = 50;`
		
		Sets the alpha property of the movie clip called `seaShell` to 50%.

_droptarget	`draggableInstance._droptarget` Returns absolute path (in slash syntax notation) of the movie-clip instance on which the draggableInstanceName was dropped	`tackClip._droptarget`

_framesloaded	`instancename._framesloaded`
	
	Checks the number of frames that have been loaded in the instance. Used to monitor the download of your movie.
		`if (_framesloaded >= _totalframes) {`
		`   _level0.gotoAndPlay(1);`
		`}`

PROPERTIES (cont'd)

Property	Syntax and Description	Example(s)

_height	`instancename._height`
	`instancename._height = value;`
	
	Sets or retrieves the height of the space occupied by the movie clip.
		`onClipEvent(mouseDown) {`
		`  _height = 200;`
		`  _width = 300;`
		`}`

_level	`_levelN;` A reference to the root movie Timeline of levelN. N is an integer specifying depth level (default 0). You must load movies, using the `loadMovie` action, before targeting them by using the `_level` property.	`_level4.gotoAndStop(5);`

_name	`instancename._name;`
	`instancename._name = value;`
	
	Specifies the movie-clip instance name.
		`sound.attachSound(this._name);`

_root	`_root;`
	`_root.movieClip;`
	`_root.action;`
	
	Specifies or returns a reference to the root movie's timeline. Specifying _root is the same as using the slash notation (/).
		`_root.tackBox;`
		`_root.shark1.gotoAndStop(4);`

_rotation	`instancename._rotation`
	`instancename._rotation = value;`
	
	Sets or retrieves the rotation of the movie clip, in degrees.
		`x = shark1._rotation;`
		`shark2._rotation = 30;`

_totalframes	`instancename._totalframes`
	
	Determines the total frames contained in the movie clip specified in the `instancename`.
		`if (_framesloaded >= _totalframes) {`
		`  _level0.gotoAndPlay(1);`
		`}`

_visible	`instanceName._visible`
	`instanceName._visible = Boolean`
	
	Determines whether the movie specified by the `instanceName` argument is visible.
	
	Boolean; enter a true or false value.
		`tackTip._visible = false`

PROPERTIES (cont'd)

Property	Syntax and Description	Example(s)

_width	`instancename._width`
	`instancename._width= value;`
	
	Sets or retrieves the width of the space occupied by the movie clip.
		`onClipEvent(mouseDown) {`
		`  _height = 200;`
		`  _width = 300;`
		`}`

_x	`instanceName._x`
	`instanceName._x = integer`
	
	Sets or retrieves the X coordinate relative to the parent timeline.
		`tackClip._x;`
		`P1._x = Math.random;`

_xmouse	`instancename._xmouse` Returns the X coordinate of the mouse position.	`x =_xmouse;`

_y	`instanceName._y`
	`instanceName._y = integer`
	
	Sets or retrieves the Y coordinate relative to the parent timeline.
		`tackClip._y`
		`P1._y = Math.random;`

_ymouse	`instancename._xmouse` Returns the Y coordinate of the mouse position.	`y =_ymouse;`
scroll	`variablename.scroll = value;` Used for creating scrolling text boxes. Set value to the topmost visible line in the text box. Default value is 1. This value is updated as the user scrolls up and down in the text box.	`text.scroll = 1;`

ACTIONS

Action	Syntax and Description	Example(s)

break	`break;`
	
	Tells the ActionScript to skip the rest of the loop.
		```x = 0;```
		```while (true) {```
		``` if (x >=100) {```
		``` break;```
		``` }```
		``` ++x;```
		```}```

duplicateMovieClip	`duplicateMovieClip(target,newname,depth);` **target:** the path of the movie to duplicate **newname:** the new name of the duplicated movie clip **depth:** the level of the movie clip Creates an instance of a movie clip when the movie is playing. If the parent movie clip is deleted, the duplicated movie clip is also deleted.	```duplicateMovieClip ("_root.shark",``` ```"shark1", 1);```

else	`else{statement(s)}`
	
	Specifies the actions, clauses, arguments, or other conditionals required to run if the initial if statement returns false.
		```if (x == 2) {```
		``` startDrag("myClip");```
		```}else{```
		``` stopDrag();```
		```}```

escape	`escape(expression);`
	
	Converts the argument to a string and encodes it in a URL-encoded format, all alphanumeric characters are escaped with % hexadecimal sequences. For example, an opening (left) curly brace ({) would be escaped as %7B.
		`escape ("Hello{[World]}");`
		
		Result:
		
		`("Hello%7B%5BWorld%5D%7D");`

eval	`eval(expression);` Accesses variables, properties, objects, or movie clips by name.	```this._x =``` ```eval(this._droptarget)._x;```

ACTIONS (cont'd)

Action	Syntax and Description	Example(s)

for

```
for (int; condition; next) {
   statement;
}
```

int: the expression to evaluate before beginning the loop sequence.

condition: an expression that evaluates to true or false. The loop will execute the commands contained in it until the condition evaluates to false.

next: an expression to evaluate after each loop—usually, an assignment using ++ or --.

statement: the code that will execute when the condition evaluates to true.

The loop evaluates the int value once, then begins a looping sequence until the condition evaluates to false.

```
for (x = 0; x < 5; ++x) {
   trace ("Neptune Resorts");
}
```

The output window would show:

```
Neptune Resorts
Neptune Resorts
Neptune Resorts
Neptune Resorts
Neptune Resorts
```

function

```
function functionName (argument1, argument2){
   statement(s)
}
```

A set of defined statements that performs a certain task. You can define a function in one location and call it from a different movie. The arguments are optional.

```
function calcTax(price,tax){
   cost = price*tax + price
}
```

getURL

```
getUrl(url [,window[,variables]]);
```

Loads a document from a specific URL into a window or passes variables to another application at a defined URL.

```
getURL("http://www.myurl.com",
"_blank")
```

gotoAndPlay

```
gotoAndPlay (scene, frame);
```

Sends the playhead to the specified frame in a scene and plays from that frame. The scene argument is optional.

```
gotoAndPlay(1);
```

gotoAndStop

```
gotoAndStop(scene, frame);
```

Sends the playhead to the specified frame and stops at that frame. The scene argument is optional.

```
gotoAndStop(1);
```

Action	Syntax and Description	Example(s)
if	```if (condition){ statement; }``` Evaluates the condition given. If the condition is true, Flash runs the statements that follow.	```if (done != true) { this.startDrag(); }```
ifFrameLoaded	```ifFrameLoaded(scene, frame) { statement; }``` Checks to see whether the contents of the specified frame have been loaded. If so, the statement is executed. The scene argument is optional.	```ifFrameLoaded(this._totalframes) { gotoAndPlay (1); }```
#include	```#include "filename.as"``` Includes the contents of the file specified in the argument.	```#include "jigsaw.as"```
loadMovie	```loadMovie (url [.location/target, [variables]]);``` Plays additional movies without closing Flash Player. Use target to specify a particular movie-clip timeline.	```loadMovie("movie.swf", _root.targetMC);```
loadVariables	```loadVariables (url [.location/target, variables]]);``` Reads data from an external file and sets values for variables in a movie or movie clip.	```loadVariables("myvariables.txt", _root.variableTargetMC);```
play	```play();``` Move the playhead forward in the timeline.	```if (x == 2) { play(); } else { gotoAndPlay (45); }```
removeMovieClip	```removeMovieClip(target);``` **target:** the target path of the movie-clip instance created with duplicateMovieClip Deletes a movie clip that was created with attachMovie or duplicateMovieClip.	```removeMovieClip(_root.shark1);```

306

ACTIONS (cont'd)

Action	Syntax and Description	Example(s)

return	`return (expression);`
	
	Specifies the value returned by the function. The return action causes the function to stop executing.
		```function calcTax(price, tax){```
		``` return(price, tax)```
		```}```

setProperty	`setProperty (target, property, expression);` **target:** the path to the instance name of the movie clip whose property is being set. **property:** the property to be set **expression:** the value to which the property is set Changes the property of a movie clip as the movie plays.	```setProperty ("shark1", _height,``` ```400);```

startDrag	`startDrag(target);`
	
	Makes the movie clip specified in target draggable. The movie clip remains draggable until a stopDrag action is applied to it.
		```on (press) {```
		``` startDrag("myClip");```
		```}```
		```on (release, releaseOutside) {```
		``` stopDrag();```
		```}```

stopDrag	`stopDrag(target);`
	
	Stops the movie clip specified in target from being draggable.
		```on (press) {```
		``` startDrag("myClip");```
		```}```
		```on (release, releaseOutside) {```
		``` stopDrag();```
		```}```

stop	`stop();`
	
	Stops the current timeline from playing.
		```if (x > 0) {```
		``` stop();```
		```}else {```
		``` gotoAndStop(50);```
		```}```

stopAllSounds	`stopAllSounds();`
	
	Stops all sounds that are currently playing without stoppng the movie itself. Sounds set to stream will continue to stream as the playhead reaches the frame.
		```on (release, releaseOutside) {```
		``` stopAllSounds();```
		```}```

ACTIONS (cont'd)

Action	Syntax and Description	Example(s)

trace

`trace (expression);`

Evaluates the expression and displays the result in the output window; similar to the `alert` function in JavaScript.

```
trace (x+=5);
trace ("Hi everyone!");
```

unloadMovie

`unloadMovie (location);`

location: the depth level or target movie clip from which to unload the movie.

Removes movie that was loaded by the `loadMovie` command.

```
on (release) {
    unloadMovie (_level2);
}
```

updateAfterEvent

`updateAfterEvent(movie clip event);`

movie clip event: allows you to specify one of the following events:

mouseMove. The action is executed any time the mouse is moved.

mouseDown. The action is executed when the left mouse button is clicked.

mouseUp. The action is executed when the mouse button is released.

keyDown. The action is executed when any key is pressed.

keyUp. The action is executed when a key is released.

Updates the display after the clip event specified in the arguments has completed.

`updateAfterEvent(mouseMove);`

while

```
while (condition) {
    statements;
}
```

Runs a series of statements in the loop as long as the loop conditions continue to be true.

```
while (x > 5) {
    trace(hammerhead);
    x++;
}
```

308

FUNCTIONS

Term	Syntax and Description	Example(s)
eval	`eval(expression);` Accesses variables, properties, objects, or movie clips by name.	`this._x =` `eval(this._droptarget)._x;`
getProperty	`getProperty(instancename, property);` **instancename:** the instance name of a movie clip **property:** a property of a movie clip Returns the value of the specified instance name's property.	`getProperty (_level0.shark., _width);`
getTimer	`getTimer();` Returns the number of milliseconds that have elapsed since the movie started playing.	`time = getTimer();` Returns a numeric value.

getVersion	`getVersion();`
	
	Returns a string containing Flash Player version and platform information.
		`trace (getVersion());`
		
		Outputs:
		
		`WIN 5,0,17,0`
		
		Indicates that the platform is Windows and that the version number of Flash Player is major version 5.

unescape	`unescape(x);`
	
	Evaluates the x argument as a string, decodes the string from URL-encoded format, and returns the string.
		`unescape ("Hello%7B%5BWorld%5D%7D");`
		
		Unescaped result:
		
		`Hello{[World]}`

HANDLERS

Handler	Syntax and Description	Example(s)
| **on** | ```
on (mouseEvent) {
  statement;
}
``` <br><br> The mouseEvent action can have one of the following arguments: press, release, releaseOutside, rollOver, rollOut, dragOver, dragOut, or KeyPress("key"). <br><br> Specifies a mouse action or keypress that triggers an action. | ```
on (rollOver, dragOver) {
  gotoAndStop(5);
}
``` <br><br> ```
on (rollOut, dragOut) {
  gotoAndStop(10);
}
``` |
| **onClipEvent** | ```
onClipEvent(movieEvent) {
  statements;
}
``` <br><br> **movieEvent:** an event that executes actions that are assigned in the statements of the onClipEvent. The action can have one of the following events: load, unload, enterFrame, mouseMove, mouseDown, mouseUp, keyDown, keyUp, or data. <br><br> Triggers actions defined in the statements for a specific instance of a movie clip. | ```
onClipEvent(load) {
  gotoAndPlay(14);
}
``` |

OBJECTS

The following tables outline some of the built-in Flash objects and methods used in this book. For more information on the built-in Flash 5 objects, please refer to the Flash 5 ActionScript Dictionary (Help > ActionScript Dictionary).

ARRAY OBJECT

Property/Method	Syntax and Description	Example(s)
| **length** | ```
myArray.length;
``` <br><br> Property of the Array object that returns the length of the array. | ```
mySharks [3] = hammerhead;
trace (mySharks.length);
``` <br><br> The output window would display 4 since there are 4 items (0 to 3) in this array. |

310
```

Array Object (cont'd)

Property/Method	Syntax and Description	Example(s)
sort	`myArray.sort(orderFunc);` Sorts the array. The orderFunc argument specifies the order that the array is sorted. The orderFunc argument can be −1 (A appears before B in the sorted sequence, or alphabetical order), 1 (A appears after B in the sorted sequence, or reverse alphabetical order), or 0 (A equals B in the sorted sequence).	`mySharks.sort();`

Color Object

Property/Method	Syntax and Description	Example(s)
setRGB	`myColor.setRGB(0xRRGGBB);` Sets the hexadecimal representation of the RGB value for a color object. The argument 0xRRGGBB is the hexadecimal or RGB color to be set. RR, GG, and BB consist of two hexadecimal digits specifying the offset of each color component.	`myColor.setRGB(0xFFFFFF);`
getRGB	`myColor.getRGB();` Returns the numeric RGB value set by the last setRGB call.	`myColor.setRGB(0x993366);`

Date Object

Property/Method	Syntax and Description	Example(s)

getDate	`myDate.getDate();`
	
	Returns the day of the month (an integer from 1 to 31) of the specified Date object according to local time.
		`day = new Date();`
		`trace(day.getDate());`
		
		The output window displays the current day of the month.

toString	`myDate.toString();` Returns a string value for the specified Date object in a readable format.	`trace(dateOfBirth.toString());`

MATH OBJECT

Property/Method	Syntax and Description	Example(s)
abs	`Math.abs(x);` Computes the absolute value of the number specified by x.	`Math.abs(-15);`
cos	`Math.cos(x);` **x:** an angle measured in radians Computes and returns the cosine of a specified angle in radians.	`Math.cos(1.57);`
random	`Math.random();` Creates a random number between 0.0 and 1.0.	`trace (Math.random());` Outputs a random number.
sin	`Math.sin(x);` **x:** an angle measured in radians Computes and returns the sine of a specified angle in radians.	`Math.sin(0.78);`
tan	`Math.tan(x);` **x:** an angle measured in radians Computes and returns the tangent of a specified angle in radians.	`Math.tan(0.52);`

MOVIECLIP OBJECT

Property/Method	Syntax and Description	Example(s)
attachMovie	`anyMovieClip.attachMovie(idname, newname, depth);` **idname:** the name of the movie in the library to attach **newname:** a unique instance name that is going to be attached **depth:** an integer specifying the depth level where the movie is being placed Creates a new instance of a movie and attaches it to the movie specified by `anyMovieClip`.	`this.attachMovie("shark", "shark"+x, x);`

MovieClip Object (cont'd)

Property/Method	Syntax and Description	Example(s)
duplicateMovieClip	`anyMovieClip.duplicateMovieClip(newname, depth);` **newname:** a unique identifier for the duplicate movie clip **depth:** the depth level where the duplicated movie exists Creates an instance of a movie clip while the movie is playing. Begins at frame 1 no matter what frame the original is playing.	`this.duplicateMovieClip` `(this._name+x, x);`
getURL	`anyMovieClip.getURL (URL[,window[,variables]]);` **URL:** the URL to load. **window:** optional argument that specifies the window in which to load the URL. Use `_blank` to create a new window, `_self`, for the current window. **variables:** optional argument that specifies the method for sending variables. GET appends the variables to the end of the URL; POST sends the variables in a separate HTTP header.	`this.getURL("http://www.` `neptuneresortsinc.com", "_blank");`
gotoAndPlay	`anyMovieClip.gotoAndPlay(frame);` **frame:** the frame number or label where the playhead will be sent Starts playing the movie at the specified frame.	`neptune.gotoAndPlay(413);` `neptune.gotoAndPlay("start");`
gotoAndStop	`anyMovieClip.gotoAndStop(frame);` **frame:** the frame number or label where the playhead will be sent Goes to the specified frame and stops.	`shark.gotoAndStop(73);` `shark.gotoAndStop("stop");`
loadMovie	`anyMovieClip.loadMovie(URL, location/target [variables]);` **URL:** the absolute or relative URL for the .swf file to load **variables:** Specifies the method for sending variables. GET appends the variables to the end of the URL; POST sends the variables in a separate HTTP header.	`this.loadMovie("puzzle.swf");`

MovieClip Object (cont'd)

Property/Method	Syntax and Description	Example(s)
loadVariables	anyMovieClip.loadVariables(URL, location[,variables]); **URL:** the absolute or relative URL for the external file to load. **variables:** an optional argument that specifies the method for sending variables. GET appends the variables to the end of the URL; POST sends the variables in a separate HTTP header.	this.loadVariables("variables.txt");
removeMovieClip	anyMovieClip.removeMovieClip(); Removes the movie-clip instance created by the duplicateMovie action.	shark1.removeMoveClip();
startDrag	anyMovieClip.startDrag([lock, left, right, top, bottom]); Allows the user to drag the specified movie clip. The movie remains draggable until explicitly stopped by calling the stopDrag method, or until another movie clip is made draggable. Only one movie clip is draggable at a time. **lock:** specifies whether the draggable movie clip is locked to the center of the mouse position **left**, **top**, **right**, **bottom**: values relative to the coordinates of the movie clip that constrain the drag of the clip	this.startDrag();
stopDrag	anyMovieClip.stopDrag(); Ends an action started with the startDrag action.	this.stopDrag();
stop	anyMovieClip.stop(); Stops the specified movie clip.	shark1.stop();
play	anyMovieClip.play(); Plays the movie clip.	shark1.play();

MovieClip Object (cont'd)

Property/Method	Syntax and Description	Example(s)
swapDepths	anyMovieClip.swapDepths(depth): anyMovieClip.swapDepths(target); **target:** the movie-clip instance that is being swapped **depth:** the depth level to which the movie clip is being swapped Swaps the depths of two movie clips.	shark1.swapDepths(shark2); shark1.swapDepths(100);
unloadMovie	anyMovieClip.unloadMovie(); Removes the movie clip that was loaded by the loadMovie or attachMovie method.	shark2.unloadMovie();

Sound Object

Property/Method	Syntax and Description	Example(s)
attachSound	mySound.attachSound("idName"); **idName:** name of the new instance of the sound Attaches the sound specified in idName to the sound object	s.attachSound("newSound"+x);
getVolume	mySound.getVolume(); Returns the sound-volume level as an integer from 0 to 100. 0 is off.	s = new Sound(); s.getVolume();
setPan	mySound.setPan(pan); **pan:** specifies the right-left balance of sound. Values range from −100 to 100. 100 uses the right channel only; −100 uses the left channel only. Sets the panning of a sound attached by the attachSound method.	s.setPan(-100);
setVolume	mySound.setVolume(volume); **volume:** an integer from 0 to 100. 100 is full volume. Sets the volume of a sound attached by the attachSound method.	s.setVolume(50);

Sound Object (cont'd)

Property/Method	Syntax and Description	Example(s)

start	`mySound.start();`
	`mySound.start(secondOffset, loop);`
	
	secondOffset: allows the sound to start playing at a specific point
	
	loop: specifies the number of times the sound will loop
	
	Starts a sound attached by the `attachSound` method.
		`s.start(5,5);`

stop	`mySound.stop();`
	`mySound.stop("idName");`
	
	idName: optional argument that stops the specified sound
	
	Stops a sound attached by the `attachSound` method. If no argument is set, this action stops all sounds.
		`s.stop();`

XML Object

Property/Method	Syntax and Description	Example(s)

firstChild	`myXML.firstChild;`
	
	Evaluates the specified XML object and checks the first child; returns `null` if the first child does not exist.
		`file = new XML();`
		`if (file.firstChild) {`
		`  trace("A first child exists")`
		`} else {`
		`  trace("Doesn't Exist");`
		`}`

load	`myXML.load(url);` **url:** the URL where the XML document is located Loads an XML document.	`file.load("file.xml");`
nodeValue	`myXML.nodeValue;` Returns the node value of the XML object.	`x = file.nodeValue;` `trace (x);`

index

Learn Macromedia's hottest software...
the Visual QuickStart way!

Macromedia tech support number: 415-252-9080

LICENSING AGREEMENT

The information in this book is for informational use only and is subject to change without notice. Macromedia, Inc., and Macromedia Press assume no responsibility for errors or inaccuracies that may appear in this book. The software described in the book is furnished under license and may be used or copied only in accordance with terms of the license.

The software files on the CD-ROM included here are copyrighted by Macromedia, Inc. You have the non-exclusive right to use these programs and files. You may use them on one computer at a time. You may not transfer the files from one computer to another over a network. You may transfer the files onto a single hard disk so long as you can prove ownership of the original CD-ROM.

You may not reverse engineer, decompile, or disassemble the software. You may not modify or translate the software or distribute copies of the software without the written consent of Macromedia, Inc.

Opening the disc package means you accept the licensing agreement. For installation instructions, see the ReadMe file on the CD-ROM.